Economics of the Undead

Economics of the Undead

Zombies, Vampires, and the Dismal Science

Edited by Glen Whitman and James Dow

ROWMAN & LITTLEFIELD
Lanham • Boulder • New York • London

Published by Rowman & Littlefield
4501 Forbes Boulevard, Suite 200, Lanham, Maryland 20706
www.rowman.com

Unit A, Whitacre Mews, 26-34 Stannary Street, London SE11 4AB

British Library Cataloguing in Publication Information Available

Library of Congress Cataloging-in-Publication Data

Library of Congress Cataloging-in-Publication Data
The hardback edition of this book was previously cataloged by the Library of Congress as follows:

Economics of the undead : zombies, vampires, and the dismal / edited by Glen Whitman and James P.
Dow, Jr.
pages cm
Includes bibliographical references and index.
1. Man-woman relationships--United States. 2. Dating (Social customs)--United States. 3. Competi-
tion--United States. 4. Capitalism--United States. I. Whitman, Glen, editor of compilation.
HQ801.E334 2014
306.70973--dc23
2014002998

ISBN: 978-1-4422-3502-1 (cloth : alk. paper)
ISBN: 978-1-4422-5666-8 (pbk. : alk. paper)
ISBN: 978-1-4422-3503-8 (electronic)

♾ ™ The paper used in this publication meets the minimum requirements of American
National Standard for Information Sciences Permanence of Paper for Printed Library
Materials, ANSI/NISO Z39.48-1992.

Printed in the United States of America

Contents

Introduction: Living Dead and the Modern Economy

Glen Whitman and James Dow

In season 5 of *Buffy the Vampire Slayer*, Buffy Summers uncovers the existence of a vampire brothel, where thrill-seeking humans pay vampires to suck their blood. Worse yet, she learns that her boyfriend Riley has been visiting the establishment and making regular donations, so to speak. [1]

These troubling events raise a host of questions. For most viewers, the question is, "What will Buffy do now? Will she stay with Riley or dump him for good?" But as economists (and dedicated fans of the show), our first reaction was, "Wait a minute. The *humans* pay the *vampires*? Wouldn't the money go the other way?"

Actually, the answer is "not necessarily." If both parties get something valuable from the exchange—sustenance for the vampires, illicit thrills for the humans—then in theory, the monetary payments could go either way. You see, it all depends on the relative size of human supply and vampire demand. . .

And so it began: a growing realization that the vampire genre is positively swollen with economic questions. And the zombie genre? Maybe more so. Economic issues take center stage in many undead narratives—and when they don't, they're still lurking in the shadows. Is there enough food to fill all those hungry mouths? Do humans have the resources, mental and physical, it takes to survive? Will people be able to cooperate with others to fight a collective threat—or will humanity descend into chaos and disorder? These are questions that the discipline of economics is uniquely positioned to address.

But it took time for the idea to evolve into a book. In the meantime, another academic discipline jumped headfirst into the pop culture field. In

2000, *Seinfeld and Philosophy*[2] marked the first of a series of "pop-culture-meets-philosophy" volumes—a trend that has grown to more than one hundred volumes and at least three different publishers. Many of the titles involved the undead, including *Zombies, Vampires, and Philosophy* (to which one of us contributed a chapter inspired by *Buffy*'s vampire brothel).[3]

After more than a decade of philosophers dominating the pop culture scene, we decided it was time for economics to have its turn. This seems only appropriate, since Adam Smith—the father of modern economics—was in fact an eighteenth-century Scottish philosopher, and his work helped economics to leave the nest of its parent discipline.

It would be tempting at this point to define economics. But that's harder than you might think. Numerous definitions have been offered since Smith's time—but every definition ends up neglecting some of the questions economists ask and some of the methods they use. In the broadest sense, economists seek to explain how people interact with both each other and the material world around them. In this sense, economics overlaps with philosophy, psychology, sociology, demographics, history, biology, and indeed all of the social sciences. Economists also tend to share a similar approach to their subject matter: systematic, analytical, with curiosity constrained by intellectual rigor.

But aside from these "family resemblances," economics defies any single definition. Embracing that fact, we have organized this book in sections, with each section reflecting a different notion of what economics is really about. For each section, we've included a short explanation of the unifying theme behind the included chapters. If one section doesn't suit your taste, sink your teeth into another.

But before you start sampling, let's return for a moment to the subtitle of this book: "Zombies, Vampires, and the Dismal Science." In a book about the undead, we couldn't resist the temptation to use the economics discipline's most famous nickname. But while many people know economics as the dismal science, few know the true origin of that phrase. It came from Thomas Carlyle, another Scottish philosopher. And Carlyle was *not* denigrating economists for their (quite real) tendency to emphasize the limits of our resources and the barriers to remaking society as a fanciful utopia. No, Carlyle was criticizing economists for *supporting the abolition of slavery*! He was incensed by the optimism of economists like John Stuart Mill, who believed that people of African origin—like people of all races—were capable of governing themselves.[4]

We tell this story because we think you'll find, possibly to your surprise, that this book presents one of the more *optimistic* perspectives you'll find on the undead threat. From Darwyyn Deyo and David T. Mitchell's argument that we should trade with vampires instead of staking them; to Kyle Bishop, David Tufte, and Mary Jo Tufte's suggestion that innovative humans might ultimately achieve victory over the zombie threat; to Brian Hollar's discussion of how humans will seek prosperity even after a zombie apocalypse, a broad theme emerges: that humans—and maybe our recently dead brethren as well—have a vast capacity to cope with adversity and somehow make the world a better place.

Part I

Soulless Mates

In this section, we explore the economics of cross-the-grave relationships. Given the growing popularity of romantic unions between humans and vampires, the time is ripe for a more penetrating study.

Romance might seem an odd place to begin a book about economics. Wouldn't the quest for love and companionship fall more naturally in the realm of psychology or sociology? But in fact, romantic partnerships exemplify one of the most popular definitions of economics: "the study of choice under conditions of scarcity." Every step in the relationship process—from searching for a lover, to making long-term commitments, to breaking up—is a choice, and every choice involves trade-offs. Relationships with the undead, in particular, have a way of forcing hard choices on those who take part in them. In romance and life in general, you can't have everything you want, and that's the defining feature of scarcity.

Ultimately, the market for romance shares much with markets in general: competition, gains from trade, offers accepted and rejected, partnerships formed and dissolved. So who knows? A little economics might improve life in the bedroom as well as the boardroom.

—GW & JD

Chapter One

Human Girls and Vampire Boys, Part 1

Looking for Mr. Goodbite

Glen Whitman

"And so the lion fell in love with the lamb . . . " he murmured. I looked away, hiding my eyes as I thrilled to the word.
"What a stupid lamb," I sighed.
"What a sick, masochistic lion."

—Edward Cullen and Bella Swan,
in Stephenie Meyer's *Twilight* (2005)

Bella and Edward. Buffy and Angel. Buffy and Spike. Sookie and Bill. Sookie and Eric. Elena and Stefan. Elena and Damon. It seems you can't crack a book, flip on the TV, or walk down a dark alley these days without finding a human girl and a vampire boy making googly eyes at each other.

Society has clearly evolved a great deal since the late 1800s, when the romantic relationship between Count Dracula and Lucy Westenra led a small group of fanatics to stake her, behead her, and stuff her mouth with garlic before tracking down Dracula himself. Until recently, romantic relationships between the living and the dead were regarded with sheer horror. But Buffy, Bella, Sookie, and Elena have blazed a trail that many young women are eager to follow. The human-vampire dating scene is taking off.

It's a competitive environment out there, and a girl who wants a vampire beau can no longer simply wait for a soulless mate to fall in her lap. You have to choose a search strategy that will enhance your odds—not merely of landing a vampire mate, but of landing a good one.

But how much advice can economists possibly offer to those interested in dating the undead? You might be surprised. The economic literature on "marriage markets" offers a great deal of insight on finding, keeping, and

3

even breaking up with undead lovers. In this chapter, I'll focus on the process of finding a mate; in the next chapter, I'll consider staying together and breaking up.

As a matter of inclusiveness, I should mention that some vampire girls might want to date human boys (for example, Jessica and Hoyt in *True Blood*), and other vampires might be interested in same-sex relationships (as in Samuel Taylor Coleridge's poem *Christabel*). I'll address my advice primarily to human girls seeking vampire boys, because that seems to be the most common case, and it avoids confusion over pronouns. But many of the lessons here apply to any relationship with the undead—and, perhaps, even to more traditional relationships.

MEAT MARKETS

Is the dating scene truly a "market"? Yes. All potential mates seek something of value, and they offer what they have in return. In that sense, a relationship is a special kind of exchange. As Nobel-winning economist Gary Becker observed in 1973, the situation is fundamentally competitive, as "Each person tries to find the best mate, subject to the restrictions imposed by market conditions."[1]

Not all markets are alike, of course. In the mating market, money is *usually* not on the table, at least not explicitly.[2] Without monetary prices, transactions take the form of barter. Each romantic partner offers his or her own qualities—looks, intelligence, personality, and so on—in exchange for his or her partner's. In the human-vampire dating market, some other attributes might also be involved; for instance, the human girl may offer a risk-free source of warm blood, while the vampire boy offers superior physical protection. Most importantly, both sides hope to benefit from the trade.

Despite its unusual features, the mating market shares key features with other markets. The most salient of these is competition. In general, more competition on the other side of the market is good for you, because it improves your options and increases your bargaining power. If vampire boys outnumber the human girls on the market, then even an average girl has a chance of snagging a truly sparkly vamp. Moreover, she can command a higher "implicit price" in terms of a potential boyfriend's behavior. If he's the kind of vampire who feeds on other girls, or he doesn't keep that fresh-from-the-crypt odor under control, there are plenty of other vampire boys ready to step in. On the other hand, if the human girls outnumber the vampire boys on the market, then some girls will have to do without. Those who do successfully reel in a vampire mate may have to make greater sacrifices, such as tolerating greater broodiness and nineteenth-century fashion choices.

If this seems hard to believe, consider the effect of the increasing ratio of women to men at American colleges and universities. "On college campuses where there are far more women than men," writes sociologist Kathleen A. Bogle, "men have all the power to control the intensity of sexual and romantic relationships."[3] This result is dependent, of course, on most of the women being heterosexual. A similar situation has occurred in nursing homes, another environment where women tend to outnumber men.

So which is it—do the interested vampires outnumber the interested humans or vice versa? The evidence is scant, but it seems to indicate that vamps will have the upper hand. The population of human girls (like the rest of the population) is increasing worldwide, and the ongoing vampire dating craze means a rising percentage of them will enter the market. Meanwhile, the vampire population is much smaller than the human population, and boys both living and dead also appear less susceptible to the current fad (note that women constituted a whopping 79 percent of the audience for the final *Twilight* movie).[4]

On the other hand, human girls tend to exit the datable age range within a decade or two, while vampire bachelors can remain highly eligible for centuries. In addition, if vampires lack a safe means of acquiring human blood or a substitute for it, they may see having a human girlfriend as their best option. Both of these factors will weigh on the opposite side of the scale, giving human girls a bit more market power. Ultimately, you'll need to assess the market conditions in your region to predict which side has the better bargaining position.

LOOKING FOR LOVE (IN ALL THE RANK PLACES)

Although the effect of competition is similar across markets, a key feature that distinguishes mating markets from many other markets is heterogeneity. Finding a romantic partner isn't like going to the grocery store and picking out one of a hundred identical bags of rice. Vampire boys differ from each other in age, beauty, wealth, psychotic tendencies, and so on. Human girls differ substantially as well. The quality of the mate matters, to both sides. To complicate matters further, not every couple is a "good fit"; we all know perfectly nice couples who just don't belong together, however much they try. So the quality of the *match* matters as well. In this respect, the mating market resembles other markets with heterogeneous people searching for good matches: the job market and the housing market. As it turns out, economists have used the same model—known as "search-matching"—to understand all three of these markets. In fact, three economists shared the 2010 Nobel Prize in Economics for their research in this area.[5]

Suppose you're a human girl interested in vampire boys. Since you can't just go pick one up at the store, you must search for one—for example, by keeping an eye out in school, night spots, and local cemeteries. On any given day, you may or may not meet a vampire. And if you do meet one, he may or may not suit your fancy—or you may not suit his. So there's a large element of randomness involved, because you can't be certain of finding a good match in a finite amount of time.

Now suppose you've just met a vampire boy named Arnold. He's reasonably good looking, but no Edward Cullen. (I'm assuming that girls do in fact find Edward Cullen very attractive, for reasons beyond my understanding.) And Arnold's nice, but a little on the broody side for your taste. Should you embark on a relationship with him? If you start dating him now, you could be taking yourself off the market too quickly. If you hold out just a little while longer, maybe you'll find your Edward! Then again, if you turn Arnold down and keep looking, you could end up searching for months or years without meeting anyone better. You might end up wistfully wishing you'd snapped up Arnold when you had the chance.

So what should you do? In the search-matching model, the best strategy is to calculate your *reservation level of romantic satisfaction*. Your reservation level corresponds to the lowest-quality boy that you'd be willing to date. You'll start a relationship with any boy who meets or exceeds this quality level and reject anyone else. (In labor markets, your *reservation wage* serves a similar purpose: it's the lowest wage offer you would accept.)

You might think a reservation level sounds a lot like "standards," and you'd be right. But many people foolishly think of "standards" as entailing strict requirements for every quality of a mate, from sex appeal to political party. Economists know better, because they know trade-offs are possible. You might, for instance, be willing to sacrifice a small amount of devilish good looks for a large enough increase in otherworldly charm. Rigid standards could prevent you from making that trade-off, thus ruling out some perfectly acceptable mates. By targeting your *overall* satisfaction, a reservation level avoids that mistake. When you raise your reservation level, you're not necessarily demanding a vampire mate who's better on every dimension—just one who's a better package all things considered.

SOME VAMPIRES ONLY SPARKLE ON THE INSIDE

What would happen if all human girls wanted the same kind of vampire boys? If every girl had the same preferences, then it would be possible to objectively rank the objects of their affection, from the dreamiest vampire to the foulest. And likewise, if vampires all wanted the same things in human girls, then the girls could also be ranked from best to worst. In that situation, economic theory says that romantic partnerships would tend to form between people of similar quality: the best vampire gets the best girl, the second-best vampire gets the second-best girl, and so on. The more smoothly and efficiently the dating market works, the closer this prediction comes to reality. Economists call this outcome *assortative matching*.

Of course, people don't really have identical preferences. We want different things, and more importantly, we put different weight on those things. Some girls want a vampire with forever-youthful beauty, while others focus on the centuries-old bank account. Some vampires care more about a girl's charm and wit, but others care more about her blood type. As a result, there's no truly objective ranking of partners. Nevertheless, to the extent that people tend to like similar things, there will be a loose ranking, and some assortative matching will result. It's no mistake that Bella chose Edward, not Count Orlok of the Nosferatu.

Why does it matter? Because it means you have to set your reservation level of romantic satisfaction carefully. A girl who's attractive to almost everyone can safely choose a higher reservation level. A girl who's less conventionally desirable may have to set her reservation level lower. It may not seem fair, but it's a reality. That means it's useful to have a realistic (neither too positive nor too negative) idea of your attractiveness to vampires with typical preferences, as well as to vampires with more idiosyncratic tastes. Keep in mind that what vampires consider attractive may differ from what humans do, which means girls who have had difficulty with traditional dating may fare better on the cross-the-grave dating scene—the best example being Sookie Stackhouse, whose limited experience with human boys was fully eclipsed by her success with vampires.

The key to calculating your reservation level of romantic satisfaction is *balance*. If you set your reservation level just right, it should exactly balance two things: (1) the loss from settling for a lower-quality partner versus (2) the risk associated with going longer with no partner at all, continuing your search, and still possibly ending up single.

Your reservation level should be affected by both market conditions and your personal preferences. Here are the most relevant factors to consider:

Your satisfaction with being single. The happier you are unpartnered, the longer it makes sense to wait. You can afford to hold out for a higher-quality vampire, which means your reservation level should be higher. And this implies another lesson: do whatever you can to increase your happiness while alone. Cultivate a life that's worth living even without an undead man at your side.

The eccentricity of your preferences. As discussed above, human girls and vampire boys with typical preferences can expect to pair off with partners of similar quality, according to the typical scale. But if you have unusual preferences, you may have an advantage. There may be vampires out there

who rank highly on *your* scale but not everyone else's. Maybe you're secretly aroused by peculiar accents from dead languages, or you dig the Civil
War–era grizzled look that other girls shun. The weirder your preferences
are, the more you can raise your reservation level, because you can capitalize
on all the quirky vampires that other (typical) girls are passing by.

The cost of search. Beyond the time spent single instead of coupled,
searching for a partner involves time, energy, money, and sometimes risk. If
you live in a place where vampires have come out of the coffin and mingle
openly with the living, then finding them shouldn't be that costly—especially
since vampires tend to be wealthy and spring for drinks. But if your town's
undead avoid the human nightlife in favor of dungeons, sewers, and graveyards—locations both unpleasant and dangerous—then the cost of search is
correspondingly high. In the former case, it's rational to raise your reservation level; in the latter case, it's rational to lower it.

Your level of impatience (or, as economists call it, your *discount rate*). An
impatient person puts relatively greater value on the present versus the future. The more impatient you are, the more it makes sense to settle for a
somewhat lower-quality match in order to shorten the wait. On the other
hand, the more patient you are, the more the future is worth to you, and hence
the greater the value of waiting for a better vampire.

The dating strategy of vampires. Keep in mind that vampire boys will be
doing the same thing you are doing. They, too, must decide whom to date and
whom to reject—meaning they, too, will have reservation levels of romantic
satisfaction. Strategically, you have to take that into account when choosing
your reservation level. The more picky vampires are, the fewer vampires
you'll meet who think you're good enough for them. That will make your
search process harder and thus provide a good reason for you to be *less*
picky.

So what should we expect about vampires' pickiness? They will consider
the same factors that you do—but they may reach different conclusions. In
particular, given their immortality and lack of aging, they will tend to be
more patient than humans. That, in turn, will tend to raise their reservation
levels, because they can wait longer for the right girl to come along. If they
don't date you, they might date your granddaughter![6]

The availability of potential mates. As discussed earlier, the number of
vampire boys relative to human girls will affect the "implicit price" of a
relationship. But the number of vampires also affects the cost of search. The
more vampires there are, the greater the likelihood that you'll meet one on
any given day. In addition, more vampires means a greater variety of vampire types—and thus a greater chance of meeting one who strikes your particular fancy. The girl who likes *Downton Abbey* has a better chance of finding
a vampire who will watch it with her, while the steampunk girl has a better
chance of finding one who also enjoys cosplay.

For that reason, you might think about moving to a place where vampires are more common. In so doing, you would be following the lead of gay men raised in small towns where other gay men are rare: they often move to the city, especially gay-friendly cities like San Francisco and Seattle. In addition, you should consider online dating, which has drastically lowered the cost of search for everyone—but especially people with specific or unusual preferences in mates. Sociological research shows that online dating has, in fact, increased the partnership rate among people who have a difficult time meeting available people of their type, including gay men, lesbians, and middle-aged heterosexuals.[7] There are now websites that cater to Jewish people (JDate.com), tall people (TallFriends.com), fans of *Star Trek* (trekpassions.com), prison inmates (Meet-An-Inmate.com), and—you'll be pleased to hear—people who want to date vampires (VampirePassions.com). Assuming the vampire dating websites feature any actual vampires, you may be in luck.

You might worry that moving to a city or cruising a website frequented by vampires would be pointless because too many other human girls would go there. As a result, you could find yourself competing for the vampires' attention—and, as we learned earlier, competition on your own side of the market tends to make you worse off. But in this case, your concern is probably unwarranted. While the greater competition from other girls might hurt you, the greater competition among vampires will help you, *plus* everyone will face lower search costs. The greater numbers will increase the variety on both sides, enhancing the likelihood of good matches for particular tastes. The result is what economists call a *thick market*, where both sides have a better chance of getting what they want.

In this respect, the mating market is much like the housing market. While home sellers and buyers cannot (usually) move houses to different locations, they can choose to enter the market at different times. For various reasons, such as the timing of school years, some people prefer to buy homes in the spring and summer. That attracts more home owners to offer their homes for sale at that time—which attracts yet more buyers to seek homes at that time. As a result, more homes get sold, and at higher prices, during the "hot season" than the "cold season."[8] And arguably, this makes both sides better off—the sellers because they get higher prices, and the buyers because they get homes that better fit their needs (more than enough to compensate for the higher price). That's the power of thick markets, and it's one that daters with unusual preferences would be well advised to take advantage of.

There is another way to expand your set of available partners. As unpleasant as it may seem, you could widen the pool to include beings other than vampires. Judging by *Twilight*, *True Blood*, and the Anita Blake series, werewolves and other shape-shifters seem like perfectly viable options. If *Warm Bodies* can be relied upon, some zombies could make the cut. And if you're really willing to stretch, you might even consider exceptional human boys. Widening your options will both lower your cost of search and increase your bargaining power.

I WANNA DO BAD THINGS WITH YOU, OR SOMEONE LIKE YOU

When discussing the search-matching model of mating, it's impossible for us to avoid the issue of "the one." If you believe that everyone has just one soul mate (or soulless mate) in the entire world, then the economic approach I've described above may sound crass, even foolish. The only correct strategy is simply to wait until you meet your one and only . . . right? But in a world with billions of people, believing in the "the one" is unreasonable. How lucky would you have to be to find that one needle in a haystack? As economist David Friedman puts it: "While many of us like to believe that our husbands or wives were uniquely suited to that role, it is not true; if it were, the chance of finding them would be remote. I at one time did some rough calculations on the subject and concluded that my present wife is about a one in two hundred thousand catch."[9]

It would be both more accurate and more beneficial, then, to think not about "the one," but "the set." There is some group of people out there (some living, some dead) who could be a good match for you. And perhaps more empowering is that, by setting your reservation level of romantic satisfaction, you are deciding the size of your set.

Chapter Two

Human Girls and Vampire Boys, Part 2

'Til Death Do Us Part

Glen Whitman

> You're immortal. She's not. It's not easy. I married my Edna Mae in aught three, and I was with her right until the end. Not a pretty picture. Wrinkled and senile and cursing me for my youth. It wasn't our happiest time.
> —*Buffy the Vampire Slayer*, "Choices" (1999)

So you've found the dead man of your dreams. The search is over, but the economic analysis has only just begun. For perspective on the inner logic of committed relationships, we turn to Oliver Williamson's Nobel-winning work on the governance of firms—and, specifically, what he called *the fundamental transformation*.[1] If you're on Team Edward, you might think the fundamental transformation is a human getting turned into a vampire. Or if you're on Team Jacob, you might think it's a boy morphing into a wolf. But if you're an economist, it's the fact that entering a new relationship—whether a job or a marriage—transforms a competitive market into a monopoly.

LET'S STAKE TOGETHER: WHY RELATIONSHIPS LAST

When you're looking for a new mate, you're shopping on a competitive market: you have many options, as do your potential partners. But as soon as you settle down, *something changes*. You start to make investments in your relationship—and, hopefully, so does he. You gain knowledge of each other's tastes and quirks, like how you love sparkly clean fangs and he prefers type A blood. You develop routines that allow you to coordinate your schedules, which can be particularly hard when one of you sleeps in the daytime. And you create memories that are special just to you, like that time you faced

11

down an army of bigoted anti-human vampires side by side. If you move in together, your new home will require a substantial investment in packing, decorating, coffin installation, and so on. Children, too, are an investment you make together. (There is some doubt as to whether human-vampire offspring are possible, but I take *Twilight: Breaking Dawn—Part 2* as the definitive statement on the matter.) If you ever broke up, some of these assets that you've created together would become worthless, and others would lose much of their value. If you want to keep them as they are, you're locked into bargaining with just one person. The situation is no longer competitive—it's a monopoly. And because the same problem affects both partners, it's a bilateral monopoly.

That change is what Williamson dubbed the fundamental transformation, and it happens in business as well as romance. When a firm looks for a new employee, there are many potential employees to choose from (and the employee can choose from many other firms as well). But after the new hire comes aboard, he starts to gain knowledge and skills that are valuable solely to this employer: familiarity with the company's routines, training in its production methods, and so on. If the firm fired him, or if he quit, they both would lose something. The value of their *relationship-specific assets*[2] gives them a strong incentive to stay together, even if their relationship should become strained.

And that is true of a romantic partnership, too. After all, why do people partner up to begin with? Because there's something they can create together that they couldn't create alone. But ironically, these shared assets can also contribute to strife within the relationship. In the competitive environment, there is little reason to argue about anything. Don't like the weird guy who just interviewed for assistant manager? Don't hire him! Don't like the creepy vampire who bared his fangs on the first date? Lose his number and nail a cross to your door! But the further your relationship has progressed, the more valuable your relationship-specific assets will be, and thus the harder it will be to walk away.

In considering the value of continuing a relationship versus walking away, you should be careful not to fall prey to the *sunk cost fallacy*. Sunk costs are costs that have already been incurred and cannot be recovered, and the fallacy is letting them influence your choices. For instance, suppose you've bought a nonrefundable ticket to see a concert (Vampire Weekend, naturally) on Sunday night—and then you get invited to a *True Blood* viewing party on the same night. In deciding what to do, the $100 you've already spent on the concert ticket is irrelevant, because you can't get it back anyway; the only thing that matters is whether you would enjoy the concert or the party more.[3] Likewise, the time and effort you've spent building a relationship are sunk costs. You're never getting them back, no matter what you do. But what does matter is what your time and effort have bought you: the shared routines, memories, home, and so on, whose value will decrease or vanish if you break up. The value of these relationship-specific assets might, indeed, be enough to justify continuing your cross-the-grave romance.

BLEEDING HEARTS: WHY RELATIONSHIPS SUFFER

Once you've taken the plunge with a new partner, the competitive market has less influence over the terms of your relationship, and either or both parties may try to change them. The employee may suddenly demand more vacation time; the employer might move him to a smaller office. Similarly, you or your undead partner might subtly alter the terms of your bargain by shirking on chores, having sex less often, or constantly tracking blood into the house. These attempts to alter the terms of a partnership after it has already begun are known as *post-contractual opportunism*. Williamson defines opportunism as "self-interest seeking with guile," which he says "includes but is scarcely limited to more blatant forms, such as lying, stealing, and cheating. Opportunism more often involves subtle forms of deceit."[4]

For a specific example, consider Elena and Stefan in *The Vampire Diaries*. Not long after they have become romantically involved, Stefan "relapses" into the craving for human blood that he had allegedly kicked decades earlier. He steals bags of blood and even feeds on another girl.[5] If he had behaved this way when they met, Elena would surely have avoided him like the plague. But in the context of their ongoing relationship, she stays by his side to help him overcome his addiction.

As Elena and Stefan's example shows, people will often tolerate even egregious violations in order to salvage their relationships. This makes sense because of the value of relationship-specific assets. And yet, over time, the attempts by both parties to have their way can eat away at the value of the relationship as a whole.

So what can be done? Sadly, many of the answers available in the business context aren't available in the romantic one. You could try to anticipate these problems and write them into a prenuptial agreement, but it's hard to foresee everything that might go wrong, and it's also difficult to enforce such agreements in exacting detail—especially if the courts won't enforce contracts with the dead. Another alternative is to use the threat of walking out and finding a new lover, like the handsome werewolf boy down the street. But threats tend to discourage emotional investment and trust within the relationship, which was the whole point of getting together.

Fortunately, there is one solution that does tend to work: the promise of repeat business. A relationship is not just one transaction, but a series of them over time. This is what economists call a *repeated game*. As it turns out, cooperation is easier to sustain in repeated games than in one-off transactions. A firm that repeatedly breaks its promises to a key employee may lose that employee's loyalty and dedication, and soon he may begin shirking on his duties and "borrowing" from the supply room for personal use. The threat of that happening gives the firm an incentive to treat the employee well to begin with. Similarly, every time your vampire mate tries to take advantage of you, he knows that you may do the same to him—and vice versa. As a result, you each have good reason to play nice in the first place, in order to avoid multiple rounds of unpleasant behavior that make both of you unhappy.

Or there might be a simpler answer. One of those relationship-specific assets is *love*—which in economic terms we might define as gaining pleasure from someone else's well-being. To the extent that you invest in love, you're cultivating an asset that will tend to protect all the other assets, because it gives each of you an incentive to maximize your combined happiness rather than yours alone.

Given the fundamental transformation, it's no surprise that almost every relationship has its fair share of strife. But that alone shouldn't cause you to throw in the towel; if it did, then few relationships would ever stand the test of time. Nevertheless, even though it's not true that *all* good things come to an end, at least some of them do. How will you know when, and whether, to call it quits?

FANGS FOR THE MEMORIES: WHY RELATIONSHIPS END

In *True Blood*, Sookie Stackhouse eventually dumps Bill Compton when she learns something new about him: that when they met, Bill intended to verify her fairy heritage and then "procure" her for the Vampire Queen of Louisiana, who wished to feed on her fairy blood.[6] Hearing this, Sookie feels too betrayed to continue the relationship.

One way to look at Sookie and Bill's breakup is through the lens of uncertainty. We all have to make choices about whom to get involved with based on incomplete information, and as a result we make some guesses. When new information reveals our guesses to have been mistaken, we reevaluate our choices. Seen this way, Sookie has learned that Bill is less honest and admirable than she had thought, which diminishes his value as a mate. She thought Bill exceeded her reservation level of romantic satisfaction (see chapter 1), but now she knows better.

Or we could look at their breakup through the lens of relationship-specific assets. Recall that many of the assets created in a relationship are memories, which you can remember fondly in the years to come. But the revelation of Bill's secret agenda *permanently changes those memories*. Sookie can't remember the good times anymore without also thinking, "When I was lying in his arms that night, he was still lying to me." The value of her memories having depreciated substantially, Sookie no longer regards being involved with Bill as superior to being single again.

Whichever of these explanations is closer to the truth, they both illustrate the simple logic of breaking up: you should break up when the value of continuing your present relationship is less than the expected value of going back on the singles market. Both of the reasons just discussed imply a sudden *drop* in the value of Sookie's relationship—apparently a large enough drop to make the difference. However, there is another possibility: what if the expected value of going back on the market *rises*?

Not long after dumping Bill, Sookie jumps into a relationship with Eric Northman, the sexy Viking vampire with whom she had exchanged smoldering glances for months. Sookie supposedly didn't ditch Bill with the specific intention of dating Eric. Nevertheless, during her time with Bill, Sookie had become much more familiar with the vampire community. Bill was the first vampire she had ever met. At the time, he must have seemed a rare find; she still perceived the availability of vampires as low, despite their having recently come out of the coffin. But soon she learned that vampires were everywhere and that many found her alluring. That discovery should have raised her expected value of going back on the singles market. So we cannot discount the possibility that Sookie and Bill's relationship was doomed even before the revelation that sunk it.

In your own undead relationships, you may never find yourself considering a breakup—in which case you probably don't need to. You chose a good match to begin with, and your subsequent relationship has only strengthened your bond (i.e., the value of your relationship-specific assets). But should a breakup start to seem worthwhile, you need to ask yourself what has changed. Have you learned new information or formed new preferences? If so, have these changes lowered the value of the relationship or raised the value of singlehood?

One reason you might contemplate a breakup is that you're constantly bickering and strategizing over the terms of the relationship—that is, you're having bilateral monopoly problems. But problems like these can in principle be overcome, assuming the fundamentals haven't changed. The question is, does your bickering actually reveal anything you didn't already know— about yourself, your mate, or both? If not, then these are probably just the trials and tribulations of any long-term relationship. But maybe you've actually learned something from all that bickering: that your mate is an intransigent jerk who hasn't compromised in centuries. Or maybe the two of you mysteriously never argue about anything, which might seem great . . . until you realize that he's been glamouring you (*True Blood*) or compelling you (*The Vampire Diaries*) to accept all of his demands. Either way, you should revise the value of this relationship downward. If it drops far enough, it's time to put a stake in it.

IMMORTAL BELOVED?

Any discussion of human-vampire relationships raises the inevitable question: will she or won't she allow herself to be turned? A century ago, when everyone regarded vampires as irredeemably evil bloodsuckers, that question would have been inconceivable. But in the modern era, where vampires are seen as sensitive immortals with superpowers and a few mild self-control issues, more and more human girls may see vampirism as a viable option.

However, becoming undead also constitutes the most extreme of fundamental transformations. Given the relative rarity of human boys interested in vampire girls, the formerly human girl will find herself with reduced options on the singles market if she and her vampire beloved should ever break up. And, of course, she will face all the usual difficulties of vampires trying to fit into human society.

Nevertheless, the human girl's transition seems almost mandatory for the relationship's long-term survival. As time passes, normal human aging will tend to push the human girl downward relative to the vampire boy's reservation level of romantic satisfaction. For comparison, consider the fact that aging men are generally considered romantically eligible for longer than aging women. This disparity between men's and women's outside options can create discord within the relationship, and sometimes older men will opportunistically dump their wives in the hope (sometimes realized) of finding a younger, hotter partner. The fact that both men and women experience aging limits this problem in traditional human-human relationships to some extent, as both partners must adjust their expectations over time. But the vampire, remaining young forever, needn't ever adjust his standards.

Love and devotion—the most important of relationship-specific assets—may keep a vampire man around, but even so, the increasing discrepancy in their physical conditions will surely put stress on the relationship. Simply put, the mortal-immortal pairing is not a sustainable relationship model. Without conversion, every such pairing is doomed by the eventuality of death. And besides, if a vampire loves his human partner enough to stay with her to the bitter end, why not give her the gift of immortality instead? A human girl might rationally wonder why her lover would refuse her that precious gift. As human-vampire relationships become increasingly common, we should not be surprised to see "turning ceremonies" emerge as the ultimate signal of undying commitment.

Part II

Apocalyptonomics

When the zombie apocalypse arrives, society will change in dramatic ways, and depending on how things turn out, the economy may have to be built anew. This theme appears not just in zombie stories, but in apocalyptic scenarios caused by alien invasion (*Falling Skies*), the disappearance of electricity (*Revolution*), and the sudden death of the male half of the human race (*Y: The Last Man*). Stories like these remind us that economics looks at more than just individual behavior. It's also about how a society is constructed, whether it's through deliberate cooperation or through independent decisions that result in an emergent order. This section uses the zombie apocalypse as a lens to see how the economy connects the individual with society as a whole.

Long-term survival after the collapse will take more than just guns and duct tape. What will stuff be worth, and how can we maximize the value of what we bring with us? James Dow shows how basic economic principles can guide us in preparing for the coming zombie hordes.

Fighting the zombies will also require the use of significant economic resources, much like preparations for war and reconstruction after natural disasters. Some people say that events like these can actually benefit society as a whole by stimulating economic activity. Are they right? Steven Horwitz and Sarah Skwire address the question of whether a zombie invasion could produce an economic boom.

After the initial panic and chaos, sooner or later humanity will start to rebuild civilization. What will it take to start improving living standards in a post-apocalyptic world? Drawing on the seminal insights of Adam Smith, the founder of modern economics, Brian Hollar explains what we will lose after the apocalypse, and how we can start to get it back.

The bottom line, of course, is who will win in the end, the humans or the zombies? Unfortunately, the movies seem undecided. Kyle William Bishop, David Tufte, and Mary Jo Tufte use the theory of comparative dynamics to analyze how things will play out and show what will be needed for the humans to triumph—if that's possible.

Finally, Jean-Baptiste Fleury and Alain Marciano look at the problem from the opposite side, from the perspective of the zombies. How do zombies coordinate their activities to accomplish collective goals, and what does this imply for humans? When it comes to cooperating with one another, perhaps zombies and humans aren't as different as they appear.

—GW & JD

Chapter Three

Packing for the Zombie Apocalypse

James Dow

THEY'RE COMING TO GET YOU

The news out of Pittsburgh is bad. The dead have come to life and nothing the police or army can do seems to stop the flesh-eating hordes as they spread across the country. Do you have your emergency zombie apocalypse kit so that you can begin to plan your escape?

Fortunately for us, that zombie outbreak near Pittsburgh was just a movie. But it could happen. And if it does, it's important that everyone has made the necessary preparations. Of course, what goes into your zombie apocalypse kit depends on how you think the zombie attack will play out. If the zombies will be rounded up in a short period of time, then you just need what it takes to hole up in your house for a week or two (although this advice never seems to work so well in the movies).[1] Alternatively, if you think the zombie apocalypse will involve the "fast" zombies of modern movies, such as *World War Z* or *28 Days Later*, I have bad news. While the movies require happy endings, in practice these zombies are just too fast and too powerful to be stopped. Prepare, don't prepare, the reality is that you'll be eaten all the same. There's no point in spending resources to prepare if this is how things will turn out.

But probably the more realistic outcome is the stories told by slow-zombie fiction such as *The Walking Dead* or the George Romero movies. In Romero's first movie, *Night of the Living Dead*, the dead arrive and attack a small group holed up in a Pennsylvania farmhouse. The movie follows their mostly failed efforts to survive the night but ends with the comforting sight of local law enforcement walking through the surrounding fields killing the slow-moving zombies. However, in the second movie, *Dawn of the Dead*, the zombies are starting to get the upper hand and order is beginning to collapse. By the third movie, *Day of the Dead*, zombies rule the world and only pockets of survivors are left. Civilization is starting over.

Unfortunately, self-help books like *The Zombie Survival Guide* don't provide much assistance for this situation (what it calls a "Class 4 Event"), and so it's up to us to look to economic theory for insight in how to prepare. It's best to assume that other humans will survive; if not, neither will we. But the existence of other humans also changes the nature of the problem. When it comes to survival for the first month after the invasion begins, the popular handbooks get it mostly right: water, weapons, canned goods, batteries, duct tape. But eventually, these things will run out. If you're planning for long-term survival, you're going to need to think further ahead. In addition to bringing things that will help you *directly*, you will also want to bring things that could bring great value *when traded to others*. That means you need to make some guesses about what things will be worth. Fortunately, economic theory can provide some guidance on the value of things in the post-apocalyptic world.

ADAM SMITH'S PUZZLE

Determining what something is worth is one of the oldest issues in economics. It can be a puzzle, because sometimes things that seem like they ought to be valuable sell for little while other, less useful things sell for more. One version of this puzzle, introduced by the famous eighteenth-century economist Adam Smith, has come to be known as the *diamond-water paradox*. The paradox is this: water is necessary for life. You literally can't live without it, and yet it sells for so little that we treat a glass of water as essentially being free. On the other hand, diamonds are frivolous baubles, and yet a single diamond can be worth more than swimming pools of water. How is usefulness so loosely tied to value?

The solution to the puzzle is to recognize that not all glasses of water are alike. You would certainly give up a diamond for the only glass of water when you're stranded in the Sahara and it's the one thing that will save your life. On the other hand, your fourth glass of water on a slightly warm day is nice, but you could do without it. This relationship between value and quantity consumed shows up in less life-saving situations as well. Your first hot dog at the ball game is great, your second is okay, and the fourth probably makes you worse off. Economists call this pattern *diminishing marginal utility*. The value (utility) you get from consuming an additional (marginal) item diminishes for each additional item you consume.

The price of a good, what it exchanges for, therefore depends on how much of it there is relative to how much people want it—in other words, *scarcity*. If water is scarce and there's only enough to satisfy basic needs, it will be expensive. If water is plentiful, consumers can satisfy their basic needs *and* shower *and* water their yards. In a competitive market, the price of water is determined by the value of the *last* bit of water used (in other words, the first bit of water people are willing to give up). If there's enough water that people will use it up to the point where they are watering their yards, the marginal value of water will be low and the price will be cheap.

In our pre-zombie world, diamonds are scarce and water is plentiful, so diamonds are expensive and water is cheap. But it may not be that way in a post-apocalypse world. What is scarce will depend on how things turn out. If you settle in a temperate climate, it's likely that water will not be all that scarce, especially given the significant drop in the human population. Food is another example. While food is essential for life, the diminished population may be able to live off what is left in stores in the short run, and given that zombies seem to prefer human flesh over animal, hunting game should be an option in the long run. So what will be both valuable and scarce? Gasoline, perhaps? I'll return to this issue by the end, but before that we need to think about the other half of the problem: what are the limits to what we can bring? If you think gasoline will be very valuable, then you might be tempted to fill up the back of your pickup truck with plastic containers full of fuel. But it's not so simple.

THE ECONOMIC PLANNER'S GUIDE TO KILLING ZOMBIES

In the most exciting part of the book *World War Z*, the author interviews Arthur Sinclair, the former director of the Department of Strategic Resources, in his home in New Mexico a few years after the war. Sinclair was responsible for the logistical aspects of running the war economy and was closely involved with the choice of which anti-zombie weapons to approve. This was a difficult question, as resources were limited, which meant the decision to build one type of weapon would rule out alternate approaches. What Sinclair and his staff recognized was that weapons were but a means to an end—a way to turn economic resources into killed zombies. They judged a weapon not on its inherent value but on how effective it was in that transformation. They summarized this information in terms of a resources-to-kill ratio (RKR), which helped them choose which weapon system to develop. Sinclair's comment from the interview: "What was so amazing to see was how the culture of RKR began to take hold among the rank and file. You'd hear soldiers talking on the street, in bars, on the train; 'Why have X, when for the same price you could have ten Ys, which could kill a hundred times as many Zs.'"[2]

Or, to return to the question at hand, why have a cubic foot of gasoline when instead that same cubic foot of space could be filled with a number of smaller and lighter items that could collectively be exchanged for more? This trade-off captures perfectly economists' notion of *opportunity cost*. The real cost of something, the opportunity cost, is the value of the next best opportunity, what you have to give up to do what you want to do. During the apocalypse, the cost of taking something with you is the value of what you have to leave behind.

The cost of foregone opportunities shows up in many economic decisions. For example, when doing the cost-benefit analysis to see if it's a good idea to start your own business, you might treat your own time as having no cost; after all, you don't have to pay yourself. But that would be a mistake. If you didn't start the business, you could work somewhere else, and so the salary you give up is an opportunity cost of starting your own business and needs to be factored into the decision.

While today weight and volume are not the prime determinants of the opportunity cost of the decisions we make (time seems to be the modern constraint), in a zombie world we need to travel light, and so weight and volume matter. The goods we bring should be scarce, valuable, and low-cost in terms of the constraints on what we can bring. However, the importance of those constraints suggests a different approach.

A TOAST TO YOUR SURVIVAL

The title of "Worst Zombie Movie Ever" is hotly contested. *Hillbilly Bob Zombie* is certainly in the running; I made it through about ten minutes before giving up (in other words, don't bother). But what brought me to it was the premise. In the zombie literature, there are a few major "creation myths." The original version was that zombies were created by voodoo priests (*I Walked with a Zombie*). In more recent movies, it's a biological cause such as a virus, either a domestic mutation (*World War Z*) or something extraterrestrial (*Night of the Living Dead*). Sometimes chemicals, often from a government experiment gone horribly wrong, are what reanimates the dead (*Return of the Living Dead*). *Hillbilly Bob Zombie* provides a novel take on the chemical story. The protagonists of the movie decide to set up a backyard still, and they find an abandoned barrel off the side of the road that seems ideal for the job. Unfortunately, the barrel formerly contained toxic waste, which ends up contaminating the moonshine and turning the drinkers into zombies. Havoc ensues. [3]

Let's face it, after the world has passed through a zombie apocalypse and civilization as we know it has collapsed, it's probably alcohol that will be in popular demand. In fact, distilled beverages may turn out to be water's highest-valued use. You may want to take advantage of this prediction. From an economic point of view, alcohol is just a technology for turning water and grain into drunken people. To make the most of this entrepreneurial venture, you want to be involved at the right part of the process, where value is high and opportunity cost is low. Bringing water and grain would take up a lot of space. Premade alcohol would take less space, but it's still pretty heavy. The better thing to do would be to bring a still, with the expectation that water and things to ferment (grain or potatoes or fruit) will be in plentiful enough supply.

Owning the means of production, what economists call *physical capital*, offers several potential benefits.[4] It leverages what you bring, since typically the value of the goods produced by the physical capital will exceed the value of the capital itself. Labor, by definition, comes with you, and raw materials are less beneficial to bring because they are bulky (high opportunity cost) and are likely to be abundant anyway due to the reduced population.

There are some risks to this strategy. One risk is that when zombies attack, they kill people but leave their goods behind. It might be that all sorts of useful capital will be left lying around, and so packing your own would be a waste. However, capital can be very specific to the goods being produced and the structure of the economy (as we will see later), and so what we find lying around may not be what is needed.

It's also important to take into account what other survivors will bring. If everyone brings their own stills, then alcohol will be in plentiful supply, and we know from the diamond/water paradox that this will make alcohol have low value in exchange, even if alcohol on average is highly valued. If you think alcohol will be in plentiful supply, then think of what else might be scarce. Guns will be valuable, which means ammunition will also be valuable. But sooner or later the ammunition will run out, so if you are packing for the long run, instead of bringing bullets, bring the physical capital needed to make bullets. Perhaps shotgun shells, which are relatively easy to manufacture and have parts that can be reused. Or find another key point in the process of transforming materials into dead zombies: perhaps you should bring the tools to manufacture gunpowder.

BRAINS

The notion that zombies like to eat brains has a firm foothold in the public imagination, but there are surprisingly few movies where this happens. Much of the time zombies are shown eating viscera—viscera being especially disgusting and hence ideal for a horror movie. It was the movie *Return of the Living Dead* that really developed the idea of brain-eating zombies. In fact, the zombies themselves show surprising ingenuity in their hunt for brains. After killing and eating the brains of the paramedics who arrived on the scene, one zombie overhears a dispatcher speaking on the ambulance's radio.

Hoping to lure additional food, he imitates an ambulance driver and moans to the dispatcher "send . . . more . . . paramedics." A fresh supply of brains is promptly dispatched.

But brains are not only tasty, they are also one of the key resources underlying the modern economy. A significant portion of the wages and salaries that people earn are actually compensation for their *human capital*—the skills they have and the things they know. The reason that skills and knowledge are called human *capital* is to remind us that we can think about the creation of these skills in much the same way as we think about the creation of physical capital. When building a factory, we sacrifice resources now in order to be able to produce more goods in the future. To evaluate whether building a factory is a good idea, we compare the value of the resources we give up now with the potential gains down the line. It's the same with education; students pay tuition now and give up the income they could have earned by working (that's an opportunity cost) in order to acquire skills that will get them better jobs and greater incomes in the future. The monetary value of the education can be determined by comparing the increase in future income with the total costs of the education.

Of course, people have known about the value of human capital for a long time. There's an old proverb and economic principle that goes, "Give a man a fish and you feed him for a day, teach a man to fish and you feed him for a lifetime." However, we need to modify this somewhat. Specialization along with trade allows individuals to focus on producing what has the biggest reward to them in the market.[5] Instead of learning how to fish, it was better for me to specialize in being a professional economist. In this way, I could earn money with which to buy fish in the market and not have to spend my time waiting around some lake. Unfortunately, I expect the demand for economists to be low after the zombie apocalypse. It will be necessary to invest in learning the skills that produce goods with the most value for *that* economy. If you think that you should plan on producing and trading alcohol, then it's best to invest in learning how to operate a still efficiently. It takes time to learn these skills, but the return could be great if alcohol turns out to be highly valued after the apocalypse. And you should do it now when the opportunity cost is low, and not later when you are giving up time that could be better spent preventing zombies from eating you.

Better still, it might be worthwhile to invest your time learning how to *make* a still. The technology is not so complicated that it couldn't be made with materials that you are likely to find lying around. Of course, found materials won't produce a perfect still, but they have one great advantage: they don't have to be carried around by you from the start. This is a major advantage human capital has over physical capital—we can carry it in our brains.

Indeed, economist Reuben Kessel argued that the reason that Jewish culture has historically been associated with education is the portability of human capital.[6] There has been a long history of persecution of Jews, and when there is a significant risk that your property will be taken away from you, it may not be a good idea to invest in physical capital. Instead of owning land that could be appropriated or that you would have to leave behind when forced to move to a new city, it's better to invest in the knowledge of how to make things—knowledge that you can take with you. Similarly, when there are zombies around, traveling light is essential, and the things we know are the lightest things of all.

Of course, what you should know still depends on what will be scarce. If you think alcohol will be expensive, know how to build a still. If you believe shotguns will be valuable but ammunition more scarce, know how to make shotgun shells. If the electrical infrastructure will be gone and batteries scarce, know how to make a water mill that can generate electricity. Find the combination of high value, low cost, and the right technology.

YOUR NEXT VACATION

World War Z ends with mankind triumphing over the zombie hordes and reclaiming the earth. However, given how bad things get, I doubt it would have turned out that way. As described in the book, "the living dead controlled most of the world's landmass, while American war production depended on what could be harvested within the limits of the western states specifically."[7] There were two hundred million zombies in the United States alone.

While killing two hundred million zombies was certainly a military challenge, there was an economic problem as well. Interestingly, Arthur Sinclair, the director of the Department of Strategic Resources mentioned earlier, recognized the exact problem (by the way, he really is the hero of the book; why Brad Pitt didn't play him in the movie, I don't know). Sinclair had framed above his desk a label from a bottle of root beer listing the ingredients; these included nine different items from nine different countries, everything from vanilla from Madagascar to balsam oil from Peru. What this label symbolized was the complexity introduced by specialization and trade. In the modern global economy, the production of goods is based on a vast web of trade where products manufactured and sold in one country can depend on capital and materials from dozens of countries. And in Sinclair's words, "And that's just for a bottle of peacetime root beer. We're not even talking about something like a desktop PC, or a nuclear-powered aircraft carrier."[8]

The root beer label was to remind him of how complicated modern production is, but it also reminds us of why his efforts likely would have failed. One of the key turning points in the war was the development of a new bullet, the NATO 5.56 "Cherry" PIE, which would explode when it hit a zombie, so that even just grazing the head could destroy the brain. However, in a world where it would be hard to make root beer, imagine the difficulties of designing and manufacturing a new bullet in Hawaii (apparently a safe haven) when most of the world is overrun by zombies. You would need lead for the bullet, copper or steel for the casing, the explosive for the tip, the primer, the factories to refine the materials, the machinery to manufacture the bullets in Hawaii, the machine tools to manufacture the machinery to manufacture the bullets. And remember, we're talking about enough bullets to kill two hundred million zombies. A world full of zombies would not allow the level of specialization and trade required to support such a sophisticated technology.

As the war against the zombies went on, the economic connections that tie the current world together would continue to break and people would need to find simpler ways of doing things.[9] If people did survive (and again, there's little point in packing for the apocalypse if they didn't), then we need to imagine a different post-zombie world. In time, the zombies would wear out and small groups of humans who managed to survive would move forward to re-create civilization. But it would be a society that could no longer support the connections of the modern economy, at least not for the foreseeable future. Mechanization would disappear and travel would become difficult. And in a world where your life is built around your local village, there is little opportunity for specialization.[10]

A post-zombie world would turn out to be one where power and transportation primarily come from animals and manufacturing is done by hand by one or two individuals rather than a factory full of workers. In fact, this world sounds a lot like the American colonies in the early 1700s.

Which brings us to Colonial Williamsburg. If you wanted the country to plan for a zombie apocalypse, you might think the most important thing would be to set up installations to preserve modern technology. However, existing books do that pretty well (although less well each year as the Internet—which would not survive the apocalypse—increasingly takes over). What is really needed is a setting that preserves the *older* technologies today; knowledge that might have been lost otherwise but will be needed after the zombies come. Colonial Williamsburg is a re-created American village with architecture and costumes consistent with the U.S. colonial era. In addition to imitating the appearances of the time, the village also features demonstrations of a wide range of colonial-era crafts. It has blacksmiths, brickmakers, coopers, gunsmiths, wheelwrights, shoemakers, and weavers, each of them masters of a technology suitable for a simpler time. Of course, you don't have to limit yourself to learning skills from that period. Modern shotguns may be simple enough to fit in with an eighteenth-century world. Alternatively, you might want to visit a Renaissance fair or a Society for Creative Anachronism gathering to learn how to make swords and armor.

While there is little evidence that Renaissance fairs or Colonial Williamsburg were actually secretly set up in preparation for the zombie apocalypse, they serve that purpose all the same. So if you're worried about surviving the apocalypse, you need to pack wisely by taking into account marginal value and opportunity cost. But it's likely that your human capital will be the most important thing you carry. So what I suggest is that you make good use of your next summer vacation. Visit Colonial Williamsburg. And pay attention.

Chapter Four

Eating Brains and Breaking Windows

Steven Horwitz and Sarah Skwire

> This is the way the world ends; not with a bang or a whimper, but with zombies breaking down the back door.
> —Amanda Hocking, *Hollowland*

The night is dark and full of terrors. You cower in your basement, behind a barricaded door, shotgun and ax at the ready. You pray they will not find you. But you can hear them coming inexorably closer. Blood-curdling moans rend the eerie hush of a city gone into hiding. The limping drag of clumsy footsteps scrapes the floorboards above your hiding place. Relentless, rhythmic thuds warn you that the basement door is about to give way. And the crash of breaking glass, as more and more of them pound the windows and fight to enter your home, announces in no uncertain terms the arrival of the zombie apocalypse.

A panicked economist hiding from zombies in the basement would find the sound of that breaking window evocative. The *broken window fallacy* is the term for a parable written by the nineteenth-century French economist Frédéric Bastiat.[1] He asks his reader to imagine a small village in which a young boy throws a brick through a window. At first, the villagers are horrified, but after a while someone suggests that maybe this isn't such a bad thing as, after all, the homeowner will now have to pay the glazier for a new window, thus encouraging his business. Although Bastiat stops there, one could also note that the glazier will then have income, perhaps to spend on a new suit, giving the tailor more income, and so on. Soon the whole village joins in and persuades themselves of the economic benefits of the broken window.

We often see this way of thinking in response to natural disasters and even social disasters like urban riots. In the aftermath of a hurricane or earthquake, it is inevitable that some commentators will try to find the silver lining in the tragedy by noting that all of the efforts at rebuilding will create jobs and generate economically beneficial spending. For example, Agustino Fontevecchia at Forbes.com wrote of Hurricane Sandy:

> Destruction wreaked by Hurricane Sandy may reach $50 billion, putting it roughly in-line with the second most devastating storm in postwar history. At the end of the day, Sandy may end up being beneficial for the U.S. economy, pushing indicators like construction spending, industrial production, and retail sales above their pre-disaster trend-lines over the next few quarters, according to Goldman Sachs. With the American East Coast getting back on its feet, and amid unquantifiable damage to individuals' lives, initial analysis of the latest natural disaster strike suggests the storm may end up being a good thing from a purely economic standpoint.[2]

We see a similar theme at work in arguments in favor of preparations for war. Even the Nobel Prize–winning economist Paul Krugman half-seriously suggested (in a 2011 appearance on CNN) that one way to help the U.S. economy recover from the crash of 2008 would be the threat of an alien invasion, as it would induce a great deal of spending on preparations that would create jobs and boost Gross Domestic Product (GDP).[3]

For the same reasons, it might seem that a zombie apocalypse would be a boon to the economy. If we imagine events unfolding in stages, the first of which would be preparations for the apocalypse, people will clearly begin their apocalypse-driven spending on weaponry or other forms of home security. They might begin to make plans for escape by purchasing plane tickets or buying vehicles that they think could survive. A thriving side market in human smuggling will likely develop as people attempt to avoid infection by crossing into safer territories without undergoing what will surely be increased border scrutiny. Max Brooks's *World War Z: An Oral History of the Zombie War* includes an interview with one such smuggler, Nury Televaldi, who notes, "Air smuggling became big business in the eastern provinces. There were rich clients, the ones who could afford prebooked travel packages and first-class tourist visas. They would step off the plane at London or Rome, or even San Francisco, check into their hotels, go out for a day's sightseeing, and simply vanish into thin air. That was big money."[4] And the big money, observes Televaldi, did not stop with his own personal profit. "I made a lot of people rich: border guards, bureaucrats, police, even the mayor. There were still good times for China, where the best way to honor Chairman Mao's memory was to see his face on as many hundred yuan notes as possible."[5] And as wealthier countries increasingly tightened their border controls, poorer countries ran side markets in providing papers to smugglers to help them evade regulations. "They practically begged us for the business. Those countries were in such economic shambles, their officials were so backward and corrupt, they actually helped us with the paperwork in exchange for a percentage of our fee."[6]

The uninfected might also attempt to become more self-sufficient in order to minimize their contact with other humans. Brooks's book records a vivid description of one such "survivalist's wet dream." "He had enough dehydrated food to keep an army fed for years, as well as an endless supply of water from a desalinizer that ran right out into the ocean. He had wind turbines, solar panels, and backup generators with giant fuel tanks buried right under the courtyard. He had enough security measures to hold off the living dead forever: high walls, motion sensors, and weapons, oh the weapons."[7] All of these options involve increases in spending, and they will certainly create new jobs in the industries that are seeing the increase in demand. Like preparations for conventional war, in which spending is driven into defense industries, those who are recipients of that spending certainly have more resources to spend on things they wish to have.

In the second stage, as the actual apocalypse begins to unfold, an increased amount of resources will be devoted to both weaponry for defense and to the search for a cure. We can imagine major investment in new forms of military equipment—from precision handguns with sufficient firepower to accurately target and destroy zombie brains to experimental bombs or chemical weapons intended to destroy masses of zombies at once. Medical professionals will be in high demand, as will producers of disinfectants and sterile gloves, hats, and uniforms. Brooks records an interview with Breckinridge Scott, the creator of Phalanx, marketed as a vaccine for the zombie infection: "It protected them from their fears. That's all I was selling. Hell, because of Phalanx, the biomed sector started to recover, which, in turn, jump-started the stock market, which then gave the impression of a recovery, which then restored consumer confidence to stimulate an actual recovery! Phalanx hands down ended the recession! I . . . I ended the recession!"[8] Just as in Bastiat's story, for certain people, business will never have been better.

In the final battle for humanity's survival, the majority of resources will be devoted to the war or to people attempting to escape to any safe zones. Arthur Sinclair Jr., director of the U.S. government's Department of Strategic Resources or DeStRes, describes the situation in *World War Z*: "The living dead controlled most of the world's landmass, while American war production depended on what could be harvested within the limits of the western states specifically. Forget raw materials from safe zones overseas; our merchant fleet was crammed to the decks with refugees while fuel shortages had dry docked most of our navy."[9] In this world, the entire structure of the economy will have shifted from the structure of the preinfection era toward one based on the zombie-industrial complex.

Seeing the expenditures related to a zombie apocalypse from this perspective should suggest the fallacy Bastiat reveals in his broken window parable.

As Bastiat observes, all of the spending that results from the breaking of the window does *not* add to society's total wealth. Instead, it at best restores us to where we were before the window was broken—but without the resources we used to fix the window. To see this, consider what would have happened if the window had never been broken.

If it costs $100 to fix a broken window, leaving that window intact means that the homeowner has $100 available to spend on *something else*. The whole flow of spending that results from the broken window would have happened anyway, but through a different sequence of recipients. In Bastiat's original rendering, the homeowner would have used the $100 to buy new shoes or new books. The cobbler or the bookseller would then have spent that $100 on something for himself, and so on. Thus, at best, all of the spending spurred by the threat and eventual occurrence of a zombie apocalypse just shifts massive amounts of economic activity to zombie preparedness, zombie fighting, and zombie cleanup—*and away from other things*. It does not create additional economic activity. As President Eisenhower said during an earlier attack, "Every gun that is made, every warship launched, every rocket fired signifies, in the final sense, a theft from those who hunger and are not fed, those who are cold and not clothed. This world in arms is not spending money alone. It is spending the sweat of its laborers, the genius of its scientists, the hopes of its children. This is not a way of life at all in any true sense. Under the cloud of threatening [zombie] war, it is humanity hanging from a cross of iron." [10]

However, seeing the zombie apocalypse as only a shift in types of spending disguises the actual *loss* in wealth that's taking place. Consider Bastiat's homeowner. If the window isn't broken, he has both a functioning window *and* the new suit he purchases with the $100. But if the window is broken and then repaired, he must spent his $100, but this time he has *only* a functioning window. He doesn't get to buy the new suit. And the tailor doesn't get to sell it to him. The breaking of the window destroys wealth by forcing the homeowner to spend resources to get himself back to where he was before, instead of increasing his well-being by acquiring the suit.

The parallels to the zombie apocalypse are clear. Once people perceive the threat of a zombie apocalypse, the expenditures they undertake to protect themselves or to search for an escape or a cure are the equivalent of payments to the glazier. Even if those expenditures are successful at heading off the apocalypse or finding a cure once it starts, they do not add to economic well-being. Had there been no zombie threat, the resources spent on staving off the undead could have instead been spent on food, clothing, technology, art, or anything else people wanted. In such a world, we would have had *both* no (threat of a) zombie apocalypse *and* all of those consumer goods. Being forced to spend resources to simply maintain the status quo against some external destructive force, whether nature, crime, an invading army, or howling hordes of the undead, is not a path to wealth. The same is true of cleaning up from any form of disaster: those expenditures simply get us back to where we were before the disaster occurred.

Given an imminent zombie apocalypse, it is certainly sensible to take precautions, to try to find a cure, and to clean up the destruction. However, that is not the same as saying an invasion of the undead would improve economic well-being. As the economist Ludwig von Mises argued a century ago: "War prosperity is like the prosperity that an earthquake or a plague brings. The earthquake means good business for construction workers, and cholera improves the business of physicians, pharmacists, and undertakers; but no one has for that reason yet sought to celebrate earthquakes and cholera as stimulators of the productive forces in the general interest."[11] Had the prospect of a zombie apocalypse loomed, Mises might well have included that in his list of disasters not to celebrate. Compared to a world free of zombies, a world plagued by the undead would be a much poorer one. As economists Wayne Leighton and Edward Lopez say of the very similar expenses we undertake to prevent our computers from being infected: "it's arguably all a waste, because antimalware products would have zero value were it not for hackers."[12] And were it not for the undead, all expenditures on fighting zombies would have zero value. These considerations point to some of the problems with GDP as a measure of economic health, and those problems are especially relevant in situations such as a zombie apocalypse.

Whether we spend resources on fixing a broken window rather than a new suit, or on laser-sighted zombie-brain-exploding guns rather than a new flat-screen TV, the effect on GDP will be the same. The same is true of the jobs created in the defense and medical industries. Those jobs are like the glazier's new income. They are simply diversions from other jobs that would have been created in the absence of a zombie threat. A zombie threat would certainly create jobs for preparation and cleanup, but those jobs would be wastes of human productivity in comparison to the work done in the zombie-free world through which those humans could be adding to wealth rather than merely maintaining it. Even though these expenditures on preparation and cleanup "count" in GDP, they do not make us better off.

There are two objections to this argument that should be addressed. The first, and less serious, one is that the death rate from zombie attacks would be so high that the fall in population would cause GDP per capita to rise. This could be true even if total GDP were falling. Economists frequently use GDP per capita as a measure of economic well-being. Is it possible that the zombie apocalypse could still make the survivors better off? As it turns out, no. This first objection assumes that the level of GDP is independent of the size of the population. But it is not.

In *World War Z* we see that even in the aftermath of a successful defense against the zombie threat, the lack of population will pose immense economic challenges. An economy recovering from the deep depression caused by the death and destruction of the zombie apocalypse will still not be able to deal with the consequences: "It is no great secret that global life expectancy is a mere shadow of its former prewar figure. Malnutrition, pollution, the rise of previously eradicated ailments, even in the United States, with its resurgent economy and universal health care are the present reality; there simply are not enough resources to care for all the physical and psychological casualties."[13] Less population is not an asset, and more population is not a liability. More people means not just more mouths consuming resources, but more hands and, ironically, more braaaaaaains to produce more resources. In addition, as economists have known since Adam Smith, the division of labor is limited by the extent of the market. A population reduced to a fraction of its prior self would have far less specialized production and would thereby be less efficient and more impoverished. The zombie apocalypse would so catastrophically reduce the human population that the shrinkage in GDP would be so large that GDP per capita would surely fall.[14]

A second, and far more sophisticated, objection to the argument that the expenditures on the broken window are a pure diversion is one raised by Keynesian economists. Their argument is that during a recession, there are idle resources lying around, such as unemployed workers and unused capital equipment. Given idle resources, perhaps the sort of spending created by the need to repair a broken window, or the desperate desire to combat a zombie apocalypse, or a government stimulus package will bring those idle resources into activity and thereby add to wealth. Unlike the diversion of spending that happens when zombie-related expenditures bid labor and capital away from their existing productive uses, the argument of Keynesians (like Paul Krugman) is that if such spending happens during a recession and activates idle resources, it will represent *new* employment of capital and labor and thereby *add* to total spending and GDP. For example, the need to mop up brains from walls and floors or cart away infected bodies, not to mention manufacturing the equipment for doing all of that, might create jobs for unemployed workers and idle machinery.

Although this argument is a commonly held position within the economics profession, we disagree with it. But before responding to it, we should note that even if this argument is true, it is only relevant if the zombie apocalypse just so happens to hit during a recession. On that much, virtually all economists would agree.

Assuming the apocalypse does hit during a recession, the Keynesian argument is still problematic. One of the assumptions in this argument is that if the government did not spend money on a stimulus package or zombie-response measures during a recession, the money would otherwise go unspent. Whether the government is able to borrow and spend that money in ways that activate idle resources will determine the success of the stimulus.

For example, if the government borrowed heavily to, say, prepare for a zombie apocalypse, it could just "crowd out" borrowing that private investors would do, and thereby just substitute one form of expenditure (and a wasteful one compared to the world without zombies) for another. There is much debate over the extent of this "crowding out," but even if it is not 100 percent, other considerations arise.

Another problem with the idle resources argument is that it treats all resources as if they are the same. If it were true that labor and capital were the equivalent of clay or Play-Doh that could be molded into whatever form was needed, then the Keynesian argument would have some truth to it. However, one of the empirical facts about labor and capital is that they are not homogeneous but heterogeneous in use. That is, workers and machines cannot be used to create any and all kinds of output; they are better suited for producing some goods and services than others. Although most can be used for more than one purpose, their uses are still less than infinite, at least not without expending other resources to refit or retrain them. What constitutes a healthy economy is not just that it uses all of the resources at its disposal, but that it uses them in ways that fit together to meet the wants of humans at lowest cost.

A zombie apocalypse would mean that real resources would have to be spent to retrain unemployed workers in the proper methods of handling infected brains and disposing of bodies. Idle equipment would require expenditures in order to be retooled for carting around the undead or cleaning up their messes. We see an example of exactly this in *World War Z* relating to property left behind by the recently undead. Zombies have no interest in their former property, thereby creating a disposal problem. That problem is solved by hiring workers and making use of machines to collect the abandoned property: "The clothing, the kitchenware, the electronics, the automobiles, just in the Los Angeles basin alone, outnumbered the prewar population by three to one. The cars poured in by the millions, every house, every neighborhood. We had an entire industry of over a hundred thousand employees working three shifts, seven days a week: collecting, cataloging disassembling, storing and shipping parts and pieces to factories all over the coast."[15]

All of those expenditures, as we argued earlier, are wasted resources compared to a world free of the threat of zombie attack. Cleaning up messes, or recycling or repurposing abandoned property, does not add to our wealth. Transforming one object to use it for another purpose requires the expenditure of real resources. All of this spending activity may well be rational given the existence of a zombie attack, but it remains a waste of resources in comparison to a zombie-free world.

Of course, it might be the case that rather than activating the resources that happen to be idle, the zombie apocalypse would instead simply pull existing resources from their currently productive uses. Instead of creating jobs for the unemployed, the zombie attack might just pull gainfully employed scientists, engineers, and construction workers away from their current jobs. The Keynesian argument assumes both that the idle resources are capable of any use *and* that it will be those particular resources that are actually used to fulfill the demands generated by the new zombie-related spending. Empirically, there are very strong reasons to doubt the first assumption, which makes the second assumption highly questionable as well. The result is that even if there are idle resources, the expenditures required by a zombie apocalypse will not add to overall economic well-being.

Even the massive quantity of currency that would be lying around in the aftermath of a zombie apocalypse is not wealth. It's a problem. As "money cop" and head of the Securities and Exchange Commission Arthur Sinclair Jr. says in *World War Z,*

> Just trying to solve the surplus bill dilemma is enough for any administration. So much cash was scooped up after the war, in abandoned vaults, houses, on dead bodies. How do you tell those looters apart from the people who've actually kept their hard earned greenbacks hidden, especially when records of ownership are about as rare as petroleum? . . . We have to nail the bastards who're preventing confidence from returning to the American economy, not just the penny-ante looters, but the big fish as well, the sleazebags who're trying to buy up homes before survivors can reclaim them, or lobbying to deregulate food and other essential survival commodities. [16]

(Sinclair fails to note that if all of this currency is still being accepted, spending this excess supply of money would, in a world with a fraction of the population and resources, generate hyperinflation.) Just as in the broken window parable, these valuable resources of goods, money, and human labor are being used up just to try to get back to where we were before the zombies attacked. Thinking that using all resources, no matter what we might use them for, is the way to achieve maximal wealth makes as much sense as thinking that the goal of doing a jigsaw puzzle is to use all of the pieces, regardless of whether they fit together to form a recognizable image or not. [17]

In the end, a zombie apocalypse has no silver lining. Should the zombies prevail, concerns about economic well-being will be moot. Should pockets of uninfected humanity somehow survive this unnatural disaster, any remaining resources would be used for rebuilding, just as they are after more natural calamities. Even these pockets of humanity, managing to truck, barter, and exchange among the broken windows and corpse pits, will not be what they once were. As one of the final speakers observes in *World War Z,* "I've heard it said that . . . even those who managed to remain technically alive were so irreparably damaged, that their spirit, their soul, the person that they were supposed to be was gone forever. I'd like to think that's not true. But if it is, then no one on Earth survived this war." [18] And even that is not the bleakest version of the zombie apocalypse. It is important to remember that not all accounts of the zombie apocalypse are as cheerful as Brooks's vision of cannibalism, smuggling, panic, slaughter, and a surviving world population that is a tiny fraction of the population from pre-zombie days. Scott Edelman's "The Last Supper" argues that an apocalyptic engagement with an ever-increasing population of nearly indestructible consuming machines, devoid of logic, dead to any desire but the desire for human flesh, can end in no way but in the tragedy of the commons, as the zombies mindlessly overconsume their food source.[19] "The streets were filled with an army of the hungry, devourers who no longer had objects of desire upon which to fulfill their single purpose."[20] In visions like Edelman's, when the zombies consume the last human, as they must, there will be no one left to fix the windows.

Chapter Five

To Truck, Barter . . . and Eat Your Brains!!!

Pursuing Prosperity in a Post-productive World

Brian Hollar

In the TV series *The Walking Dead*, the characters find themselves living in a zombie-filled, post-apocalyptic world of increasing poverty. A zombie epidemic has broken out and nearly all of the world's population has turned into flesh-eating "walkers." Anyone bitten by a zombie soon becomes a zombie himself. Nearly all social institutions have broken down, and there has been an almost complete breakdown in communication and interaction among the various small bands of survivors. Whenever any groups of the living do meet, they immediately distrust one another, and these encounters often end in violence. To make matters worse, zombies vastly outnumber survivors, forcing the living to expend nearly all of their resources fighting the undead, defending against other survivors, and doing all they can merely to stay alive. This leaves precious little time, energy, or resources to devote to productive activities, putting the survivors at perpetual risk of worsening poverty relative to their pre-apocalyptic lives. After the initial panic of a zombie apocalypse, the survivors will eventually start looking for ways to return to their prior level of prosperity. But how? For help in answering that question, we should turn to the father of modern economics, the Scottish Enlightenment philosopher Adam Smith, who taught us that specialization, division of labor, and trade are the keys to creating wealth. [1]

WHY WOULD A ZOMBIE APOCALYPSE LEAD TO POVERTY?

No Production

In the world of *The Walking Dead*, electricity and running water are no longer available. Roadways are blocked by abandoned cars and industries no longer operate. Flesh-eating zombies freely roam the streets and countryside. All mass production has stopped, and people are left with only what goods they can find abandoned as people fled their homes. With no new production occurring in this economy, the survivors slowly consume the remaining goods leftover after the zombie outbreak struck. All forms of infrastructure are in a state of disarray with no one left to maintain them. Without new production, the survivors find everything quickly falling into a state of complete disrepair, with the whole world turned into one gigantic ghost (zombie?) town.

Without the production of new goods, the survivors will eventually run out of supplies. They will have to either figure out how to start producing replacement goods or else discover how to get by without simple goods we take for granted—toothpaste, soap, pencils, paper, books, toilet paper, clothing, and bread. Food will increasingly become a problem as perishable foods spoil and less perishable foods are eaten. With zombies chasing them at every turn, survivors will be forced to live a nomadic lifestyle, making agriculture and raising livestock tremendously difficult. (Zombies happen to eat animals, too.) Unless they can secure farmland against zombies, survivors will ultimately have to turn to hunting as their primary source of food. But this won't give them the diversity of food they enjoyed in their pre-apocalyptic lives. Without a variety of fruits, vegetables, and other foods, survivors may find themselves malnourished and forced to eat the same types of food again and again.

This post-apocalyptic scenario highlights how quickly people will become poor if they are not able to replenish their supplies by producing new goods. Clothing will wear out, cars will break down, and most goods will wear down and break. Eventually, abandoned homes and stores will be completely raided by survivors until nothing is left. If people do not figure out ways to produce new goods—particularly food, shelter, and clothing—their standard of living will rapidly decay to the point where they are living lives not much better off than in a primitive society—and this only if there are enough animals left to hunt and support the surviving human population.

No Exchange

Besides the perpetual threat of zombies trying to eat everyone in sight, one of the starkest contrasts between the world of *The Walking Dead* and "real life" is the minimal amount of exchange taking place between groups of people. In the zombie world, people find they are essentially living their own version of a Robinson Crusoe existence—cut off from the society they once knew and forced to produce (or scavenge) everything on their own. The characters form small communities, similar to tribes, whose members provide support to one another and undertake some degree of specialization of duties. But unlike in modern America, there is very little trade with strangers. The primary exchange seen in the first three seasons of the show is among individuals within groups who form close bonds with almost family-like familiarity. While this type of social relationship is critical for innate social needs, forming these bonds is also incredibly time-intensive and illustrates the scarcity of opportunities for cooperation with others in a zombie-filled world.

Over 230 years ago, Adam Smith recognized that trade is a critical component for enhancing the standard of living of individuals living in a society. Trade arises, Smith said, from a natural human "propensity to truck, barter, and exchange one thing for another."[2] By definition, any people engaging in a voluntary exchange do so because they consider what they are trading less valuable than what they are receiving. Imagine one man with two guns and another with two first-aid kits. Both men would rather have one of each, and trading would make both of them better off. Your first gun is worth more than your second first-aid kit, and vice versa. Absent fraud or coercion, trade enhances the well-being of both parties engaging in any particular exchange. This increase in well-being is one of the primary means by which wealth is created in an economy.

Trade further enhances wealth creation by allowing people to specialize by focusing their energies on the tasks they are most skilled at doing. Individuals then trade the product of their specializations for other goods (such as food, clean water, shelter, etc.) that other people have specialized in producing. This ability to specialize increases the total wealth of society by allowing people to focus their time doing what they are most productive at doing and improving their skills over time. This allows society to produce much more than it could without specialization. For example, in *The Walking Dead*, various characters specialize in different tasks. Rick leads. Daryl hunts and tracks. Herschel provides medical care. Michonne fights. Glenn moves quickly and sneaks around quietly. By taking advantage of each character's different talents, specialization and trade allow the group to accomplish far more together than they can apart. But the extent of specialization is, unfortunately, limited by the small size of the group.

When voluntary exchange is impeded—whether by governments, natural disasters, or roving hordes of zombies—people are worse off than they could be if they had greater ability to specialize and trade. If all individuals in a society face systematic barriers to exchange, their standard of living will rapidly decline. This has occurred numerous times in human history and summarizes the situation we see in *The Walking Dead*, as zombies make any form of trade, transportation, or communication between survivors incredibly difficult.

In a healthy economy, individuals will exchange with strangers on nearly a daily basis—buying and selling from others with little consideration about the risk involved in trusting someone they do not know. Indeed, this can be viewed as the distinguishing mark of a modern society. Institutions we often take for granted—a legal system protecting against fraud and enforcing contracts, a police force to enforce laws and protect public safety, ready access to a universally acceptable form of currency, reasonable expectation of security and trust when interacting with others—all help lower barriers to exchange. And all of these institutions collapse once the zombies come. Strangers in the show are typically viewed as a threat, which greatly inhibits everyone's ability to trade with one another.

No Money

Not only is there little exchange going on in *The Walking Dead*, but there is also nothing resembling money in the show. In fact, the show never mentions money of any kind at all. Without money, people can only trade by bartering—that is, exchanging one good for another—a highly cumbersome method that Smith characterized as "very much clogged and embarrassed in its operations."[3] For barter to work, you have to want what someone else is willing to trade at the same time he or she wants what you are willing to trade. Bartering is inefficient because it only allows you to trade with people who both want what you have *and* have what you want. Money gets around this by allowing you to sell your goods to someone who wants them and then use the money you made to buy goods from someone else.

For example, imagine a survivor in the zombie apocalypse who has lots of canned food but is running low on ammo. He encounters a family that has lots of ammo, but isn't interested in his canned goods. In Smith's word, "No exchange can, in this case, be made between them. He cannot be their merchant, nor they his customers; and they are all of them thus mutually less serviceable to one another."[4] Without money, the survivor has to first figure out what the family with ammo would accept in trade for it, then find someone with that good who is willing to trade it for canned goods. Suppose the family needs medical supplies. With luck, the man with canned goods manages to find a woman who has extra medical supplies and needs canned goods. After making that trade, he must then go back to the family with ammo and hope the family is still willing to trade the ammo for the medical supplies. Money simplifies this process tremendously. With money, the survivor only has to find someone willing to buy his canned goods and someone else willing to sell ammo. Money helps make trade easier by allowing people to trade any good for money and then trade money for any other good. This eliminates the need to spend time and energy finding someone who wants to trade the goods you want for the goods you have.

Money is also much easier to store and transport than most other goods in an economy. To illustrate, imagine raising a herd of pigs in the zombie world that you plan to use for food and to trade for ammo and medical supplies. In order to grow your herd, you have to expend many resources (food, water, land, labor, etc.) simply keeping your herd alive and well fed prior to the time of trade. Without money, it would be incredibly difficult to amass much trading power through livestock. A sudden zombie attack could force you to flee at a moment's notice, possibly losing your entire herd to hungry zombies. If you were fortunate enough for your herd to live long enough to trade for other goods, you would still have the problem of safely transporting your livestock to the location of trade, facing many risks along the way. In contrast, money holds its value over time, is easily portable, and can be exchanged for nearly any other good.

So this raises the obvious question: why there is no money in *The Walking Dead*? Didn't the characters have experience living in modern America before the zombie outbreak? Why don't they just choose something to use for currency? Why not continue to use dollars as money?

The difficulty is that money has to be something other people will recognize and accept as having value. In other words, everyone thinks money has value because everyone *else* thinks money has value. In a society without a central government, it would be difficult to kick-start a process of developing a currency others will accept. Instead, people would likely turn to some commodity that has inherent value for use as money. As Smith put it, each person will tend to collect "some one commodity or other, such as he imagined few people would be likely to refuse."[5] One advantage of this sort of commodity money is that because the commodity has intrinsic value itself, it can always be consumed by its owner or bartered for something directly if others don't accept it as a form of currency.

Besides inherent value, other characteristics of good commodity money include divisibility, uniform quality, and high value relative to weight. Possibilities of potential commodity money in *The Walking Dead* might include gasoline, bullets, canned food, batteries, and so on. Gas is divisible, but probably has low value relative to weight. Bullets are divisible and have high value relative to weight, but are not of uniform quality. Canned goods and batteries are getting closer to the mark, but would have to be checked for quality prior to trading, which could become time consuming when it comes time to trade.

A historical example of commodity money is cigarettes being used as money by Allied prisoners in German prison camps during World War II.[6] Cigarettes met all three criteria of commodity money—divisibility, relatively uniform quality, and high value to weight. They also had the inherent value of being able to be smoked and enjoyed if a prisoner could not find something to trade for them. Also, if another prisoner would not accept them as currency, an owner of cigarettes could still trade them through barter just as they would any other good.

So why has no commodity money emerged in *The Walking Dead*? In this post-apocalyptic world, there is little contact between survivors, and when there is contact between strangers, it tends to be violent. This low frequency of interaction with others and the high risk of these encounters may create a situation in which a form of commodity money never has the opportunity to emerge. However, this may be one element that the show actually gets wrong in its storyline. There is no reason to expect the natural human propensity to "truck, barter, and exchange" to suddenly disappear in a post-apocalyptic world. When strangers meet, they would likely be much more predisposed toward trading than the show portrays.

RAISING YOUR STANDARD OF LIVING IN THE LAND OF THE DEAD

In *The Walking Dead*, characters continually find themselves lacking basic resources. They continually attempt to improve their impoverished situation by breaking into abandoned stores and homes in search of supplies. One example of this is when a newborn baby's mother dies during childbirth. With no one to nurse the infant after her mother's tragic death, two of the main characters risk encountering hungry zombies and hostile strangers in order to search for baby formula—something the group simply has no way of producing on its own.

Examples like this underscore that in order to increase your own standard of living, you need to increase your access to goods and services. There are four primary ways to do this: producing them yourself, trading for them, scavenging for them, or plundering them from others. Scavenging and plunder do not increase the total amount of goods available in the world. Trade can make people better off by allowing both parties to exchange something less valuable for something more valuable, as discussed earlier. However, if there is nothing new being produced, then there is only a fixed amount of things in the world to be traded. Without new production, there is a limit to how much better off trade can make people. Put another way, an increasing standard of living ultimately relies on a society's ability to become more productive over time.

In looking at the ways to increase their own personal standards of living (production, trade, scavenging, and plunder), individuals will use whichever method of acquisition gives them the most gain for the lowest cost (in terms of effort and/or resources). Immediately after the zombie outbreak, scavenging and plunder will seem like the most viable options—particularly with so many resources left behind as people abandon their homes. As discussed earlier, trading in a zombie-infested world involves inherent risks, as do scavenging and plunder. Given the limited set of skills, resources, and time available, the survivors will often find it more efficient to risk fighting zombies to obtain abandoned resources than to risk interaction with other survivors or attempt to produce things on their own. While fighting mindless zombies is a big risk to undertake in order to obtain supplies, it seems small in comparison to the risk of trusting other survivors, who are armed, intelligent, and often trying to kill you.

Production

So if trading, scavenging, and plunder carry such high risks from both the living and the undead, why don't the survivors engage in more productive activities? After the most valuable resources have been scavenged or plundered, the calculus for improving one's welfare will eventually make trade and production seem more worthwhile—particularly after survivors start banding into groups for mutual protection. This shift can arguably be seen in the progression of the show. Until the survivors discover temporary safe havens—first on a countryside farm and later in a prison—they are living a highly nomadic lifestyle, and thus are only able to keep the resources they can carry with them in their vehicles. The quest for the characters to find a place to call home represents the desire for safety (reduced cost of defense), accumulation (insurance against future scarcity), and productivity (ability to start producing things to improve their lives). Even in the midst of a zombie apocalypse, the natural motive to improve one's circumstances remains.

Every time the characters find safe refuge, they shift toward productive activities. One example occurs when the group moves onto a countryside farm and, for a brief time, experiences a period of relative peace. The property is an operational farm, complete with livestock, crops, and access to safe water. The group finds itself with plenty of food to eat, an area to train members on how to use guns, good shelter and cooking equipment, and access to medical supplies. While on the farm the survivors are able to relax, repair equipment, contribute to the operation of the farm, make scavenging forays into town, and recover their health. Until the farm is overrun by a horde of zombies, it looks like a promising place to begin rebuilding their lives.

Later, they discover and move into an abandoned prison. Ironically, the prison offers a place of sanctuary for the band of weary travelers. The same fences originally designed to keep prisoners in serve equally well for keeping zombies out. The group immediately begins securing safe areas within the prison, taking advantage of the shelter, the supplies within, and the cells as a home to call their own. To secure the prison, the group has to systematically go through sections of the prison, clearing out zombies and making the prison a more livable and secure environment. Just as a pioneer improves land by first occupying and eventually clearing it out and building on it, the group occupies the zombie-infested prison, eradicating the zombies within and gradually improving the defenses and living accommodations. Unfortunately, this comes at the incredibly high price of two group members' lives and the limb of another. Still, the group members entrench themselves in the prison and prove willing to engage in high levels of violence in order to protect their new home from the threat of others—both living and undead.

But perhaps the best example in the show of people banding together in an effort to promote prosperity and well-being is in the town of Woodbury. This is the only setting in the show that has functioning electricity, ample supplies of food and water, medical treatment, secure perimeters with rotating guards, and so on. While it is later revealed that the town has a hidden darker side, Woodbury still represents the highest standard of living seen on the show. At one point, someone offers a character an iced beverage while telling her the town has generators that allow them to keep things cold and fresh. The town of Woodbury provides its residents the closest thing to a pre-apocalyptic existence any of the characters have yet encountered.

Woodbury represents the three main reasons Adam Smith identifies as to why the division of labor contributes to productivity: "first to the increase of dexterity in every particular workman; secondly, to the saving of the time which is commonly lost in passing from one species of work to another; and lastly, to the invention of a great number of machines which facilitate and abridge labour, and enable one man to do the work of many."[7] Or, in modern language, improvement of skill, saving of time, and encouragement of innovation. Examples of this division of labor in Woodbury include a scientist providing technical expertise, the governor providing political leadership, a doctor providing medical services, teachers providing instruction to the children, and henchmen providing law enforcement and military protection. One of the elderly members of the town even contributes to the town's knowledge accumulation by allowing a scientist to observe him turning into a zombie after dying of old age. As each member of the community focuses on doing specific tasks, it frees up other members to focus their time on doing the things they do best. The scientist doesn't have to give up time researching in order to stand guard. Woodbury's leader doesn't have to take time away from leading in order to grow food. This focus also allows people to develop better skills in their areas of specialization and figure out new ways of performing their duties that extend what they can do and save both time and resources.[8]

So what is it about Woodbury that allows it to achieve a higher standard of living than other survivors were able to enjoy on the farm or in the prison?

A number of factors contribute to the differences. These include a clear political structure that clarifies decision making within the small society. Alongside this, there is a semblance of law in the town, including forced curfews when danger looms. Both the political system and legal structure give residents of Woodbury confidence that they can rely on the productive contribution of others and that their own contributions will add to the overall welfare of the town. These social structures allow each resident the ability to specialize, collectively making the town far better off than if residents were left to fend for themselves against the zombies. The larger population of the town allows greater degrees of specialization, division of labor, and trade, resulting in greater productivity than the smaller group on the farm is able to enjoy.

But there are limits to how much Woodbury's small population of seventy-five residents can specialize. As Smith argued, "the extent of this division [of labor] must always be limited by . . . the extent of the market."[9] The extent of any market is limited by population density and transportation costs. Unfortunately, zombies have a huge negative effect on both of these factors. Not only have the zombies killed most of the world's population, but their constant presence also makes the transportation of goods and services between surviving populations extremely dangerous. Unless survivors are able to figure out ways to trade between different communities, their markets will be limited to small populations and their ability to improve their lives through specialization will be drastically reduced. Rebuilding trade and communication networks should be one of the survivors' top priorities so they can extend their markets and unleash humanity's full potential to begin to flourish again.

Innovation

In the show, the group quickly discovers that zombies are attracted to sound, and they therefore shift from guns as their primary weapons to quieter weapons such as knives, machetes, and even screwdrivers. One character's samurai sword represents perhaps the best use of a weapon in the show. Not only is it silent, but it also slices off the heads and limbs of zombies with ease. The sword-wielding character shows further innovation by using her sword to cut off the arms and jaws of two zombies and then keeping them on a chained leash. Not only do they help her carry supplies, but their smell also helps mask her presence from other zombies.

Innovation is another key driver of increasing prosperity. As mentioned earlier, Smith saw the ability to innovate as one of the key benefits of specialization. As new ways of doing things are discovered, this allows a society to do more with fewer resources, increasing the productive potential and standard of living for that society. *The Walking Dead* captures this process in a remarkable way, showing the progression of characters coming up with new ways of doing things, often through trial and error. Examples of this include discovering that zombie guts mask the smell of the living (allowing them to walk among zombies without attracting attention) and creatively using zombies as weapons against other living humans.

But in order to increase their standard of living, survivors need to channel their creative energies to innovating in productive, rather than destructive, ways. The example of chained zombies being used as laborers gives a glimpse into how this might manifest itself. Survivors could use similarly "modified" zombies in the same way as pack animals and farm animals are used to save labor. Imagine zombies being used to pull plows to grow agricultural products, chained together to pull wagons for transporting goods, attached to a wheel to pull up water from a well or to generate electricity, and so on. Beyond zombie laborers, other potential innovations could include building treetop cities (zombies in *The Walking Dead* can't climb) to lower defense costs; developing more walled towns like Woodbury; coming up with methods of communication with other survivors (such as smoke signals, some sort of pony express, carrier pigeons, or electrical signals); developing traps to begin eliminating the zombie population (several examples of this are seen in the show); developing floating cities that can anchor offshore and move along the coastline to escape zombies and to trade and fish; and so on. These innovations are ultimately only limited by human imagination, physical resources, and the problems people are trying to solve. As survivors continue to discover innovative ways to do things, life will slowly start to get easier for them and their levels of prosperity will begin to improve.

RISING FROM THE WRECKAGE

The Walking Dead highlights many key lessons from economics that help explain how individuals, groups, and nations can increase their standard of living—and why a societal collapse would almost certainly lead to a life of poverty for anyone who survives. Survivors must continually expend resources protecting themselves against zombies, leaving little ability to focus on being productive. The ever-constant presence of zombies decreases the amount of trade, specialization, and division of labor among the living, leading to a further decrease in productivity. As survivors form larger communities, the power of specialization will allow them to gradually make themselves significantly better off than they would be living in isolation. However, until abandoned resources become too scarce or too difficult to obtain, scavenging and plundering abandoned supplies will likely continue to be a significant way for survivors to increase their wealth.

In the short run, a zombie apocalypse would not only lead to a loss of people, but also a drastic reduction in the standard of living of most societies. But in the long run, *The Walking Dead* also shows a ray of hope for people who unleash their "propensity to truck, barter, and exchange." The people who successfully form into larger communities and networks of communities, with greater degrees of trade, specialization, and division of labor, will be those who most quickly rebuild society and once again begin to improve the quality of their lives.

Chapter Six

What Happens Next?

Endgames of a Zombie Apocalypse

Kyle William Bishop, David Tufte, and Mary Jo Tufte

Zombies exist in a variety of stories; as such, one cannot definitively speak about how they behave and function. The most familiar narrative is the zombie apocalypse, in which the actions of the undead destroy civilization, a story structure essentially invented by George A. Romero when he adapted the book *I Am Legend* into *Night of the Living Dead*. He fused the vampire's procreation through conversion with the existential threat of ghoulish consumption. While Romero's resolution implies a victorious human population, later zombie films explore the apocalyptic potential. Because at least some killed humans reanimate as zombies, humans are likely to lose. In the original *Dawn of the Dead*, social infrastructure collapses, and the remaining humans struggle to survive by hiding, fortifying, and scavenging. In many narratives, humans' best hope is stalemate—the zombie population persists and the humans stay hidden and safe. But what might happen after the movie ends?

Most zombie narratives, especially films, focus on a finite period of time: the tale ends with the deaths of protagonists as with the remake of *Dawn of the Dead*, an ambiguous stalemate as in *Land of the Dead*, or the potential survival of a few humans as in *Resident Evil*. Relatively few movies depict a "return to normal"; examples include *Shaun of the Dead* and *World War Z*. Cinematic depictions of a zombie apocalypse appear more interested in showing how such scenarios begin and develop. Indeed, these short-arc narratives often leave audiences hanging, wanting to know how it will all end. Surprisingly, an understanding of economics, complemented by biology, can lead filmmakers, screenwriters, and curious fans alike to the probable resolutions of apocalyptic zombie scenarios.

Interestingly, *The Walking Dead* introduces an important new wrinkle: zombies don't need to beget zombies because humans carry an infectious agent that leads to reanimation, even when death is natural.[1] This bit of biology matters to the economics because some nonfictional infections are known to influence decision making, and latency plausibly makes that influence harder to combat. Economists view choices as the interaction of internal subjective value (sometimes called *utility*) with external objective constraints. For example, the way we value cookies comes from something inside us, but our choice to buy them or not is also influenced by the price other people put on them. Infection is relevant because it suggests a potential change to those internal valuations (e.g., you like cookies less because you're infected) rather than to the external constraints (e.g., you buy fewer cookies because the price went up). So, the presence of an infection means the visceral antipathy of humans and zombies may not be written in stone at all.

Students of economics are versed in *supply and demand*—a model of the interaction of opposed actions. For example, zombies' desire for flesh can be modeled as a kind of demand. Zombie hordes "pay" for flesh with damage to themselves, and when that price is lower they consume more. Perhaps unwittingly, humans supply flesh, while requiring increasing costs of the zombies to obtain larger quantities. Equilibrium is the outcome of those opposing actions: some quantity of humans is eaten, and some price is exacted from zombies. Figuring out how that outcome responds to behavioral changes is called *comparative statics*. Extending the example, if humans develop better techniques to fight off zombies, such as learning to avoid unnecessary gunfire that will attract zombies, this could be modeled as increasing the cost of flesh (supply shifting to the left). The equilibrium at the intersection of supply and demand then moves up and to the left. The model therefore predicts that avoiding gunfire leads to less consumption of humans as a higher price is exacted from zombies, who are easier to deanimate when they are not attracted in large groups. In such comparative statics, we compare a static (or stable) situation before the technique was adopted to a second static situation after it was adopted.

What's missing from this example is any explanation of what happened over the period of time it took to start avoiding gunfire. More complex models fill voids like this with sequences of actions that play out over time. In zombie narratives, it's common for the initial zombie attacks to be met with ineffective techniques. Usually these failures create more zombies, often including recently familiar humans. The zombie attacks then become more pervasive, and humans respond with new techniques. The situations in these narratives are dynamic instead of static. To study them, modelers focus on the *steady state*—a situation in which changeable variables stop changing.

The study of the sequences of behavior that lead to steady states is called *comparative dynamics*.

To model the unspoken endgame of an apocalyptic zombie narrative, we need a model with comparative dynamics. In fact, such a model already exists.[2] Munz, Hudea, Imad, and Smith (2009) created a mathematical model of a zombie outbreak in a paper that has been heavily cited in both the scholarly literature and over a hundred blog posts. What they did was use comparative dynamics to figure out how many possible endgames exist for narratives with typical zombie behavior. However, their model is hobbled by untenable assumptions about both zombie and human behavior, and these assumptions lead directly to their dire conclusion: that once zombies appear, doomsday is the only plausible endgame. Using insights from economics and biology, we will argue that Munz and his colleagues' conclusion is incomplete, and that other endgames are also possible—including both stalemate and total victory over the zombies.

COMPARATIVE DYNAMICS OF THE ZOMBIE APOCALYPSE

Munz, Hudea, Imad, and Smith model the comparative dynamics of an infectious agent, an infectible host, and perhaps an infected but uncompromised carrier. In their view of the narratives, zombies are the infectious agent, humans can be infected and become zombies, and the carriers are corpses that may reanimate. They come to a startling conclusion: if there are any zombies at all, humans will eventually lose. They show there are only two steady states: an *unstable* zombie-free one with only humans and a *stable* one with only zombies that they call "doomsday." A word of caution is in order about terminology. In comparative dynamics, unstable doesn't mean impossible, but rather *possible unless disturbed*. So a zombie-free society (like our own) is sustainable, and it is one possible endgame. But the advent of zombies disturbs us away from that steady state, and because it wasn't stable, we eventually make our way to the other stable steady state—doomsday.

The contribution of Munz, Hudea, Imad, and Smith has two related weaknesses: one related to epidemiology and the other related to the absence of economic decision making. Both of these weaknesses serve to strengthen their conclusion that only the doomsday outcome is stable. The epidemiological issue is the assumption that corpses never stop reanimating: in their model, there's a chance any corpse will reanimate at any time. This view is consistent with films such as *Night of the Living Dead*, in which radiation reanimates the recently deceased; *Zombie*, in which vintage corpses also reanimate; *Dawn of the Dead*, in which corpses reanimate because "there's no more room in hell"; or AMC's *The Walking Dead*, in which living humans are already infected with the zombie virus. However, not all zombie narratives support this assumption; in *World War Z*, for example, zombies only arise from dead and infected humans. But the difficulty runs even deeper: Munz, Hudea, Imad, and Smith also assume that all deanimations are transitory, meaning that even a killed zombie will arise again. This strange assumption leads straight to their forecast of doom. The usual "rules" say a zombie can be deanimated "by a shot to the head or a heavy blow to the skull. . . . Kill the brain, and you kill the ghoul."[3] This insight occurs commonly across a variety of narratives,[4] and when Munz's model is corrected so that properly dispatched zombies remain dead, it turns out other endgames are possible, including both total victory over the zombies and stable coexistence of humans and zombies—depending on the parameters.

Furthermore, most zombie narratives focus on humans' ability to change their behavior in ways economists find sensible. They learn to avoid attacks in which death and reanimation are likely. They hide and fortify—in a farmhouse, a shopping mall, a bunker, a pub,[5] or even in a reality show's house (as in the miniseries *Dead Set*). Those in *Land of the Dead* and *World War Z* use military equipment to limit direct contact and avoid being overwhelmed by hordes of zombies. For others, the zombie threat is mitigated by imprisonment, as in *The Walking Dead* or *World War Z*. Furthermore, to ensure zombies will "stay down" when deanimated, special care must be taken (as in the "double tap" from *Zombieland*). Introducing these possibilities into the comparative dynamics allows yet another endgame: one with cyclical movements in both zombie and human populations.

IS DOOMSDAY INEVITABLE? A DISSENTING VIEW

A straightforward way to summarize comparative dynamics is with a diagram. We're concerned about the evolution of the populations of humans and zombies. The real world has humans but no zombies—and we appear to be approaching a steady state in human population,[6] with demographic forecasts suggesting a plateau of about 9.6 billion humans will be reached within the next few decades.[7] This scenario is summarized in figure 6.1.

The arrow shows dynamics: the human population will increase with the passage of time (as long as the zombie population stays at zero). Eventually we'll reach the zombie-free steady state of Munz, Hudea, Iman, and Smith.

When Munz et al. say this state is unstable, they do not mean the path along the arrow can't happen. Instead, they mean that if somehow zombies come into existence—so the world's position is bumped a little bit "north" of the arrow—then this particular arrow ceases to be relevant because we'll now move in some other direction. That *is* the comparison in comparative dynamics: in one situation the arrow points this way, and in different circumstances the arrow points some other way.

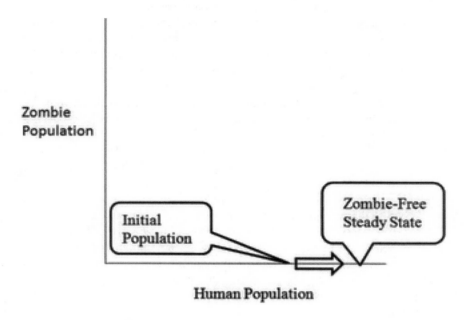

Figure 6.1.   The Unstable Present

Part of what makes zombie narratives interesting is that the circumstances following a fictional outbreak do not point along the familiar path toward a zombie-free steady state. Instead, established social structures begin to collapse.[8] In the movie *World War Z*, hardly hours pass before people resort to looting, rape, and kidnapping, and both versions of *Dawn of the Dead* famously depict the ransacking of stores in shopping malls. Then governmental institutions fail; while they may try to contain zombie outbreaks with military strikes, most zombie narratives follow the original *Day of the Dead*, in which such measures are futile. Eventually, even the personnel give up: *Survival of the Dead* shows impotent and even dangerous soldiers, while *World War Z* depicts lawless police.[9] And although survivors rely on the media longer than any other institution, eventually it falls silent too, as seen in the original *Dawn of the Dead*. These narrative features are summarized by a movement in the direction of the new arrow in figure 6.2. The zombie-free steady state is still there, but we're no longer heading toward it. That's what is meant by unstable: there's a path that leads to the zombie-free steady state, but once we're off that path, the other paths lead away. Instead, we're heading toward a different steady state—doomsday. As time passes, the human population falls as we move to the left on the diagram, and the zombie population increases as we move upward on the diagram. (Even when zombies are present, the human population may continue to grow for a while because human reproduction still outpaces zombie conversion and then starts to shrink once the zombie population gets large enough. But for simplicity, we've left this out of figure 6.2.) This is what makes the doomsday steady state stable: the path might be wobbly, but the general direction will be up and to the left, and because each human death potentially creates another zombie, one way or another, eventually every human will succumb. Figure 6.2 depicts the doomsday steady state of Munz, Hudea, Iman, and Smith; just imagine the arrow extending all the way across as human population goes to zero.[10]

But is doomsday inevitable? Does the arrow shown in figure 6.2 have to extend all the way across? No; it depends on certain restrictive conditions. If we follow Munz et al. in assuming that even zombies with their brains blasted out can reanimate, then doomsday is indeed the only stable outcome. But let's drop that assumption and suppose that zombies can be permanently dispatched. Even so, doomsday will still occur if humans aren't good enough at killing zombies. Imagine a random encounter of a human and zombie. The human has some chance to deanimate the zombie, and the zombie has some chance to bite and infect the human. If the human kill rate is less than the zombie bite rate, then the zombie population will inexorably climb—and the human population will fall—until doomsday arrives.

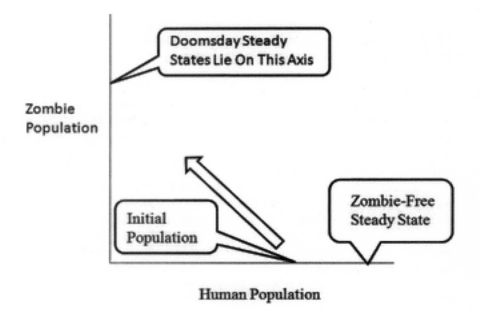

Figure 6.2.   The Path to Doomsday

On the other hand, what if the human kill rate exceeds the zombie bite rate? In that case, the outcome depends on whether any dead human might become a zombie (perhaps because of a latent infection, as in *The Walking Dead*) or if only bitten-and-infected humans become zombies (as in *World War Z*). In the former case, we will never be rid of zombies, because no matter how many we kill, more will rise from the dead and take their place. However, provided humans are good enough at killing zombies, a "stalemate" endgame in which humans and zombies coexist is possible. The number of zombies dispatched by zombie hunters exactly balances the number of zombies who rise, leading to a constant zombie population, and likewise, the number of new human births are sufficient to overcome the losses due to natural death and zombification. The stalemate endgame is depicted in figure 6.3.

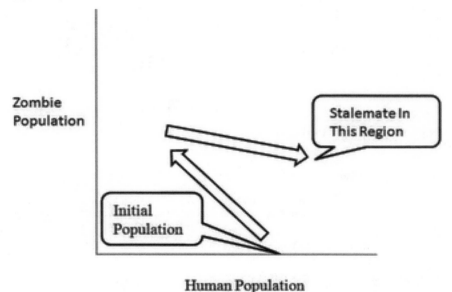

Figure 6.3.   The Path to Stalemate

In the latter situation, where only bitten-and-infected humans become zombies, another endgame becomes possible: total human victory. In this situation, humans kill the zombies faster than the zombies can replace themselves until, eventually, the last zombie is deanimated. The "total victory" endgame is depicted in figure 6.4. The possible endgames with zombies are summarized in table 6.1.

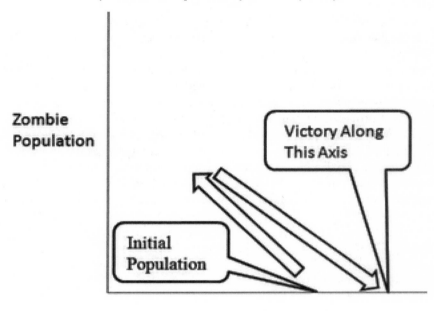

Figure 6.4. The Path to Victory

Table 6.1. Endgames of the Zombie Apocalypse

	Human kill rate is less than zombie bite rate	Human kill rate is greater than zombie bite rate
Any dead human might reanimate	DOOMSDAY!	STALEMATE!*
Only bitten-and-infected humans might reanimate	DOOMSDAY!	VICTORY!

* Requires that the human kill rate be sufficiently larger than the zombie bite rate.

FLEXIBLE RESPONSES FROM HUMANS . . . AND ZOMBIES

But all of the above scenarios—from doomsday to stalemate to total victory—assume zombie and human behavior are fixed. That is, the human kill rate, the zombie bite rate, and the corpse reanimation rate are all treated as fixed instead of variable. But this kind of unchanging behavior is not consistent with most zombie narratives. Instead, a general theme is that while globally humans may be heading toward doomsday, locally things may be different: what remains when central authority is lost is a tribal system that sometimes evolves into a city-state with a barter economy. More specifically, zombie narratives frequently involve the establishment of a safe zone with more limited human populations and no zombies (e.g., Fiddler's Green in *Land of the Dead* or Hershel's farm, the prison, Woodbury, the Alexandria safe zone, and the Hilltop community in *The Walking Dead* comic) that may grow and thrive. Furthermore, humans in zombie narratives often discover better ways to defend themselves (reducing the zombie bite rate), better methods of killing zombies (increasing the human kill rate), and better strategies for preventing reanimation, such as beheading the dead (reducing the reanimation rate). In short, humans are innovative. That means we could start on a seemingly inevitable path to doomsday, but then change our behavior in ways that make stalemate or even victory possible. Often, zombie narratives feature what appear to be population fluctuations: the local zombie population is diminished, humans establish a safe zone and thrive, the zombie population somehow reestablishes itself, and the cycle begins again. This cycle is exemplified in *Land of the Dead*. At the beginning of the film, human society has somewhat reestablished itself, with the wealthy living in Fiddler's Green while the poor eke out a meager existence in the streets. Zombies are not initially a direct threat, but they eventually resume their assault on humanity—successfully—and most humans die or are reanimated, swinging the pendulum back again. What could explain these fluctuations?

For humans, it's best if zombies never exist at all (as in figure 6.1), but if they do, then a return to a zombie-free world (as shown in figure 6.4) is second best, and stalemate (as shown in figure 6.3) is third best. But consider the case of zombies. If they eliminate the human population (as in figure 6.2), what is left for them to do? This query isn't mere flippancy: any creature that consumes all its prey . . . dies, so will zombies *persist* if the humans are gone? This issue goes unanswered in most zombie narratives. Films such as *28 Days Later* feature living, breathing zombies that must eat to survive, which means if they keep killing humans, they will lose. Romero-style zombies are just the opposite: since they are biologically dead, they don't need food at all (as established in *Day of the Dead*), and their unnatural existence will continue, presumably, forever. In sum, the doomsday equilibrium is best only for zombies from certain types of narratives.

The recent trend in zombie narratives has favored the kind of monsters that will fail if they consume all their human prey. *The Walking Dead* comics explore what might happen to zombies that consume too little, becoming slow and lethargic "lurkers" rather than "walkers." In the film *World War Z*, zombies fall into a dormant state when no human prey is near. In *The Zombie Survival Guide*, zombies continue to rot, and their bodies eventually degrade to the point where animation is no longer physically possible. One thing

seems consistent across all the newer zombie narratives: they need to continue to kill and, as a by-product, infect humans to create new zombies, thus
procreating their "species." Once all the humans are dead, the zombies have
no more prey and no more victims to infect. They may fall into dormancy or
rot to pieces, but either way, the zombie population will decline to zero: the
worst outcome for the zombie horde.

In other words, doomsday is the worst endgame for both humans and
zombies. Consider a scenario that strictly follows Munz, Hudea, Iman, and
Smith: patient zero turns into a zombie, and ultimately all humans are
doomed; once all humans are gone, the zombie population will likely diminish or disappear as well. The possibilities of this scenario might make for an
interesting book or film, but if things always turned out in such a predictable
way, such narratives wouldn't sell. Instead, what fans hope for is at least the
possibility of avoiding doomsday, and this possibility is exactly what is
implied by both economics and biology.

Economics has a long tradition of models such as Munz, Hudea, Iman,
and Smith in which the math is fixed in spite of the obvious fact that human
decision-making flexibly adjusts to worsening situations. That tradition
started to unravel in the 1970s when opposition to this sort of model arose in
the form of the Lucas critique, named after economist Robert Lucas.[11] Although Lucas's criticism was specifically directed at then-current macroeconomic models of the business cycle, his argument has broader significance.
In essence, Lucas argued that the traditional model with fixed parameters
leads to an unacceptably unrealistic description of flexible decision makers.
In the context of a zombie apocalypse, the Lucas critique predicts that humans will adapt and learn in their new environment. Currently, humans have
little in the way of zombie-fighting skills, which is rational considering there
are no zombies to fight. However, when predicting the effect of introducing
zombies, one wouldn't want to continue with that assumption, because humans will rationally respond to their new environment by acquiring new
skills that could change the final outcome. Of course, a common theme in
zombie narratives is that humans may just not be that bright, as in the mall
scenes in the original *Dawn of the Dead*.[12] Note that in asserting that humans
may respond rationally, the Lucas critique does not guarantee that this will be
sufficient.

The Lucas critique may have even broader implications because it doesn't
necessarily presume *thinking* behavior, but only *adjustable* behavior. This
perspective raises a question: can zombies change their behavior? In short,
do they even have the ability to consume less? The zombies of *28 Days Later*
seem to retain this ability, but they are living creatures, not reanimated
corpses. In the film version of *World War Z*, zombies are only seen biting
victims, but this may be driven more by the film's rating. In *Warm Bodies*, a
zombie's consumption of a human male changes his behavior toward the

victim's girlfriend. Alternatively, in Romero's films, zombies will eat their victims until (1) they are stopped or (2) their meal reanimates. The question is, what truly drives the zombies: an unchanging drive to consume humans or a biological imperative to perpetuate their "species"? As humans take action to reduce the reanimation rate, might other behavioral changes take place in zombies that change the transmission rate?

Biology suggests we shouldn't be surprised if this happens. In the real world, the reanimation rate is zero. If an infectious agent evolved that could cause reanimation, would it be biologically successful? The answer is no since it would lead to a doomsday outcome. The endgame for an infectious agent whose reanimation rate and infection rate are too high is zero humans, and probably zero zombies to carry the infectious agents. But this is not how infectious agents work in the real world—no extant cases of infectious agents exist that consume everything and then disappear. It is anthropic, yet nonetheless true, that we've never observed a zombie vector that can get us to doomsday, because if we did we wouldn't be around to describe it (the same can be said for extant high-mortality infectious agents like the Ebola virus). To be realistic, a zombie narrative featuring an infectious agent requires imperfection in the killing ability of that agent. An infectious agent that thrived because it increased the reanimation rate from the zero of our real world to the positive rate of the zombie narrative would also need to be able to change the transmission rate to preserve itself. In short, while doomsday may be the endgame for Romero-style zombies, the zombies from more contemporary narratives featuring infectious agents collectively don't "want" to go there.

So, economics and biology are complementary, and both suggest the existence of another endgame. What might that look like? In economic terms, zombies face a tragedy of the commons: each individual zombie wants to eat more humans, but if they all do this, then no zombie will have any humans left to eat.[13] In biology, zombies and humans are clearly in a predator-prey relationship,[14] which may end in a tragedy of the commons, but this result is rare in the real world. Why? Because excessive predation causes some of the predators to die off, allowing the prey to thrive again. This theme was not explored in early zombie narratives, probably because the zombies are already dead, but it has been appearing more often recently. In *Land of the Dead*, zombies cease being a direct threat, engaging in "remembered" behavior instead (see also the novel *Zone One*). In addition, the lurkers of *The Walking Dead* or the dormant zombies of *World War Z* suggest a zombie "life cycle" yet to be explored. Therefore, in addition to the endgames already discussed (doomsday, total victory, and stable coexistence), another possibility exists in which human and zombie populations cycle as humans adjust their behavior, then zombies adjust their behavior, then humans adjust again, ad infinitum.

ONE MORE POSSIBILITY: THE ZOMBIE-HUMAN-PARASITE LIFE CYCLE

Delving further, predator-prey situations exist in which an infectious agent carries out its life cycle by inhabiting both predators and prey. What if a "zombie vector," as *The Walking Dead* television show proposes, carries out its life cycle in both zombies and humans? Nature offers examples of infectious agents that modify behavior to accentuate the predator-prey relationship for their own benefit.[15] For example, the *Toxoplasma gondii* parasite causes infected mice to become fearless around cats, thereby increasing the likelihood of their being eaten by the cats. This helps the parasite complete its life cycle, as the parasite is spread through cat feces. Parasitic behavioral manipulation has been documented in humans.[16] Most zombie narratives feature the idea that the condition can be transmitted by bite, like an infection, and *The Walking Dead* has added the notion that humans carry the agent. What would the endgame look like if the behaviors of humans and zombies were influenced by a parasite that passed back and forth between them?

We envision a scenario in which humans and zombies coexist, with the zombie vector producing behavioral changes that appear suboptimal to humans in the zombie-free real world. These suboptimal behaviors include such things as (1) keeping zombies alive in hope for a cure, (2) sneaking bite victims into zombie-free zones, (3) stalling when the reanimation process starts, (4) engaging in risky behaviors such as unprotected sex with the infected, and (5) exhibiting other suspect behaviors, such as infighting within human subpopulations, engaging in behavior that attracts zombies, or suicide by zombie.[17] The zombie vector could be the driving force behind these behaviors. Although they seem suboptimal to us, they may be optimal for a human infected with a zombie vector because these behaviors enhance the fitness of the behavior-modifying zombie vector. This scenario would be a world in which neither humans nor zombies ever win, but in which both humans and zombies avoid their worst outcomes—in essence, a fluid stalemate. The situation might involve cycling, or it might resemble the stalemate outcome in which zombie and human populations stabilize. Either way, it would be supported by unusual human behavior that is the new normal. Contemporary narratives are only beginning to explore this possibility, most fully in *The Walking Dead* comic books, *Zone One*, and *Warm Bodies*.

A zombie invasion would assuredly cause great damage to human society. But contrary to the doomsayers in both Hollywood and the ivory tower, we suggest that the eradication of the human race is not the *only* plausible endgame. If humans are not only bad at killing zombies but also incapable of learning and adapting to their environment, then yes, doomsday is the most likely outcome. But if humans demonstrate the innovative thinking that is the hallmark of our species—and if zombies display the behavior we expect from real-world disease vectors—then other outcomes are indeed possible. We could achieve total victory, or failing that, at least a stable coexistence. There is a light at the end of apocalypse.

Chapter Seven

Order, Coordination, and Collective Action among the Undead

Jean-Baptiste Fleury and Alain Marciano

Grand Central Station (New York City), 7:30 a.m., peak of the peak hours. Thousands of people are running at various paces in every possible direction in a seemingly chaotic fashion. At more or less the same time of the day, the same occurs in Charing Cross and Victoria stations (London, England) and Gare du Nord (Paris, France). Yet no major accident or conflict or problem alters the course of these human beings as they dodge their way through the dense crowd, barely touching each other, without any discussion or formal communication with one another. A certain order underlies the apparent chaos of human interactions, and it exists only because individuals follow general and implicit rules—like politeness. Similarly, in more sophisticated situations such as market transactions, individuals do not usually fight each other, and transactions proceed in an orderly and peaceful way. Accidents occur, but they are exceptional compared to the vast number of transactions that take place. Apparently, living human beings are able to interact and to coordinate themselves with others *spontaneously*, that is, without resorting to any formal, explicit agreement between them or following a central plan deliberately designed by a (great) architect. At least, sometimes they are. At the same moment and in the very same places, individuals purchase train tickets, coffee, food, and many other goods and services that are produced by the coordinated behavior of people within companies small and large, from Amtrak and Starbucks to the local burger joint. But unlike the coordination without command discussed above, the concrete production of goods generally requires a top-to-bottom process, with a chain of command linking the CEO to the retail clerk. Thus, planned organizations are embedded within a self-organized, unplanned order.

The post–zombie infection society also *seems* to be one of total chaos, in which only humans appear to be capable of maintaining a form of order. This is what strikes us, at first sight, upon seeing thousands of zombies roaming toward a commercial mall in George A. Romero's 1978 *Dawn of the Dead* and its 2004 remake by Zack Snyder. But if we shift our point of view away from the humans and toward the zombies, we can easily see that in these accounts, as well as in many others, zombie flocks show characteristics of an unplanned order similar to those observed among living beings. Zombies often brush against each other without colliding, almost never fight each other, and never attempt to eat each other. Zombies follow implicit rules, too. Furthermore, as we will argue later, zombies are sometimes capable of engaging in forms of deliberate planning and purposeful collective action as well. Thus, like human societies, zombie societies exhibit more order than is commonly assumed; in particular, two levels of coordination—spontaneous order and deliberate organization—coexist. This is what this chapter aims to analyze by using a political economy approach.

Departing from the common definition of economics as the science of choice under conditions of scarcity, political economists study a broader phenomenon: the coordination of individuals in a society so as to achieve individual as well as collective goals. Such study of social order started in the eighteenth century with the works of the founders of economics, David Hume, James Steuart, Adam Ferguson, and Adam Smith, and it has remained a central concern of the discipline. Political economists have developed two concepts to model coordination among (living) human beings: spontaneous order[1] and deliberate organization.[2] They argue that many social phenomena, for instance, money, law, social norms, and language, as well as nonhuman phenomena such as the formation of beehives and anthills, possess an order that "nobody has deliberately designed."[3] To use a famous saying from the Scottish philosopher Adam Ferguson (1613–1679) and popularized by twentieth-century economist Friedrich Hayek, they are *the result of human action but not of human design*. In contrast, there are situations in which order does not result spontaneously from individual actions. In those cases, human design is necessary and coordination must be deliberately organized.

Challenging the die-hard cliché of rampant violence and chaos among zombies, we use this frame of analysis to understand coordination among zombies. First, we contend that, within large masses—or flocks—of zombies, coordination results from bottom-up, unplanned processes rather than from top-down, constructed, commanded processes. Order exists without a formal organization and rests on a limited set of simple rules of behavior, which have interesting survival properties for the zombie group. But, at this level, zombies cannot reach goals that go much beyond their primal instinct to eat living human flesh. These large masses of zombies cannot engage in forms of purposeful collective action, precisely because there is no organization. Among the living, collective action through organization occurs, for instance, within a firm that gathers many individuals and organizes the division of labor. We contend that deliberate organization also occurs within some zombie societies. But this only happens within groups that, like their human counterparts, follow the lead of an entrepreneur in order to achieve ambitious goals. Many contributions, such as Romero's movies, confirm our analysis.

ORDER WITHOUT PURPOSEFUL COLLECTIVE ACTION: THE ZOMBIE MOB

Let us forget for a moment the more organized groups of zombies (see the next section) and start with the large flocks of roaming zombies, like those depicted most famously in Romero's movies, in *The Walking Dead* TV series, and in many other movies and books. In these contributions, zombie flocks exhibit a complete absence of organization. These groups are not sustained by or based upon a structure or any hierarchy. All differences have faded away and seem totally secondary. In particular, gender and racial differences—think of Romero's early movies, in which zombies are all white-faced—have disappeared; sex is (almost) nonexistent among zombies; families no longer exist and there is no basic kinship group among zombie masses. To some extent, these zombie groups are made of absolutely independent individuals and form a perfectly individualistic society. This extreme individualism and the related lack of structure seem to imply chaos and disorder. But this is not the case. Like what happens at rush hour in Grand Central, groups of zombies are ordered, even if disorganized.

Actually, the very fact that zombies gather in large and stable flocks, as most accounts will confirm, is evidence of an ordered society. If zombies were not ordered, they would wander chaotically and scatter into the wilderness, like particles of smoke into the air. Groups would form only occasionally and would be short-lived. But such chaotic behavior would seriously undermine zombies' ability to hunt and eat human flesh. Due to limited agility and cognitive abilities, a zombie is not much of a threat when hunting alone. Many action sequences in *The Walking Dead* TV series illustrate this point: Rick and his friends are generally pretty effective when it comes to fighting with roaming individuals as well as small groups of zombies. But when attacked by hordes of "walkers," as in the last episode of the second season, Rick and his friends are quickly overwhelmed and eventually escape only at great cost. As confirmed in many accounts, such as Romero's *Night of the Living Dead*, flocks of zombies are most dangerous to humans: they can exert tremendous collective pressure so as to break down manmade barriers and barricades. Thus, zombies tend to gather in stable groups, which help them maximize their chance of success in case of confrontation with humans.

The most obvious instance of order within these large groups of zombies relates to food—which is the most important issue for zombies. In that matter, zombies follow a simple and informal rule of conduct: they eat their share on a first-come, first-served basis. Indeed, we do not know of any example of zombies fighting or competing with each other when they try to find living food to sustain their hunger. They never eat each other's food. Sometimes, they may share a victim—one chewing on the head, another on the leg, and so on—but only if there is room for them to do so. When arriving too late on prey, one zombie will not attempt to force its way through against his fellows, but will instead wait his turn or go chasing another human with others. This rule of conduct comes from a deeper rule of behavior that coordinates zombie groups: a zombie will never attack or harm another zombie purposefully. It might appear counterintuitive, but groups of zombies exhibit a complete absence of violence toward one another: zombies are docile and peaceful to their fellow ghouls, and they walk in an orderly fashion.

Once again, such a rule of conduct has high survival value: imagine, for instance, that a zombie joins others in hunting humans but eventually attacks his fellows in order to secure more food for himself alone. In such a case, the stability of the group would be called into question. But cost-benefit analysis shows that zombies do not have much interest in doing so. Attacking another zombie could be, at the individual level, pretty devastating. Although not very agile, the living dead are endowed with tremendous strength, which leads to the conclusion that such strength is unlikely to come from inherited characteristics of the living individual they were, but rather from the virus that infects these bodies. Thus, it is likely that zombies have more or less the same strength, be they men, women, or children. Attacking a fellow zombie could last a long time and result in severe damage that would subsequently minimize its ability to hunt humans.

Obviously, these rules of conduct that zombies—more specifically *modern*, post-Romero zombies—follow were not imposed by any great architect, nor did zombies gather to discuss the basic constitutional provisions to follow within the group! The main reason is that *formal* communication among zombies is almost impossible. Most zombies cannot speak because of their damaged brain functions. Even if zombies were to some extent capable of learning, they would still have great difficulty in communicating through a formal and explicit language to each other in the context of a large flock that involves many interactions. If learning and communicating abilities could be found among zombies, they would tend to result in a different kind of group, a more organized one, as we will argue in the next section. Among zombies in large groups, communication is largely informal: these groups are characterized by an order that is perfectly spontaneous and does not result from any agreement or social contract.[4]

When they try to explain the conditions under which spontaneous coordination is possible among living beings, economists first resort to a process that consists of repeated interactions: by meeting the same persons regularly in the same conditions, individuals are able to observe how others behave, progressively understand the type of rules they follow, and learn about the merits of coordination and how to coordinate with others. But in the case of large zombie flocks, this type of explanation does not seem relevant, because their cognitive skills are too limited. Zombies gathering in big flocks are generally incapable of learning from the behavior of others.

This leaves us with a second type of explanation that is based on the existence of a certain propensity to coordinate with others. Where would it come from? Three main sources can be identified. First, it might come from zombies' past lives as humans. Indeed, the ability to coordinate with others is sometimes described as a moral feature characteristic of human beings. Authors like Charles Darwin and Friedrich Hayek believed that it was biologically innate, an instinct resulting from a natural selection process that started in the very first stages of the evolution of species and was passed on from generation to generation. Some of this initial hardwired human ability may have been passed on to their zombie counterparts, the same way that zombies, like humans, can walk.

Second, zombies might draw their propensity to coordinate with others from reminiscences of their past life as *socialized* human beings. Think, for instance, of the zombies that still play instruments in a zombie parade band in Romero's *Land of the Dead*, and of the zombies that go to the mall in Romero's *Dawn of the Dead*, out of "a kind of instinct, a memory [of] what they used to do" because "this was an important place in their lives."

Third, the zombies' propensity to coordinate might originate from the virus that causes zombie-ism. As infected bodies, zombies crave only living human flesh and seem to be able to smell dead meat in order to know what to hunt and what not to. In *The Walking Dead* TV series, for instance, humans are able to use this characteristic to hide from zombies when they cover themselves with dead human meat and blood. Being able to recognize a fellow zombie helps zombies coordinate without having to engage in costly attempts to communicate. Moreover, the virus causes the infected to behave in new ways. For instance, the members of the Zombie Research Society note that

> zombies allow themselves to be freely injured as a selfless gesture that benefits their fellow ghouls . . . Though it's general[ly] believed that the undead don't technically work together in battle . . . any single zombie can function as the perfect decoy, sucking precious time, energy and resources from a survivor,

even as the initial attack fails. This ensures that future resistance will be weaker, substantially increasing the odds that zombie number two, three, five or ten will eventually succeed.[5]

The "zombie ant-pile pyramid" seen in the movie *World War Z* provides further illustration of such complex coordination that is certainly provoked by the virus: these are not behaviors that living humans exhibit. We do not form ant piles. But the coordination process leads them to form a consistent and unified front line; in this way, zombies attain what economists call a "critical size," that is, the minimum capacity of a group to sustain competition.

These coordinating capacities enable zombies to form ordered and stable flocks better able to survive the competition with humans given their initial limitations. But these abilities do not enable them to do much more. For instance, if zombies eat the human population at too fast a pace, they will face the exhaustion of their primary source of pleasure without changing their behavior accordingly. Similarly, if a zombie eats a human to the bone, it cannot infect the body and, thus, does not allow for an expansion of the zombie population. Their propensity to coordinate enables them to survive, not necessarily to grow.[6] Thus, in spite of spontaneous coordination, large zombie groups are generally not organized and face the limitations of their compulsory need to eat living flesh right here, right now, a need that isn't even a prerequisite for them to survive. If zombies want to attain goals that are not exclusively oriented toward the satisfaction of their immediate needs, they need some form of collective action, through an organization. But such a structure will not emerge spontaneously—just as, in human society, Apple and Google did not emerge out of the blue. To diversify their goals and extend them beyond one period of time, to engage in purposefully collective action, zombies need to follow an entrepreneur.

FROM SOCIAL ORDER TO COLLECTIVE ACTION: THE ZOMBIE LEADER

What we have said earlier about spontaneous order among flocks of zombies is true for the vast majority of cases. Yet there are a few important exceptions. Examples of organized groups of zombies do exist in the literature and the movies. The zombies described in *American Zombie, Land of the Dead*, and *The Omega Man*[7] live in organized, formal groups. Similarly, in Robin Becker's *Brains: A Zombie Memoir*, a small number of zombies progressively gather and eventually get socially organized. These forms of collective action deserve study. How is it possible that zombies, who appear brainless, myopic, and unable to communicate with each other, engage in actions that require precisely those capacities they do not possess?

A first part of the answer lies in the existence of some zombies who have kept part of their pre-infection abilities intact. Sometimes they can talk (in *Warm Bodies, I Am Legend* [the novel and the movie], and *The Omega Man*), shoot guns and use other types of weapons (in *Brains: A Zombie Memoir*, *Night of the Living Dead, Day of the Dead*, and *Land of the Dead*), and so on. However, these abilities, although potentially fruitful and productive, relate to behaviors that remain, for the zombie, secondary to his main activity of eating living flesh. In other words, although gifted differently from other zombies, they do not differ in behavior so far. Thus, further explanation is needed. For the group to become formal and reach a collective goal, an agent of collective action—in other words, a leader—is necessary. This is exactly what we observe when organized groups of zombies exist. Even if it may seem surprising at first sight, the figure of the vampire-zombie leader is actually widely accounted for in the movies and the literature. Leaders play an important role in Richard Matheson's *I Am Legend*, in *Brains: A Zombie Memoir*, in Romero's movies *Day of the Dead* and especially *Land of the Dead*, and, more recently, in *Warm Bodies*. Sometimes, the undead leader appears to be a vehicle for the devil himself, as in Lucio Fulci's *City of the Living Dead* and John Carpenter's *Prince of Darkness*.

These zombie-leaders are crucial. It is only they who make purposeful collective action possible. Actually, they are not only leaders, they are *entrepreneurs* and more precisely *institutional* entrepreneurs, or agents of collective action. Perhaps surprisingly, few economists have analyzed the role of entrepreneurs. Those who have—including Richard Cantillon, Jean-Baptiste Say, Alfred Marshall, Frank Knight, Joseph A. Schumpeter, William Baumol, and Israel Kirzner—do not fully agree about what entrepreneurs do, who they are, and how they act. Nonetheless, we will sketch a few interesting theoretical elements that may help us understand the entrepreneurial behavior of zombie-leaders.

First, without doubt, entrepreneurs differ from "normal" individuals because they are innovators. While typical individuals—even managers and CEOs—repeat what they are used to doing and work within the limits of what is already known, entrepreneurs can act in a genuinely *new* fashion that radically alters the path the society was following.[8] For instance, to mention but two names, James Watt certainly qualifies for the title, as does Steve Jobs. Though it is relatively easy to call someone an entrepreneur or innovator, it is trickier to explain how the person came up with such brilliant ideas. In effect, entrepreneurs are exogenously endowed with a specific capacity that few others possess: a wild spirit, a vision (Schumpeter),[9] or an alertness (Kirzner).[10] Similarly, in the case of zombies, we know little about the origins of the capacities of the zombie-leader-entrepreneur. We simply observe that they exist and are able to "innovate"—that is, to go against their primal instinct to eat living bodies and to think about future effects of their actions.

The zombie-leader has the capacity every other zombie lacks: the capacity to think intertemporally, that is, to think of strategies that play out over time in order to alter the course of things.

And generally, the collective goals are far more ambitious than the hunting-eating routine of large flocks of zombie. Some of them strive to cure themselves and their group from the zombie virus. For instance, in Becker's *Brains: A Zombie Memoir*, zombie college professor Jack Barnes wants to reach Chicago to meet with the inventor of the zombie virus and ask him how to cure it. Similarly, in *Warm Bodies*, the leader R also manages to lead his group of zombies to a collective cure.

Other times, the collective purpose is less favorable to mankind. In Matheson's *I Am Legend*, vampire-zombie leader Ben Cortman is mainly concerned with how to infect Robert Neville—the last human living on earth—and he devises intertemporal strategies to do so. Once, when Neville gets back home after sunset, Cortman takes a shortcut and tries to trap Neville before he is able to lock himself safely inside. And when the strategy fails, because Neville is too quick, Cortman devises another plan: to convince some women to perform lascivious acts to lure Neville into joining them in becoming vampire-zombies. In Romero's *Day of the Dead*, the zombie test subject Bub is trained by the scientist nicknamed Frankenstein to go beyond his instincts. Bub eventually hunts down and kills his torturer, the military chief Rhodes, by wounding him with a gunshot rather than eating him and then trapping him so that other zombies can eat the soldier. Finally, in both Fulci's *City of the Living Dead* and Carpenter's *Prince of Darkness*, evil forces are not able, from the world of the dead, to directly invade the world of the living. They need to take control of bodies in order to fulfill their plan, that is, to create the conditions for their own return to earth. The zombie leader, possessed by the devil, is determined to kill humans, infect their bodies, and lead them so as to open the gates of hell through a dimensional portal.

Yet devising future strategies is not enough; to be an entrepreneur also means trying to make the change effective. The economic literature envisages various mechanisms for entrepreneurship, one of which is collective action. The entrepreneur acts as an agent of change by organizing the behaviors of individuals, channeling and structuring them into collective action, and sometimes organizing a division of labor. In the case of zombies, this means diverting the normal zombies from their immediate and basic goal—eating—toward a collective and more remote objective the zombie-leader has chosen.

For instance, the hero of Becker's *Brains: A Zombie Memoir*, Barnes, forces the members of the small group he has gathered around him into *saving* food for a future use. In Romero's *Land of the Dead*, Big Daddy is remarkable for being "able to call zombies from his core group away from distractions, which included the undead's instinct to devour the flesh of living creatures."[11] Even living beings understand that. At the end of the movie, the human hero, Riley, prevents another human from killing Big Daddy. Riley, watching Big Daddy leading his group "to the future," as the script tells us, concludes: "All they want is somewhere to go. Same as us."

As part of the mechanism of change, the leaders must be capable of communicating this distant goal to the members of the group. From this perspective, Big Daddy is remarkable because of his capacity to establish formal communication with other zombies through gestures and body language. Similarly, in Matheson's *I Am Legend*, Cortman can speak; every night he shouts Neville's name in front of his house. In *Warm Bodies*, R and his friend M lead a team to hunt for food in human territory using rough communication. After R falls in love with Julie, he stops craving food and hunting humans; instead, he starts to think about strategies to prevent Julie from going back to the humans. R, who discovers that love and the memories of cherished ones can bring zombies back to life, eventually leads his group to a collective cure by teaching M and the others his discovery. Finally, communication enables the zombie leader to organize the division of labor among members of the group, as is illustrated by Big Daddy's entrepreneurial role. When facing an obstacle, like a door or a fence, zombies usually only flock and use incredible pressure to take it down. But Big Daddy is able to command in a very rudimentary way (body language and gestures) the butcher zombie to chop down the wooden door with his knife.

In short, zombies sometimes form small groups and even societies, thus taking collective, purposeful action despite their cognitive limitations. The explanation can be found in the role of the zombie entrepreneur, who exhibits very special traits, the most important being his ability to postpone consumption in time. Whether he uses lieutenants or assumes the leadership all by himself, the leader generally finds it easy to control the zombie masses because of their inherent docility. What makes zombie societies particularly dangerous is the absence of free riding among them, which in many (if not all) accounts contrasts with the simultaneous breakdown of human societies, crippled by free riding and conflicting personal opinions and aspirations.

DAWN OF THE DEAD SOCIETY

Zombies can form societies with various degrees of coordination. The most intriguing characteristics of zombie societies are their lack of violence and their lack of coordination problems, even when they have no collective plan. And under the leadership of a zombie entrepreneur, the mass of zombies can organize into a coherent group moving toward collective goals that depart from the immediate consumption of living flesh. Thus, the accounts of apocalyptic states of nature found in most movies involving the living dead do not merely describe the end of human societies. Of course, human societies are shown dislocating in many groups and, in Romero's accounts, eventually disappear due to free riding and the inability of group members to pursue a common goal. But these accounts also depict the dawn of a new society, building on the ashes of mankind: a dreadful zombie society of order, not chaos.

Part III

Blood Money

The economist Alfred Marshall famously described economics as "a study of mankind in the ordinary business of life."[1] This is pretty much how the man on the street thinks about economics: it covers the money parts of our lives—the companies we work for, the goods we buy, the money we invest. It's a nice definition, but we object to the part that limits us to the study of *mankind*. Or, at least, we would like to extend the definition of mankind to include our recently deceased brethren. In this section, we step away from the apocalypse and instead imagine a world where the undead have adapted to modern civilization and join us in everyday economic activity.

Judging by the popular literature, modern-day vampires seem to have lives of wealth and luxury. How did that happen? James Dow looks at how vampires got so rich and whether we humans might use their investing strategies to improve our own financial behavior.

What happens when zombies become just an everyday threat, much like car accidents and house fires? Eleanor Brown and Robert Prag argue that if people face an ever-present risk of zombification, they may wish to buy insurance against such an event. How will insurance companies—and their regulators—respond?

The undead are justly famous for their consumption—not just of blood and flesh, but also of consumer products. Lorna Piatti-Farnell makes the point that the goods we consume represent who we are and how we see ourselves. The behaviors of vampires and zombies, in their different ways, capture some scarily realistic aspects of our consumerist culture.

What's the best way to fight the bloodsuckers among us? That will depend on the vulnerabilities of the vampires, but also the availability of different weapons. Charlotte Weil and Sébastien Lecou take a look at the market for anti-vampire weapons, bringing to bear the theory of industrial organization, and pose the question of whether the Transylvanian Trade Commission should approve the proposed merger of two firms that make competing types of bullets (wooden and silver) for killing vamps.

While most horror fiction puts humans and the undead in adversarial roles, we might wonder, because of each race's unique skills, if there aren't ways they could help each other. In this spirit, Darwyyn Deyo and David T. Mitchell examine opportunities for trade that might benefit both humans and the undead.

As we suggested in the introduction to this volume, if there is human-vampire trade, the odds are good that it will involve blood. Enrique Guerra-Pujol examines what's needed to create a successful market that will keep the blood flowing and suggests that the absence of legal blood markets might explain much of the ongoing violence between humans and vampires.

Finally, as the undead become a productive part of the modern economy, the tax authorities will naturally want their cut of the action. Joseph Mandarino provides helpful guidance on the tax implications of zombie labor in the economy. However, Mandarino asked us to point out that the IRS has not yet made definitive rulings in these matters, and so this chapter is *not* meant as tax advice for anyone living or dead. Questions should be addressed to your tax lawyer, accountant, or shaman.

—GW & JD

Chapter Eight

Investing Secrets of the Undead

James Dow

When I was a kid, vampires didn't sparkle. Mostly they lived in earth-filled coffins and skulked around dank cellars, drinking human blood when they could and rat blood when they couldn't. However, the modern vampire would not put up with such a pedestrian life. Anne Rice's Lestat is a rock star who travels the globe and enjoys all the trappings of the rich, while the vampires of the fantastically successful *Twilight* novels (those are the sparkly ones) are prominent and wealthy members of their community. Indeed, in 2010, *Forbes* listed Carlisle Cullen, the head of a vampire clan in *Twilight*, as the richest fictional character in the world (if you were wondering, Scrooge McDuck, Richie Rich, Tony Stark, and Jed Clampett rounded out the top five).[1]

But while the lives of the rich and famous vampires are certainly interesting, we might wonder if there are practical lessons for those of us who are still living. How *did* the vampires get so rich, and more importantly, what lessons can human investors learn from them? Unfortunately, most novels do not spend much time on the tax returns of their characters, and so we have to speculate about the sources of their wealth.

The books do give us some clues. Bella, the heroine of the *Twilight* novels, talks about the finances of the family she is marrying into: "Money meant next to nothing to Edward or the rest of the Cullens. It was just something that accumulated when you had unlimited time on your hands and a sister who had an uncanny ability to predict trends in the stock market."[2]

Being able to see into the future is surely a useful skill, although not much help to us. A slightly different approach was suggested when the question was raised by Sookie Stackhouse, the heroine of the "southern vampire" novels and the HBO show *True Blood*. In a passage talking to the vampire Bill:

"Sixty thousand dollars isn't a lot of money to a vampire, surely," I observed. "You all seem to have plenty of money."

"Vampires rob their victims, of course," Bill said matter-of-factly. "Early on, we take the money from the corpse. Later, when we're more experienced, we can exert enough control to persuade a human to give us the money willingly, then forget it's been done. Some of us hire money managers, some of us go into real estate, some of us live on the interest from our investments."[3]

This doesn't help us much, either, since it would be difficult to persuade someone else to just give us money willingly. Well, unless we're Bernie Madoff. But a better solution is the explanation hinted at by Bill the vampire and suggested by the *Forbes* article. In fact, it was put bluntly in an article in the *Wall Street Journal* on the recent vampire craze: "Above all else, vampires are rich. (The source of vampire wealth is obscure, since few of them appear to be gainfully employed. The assumption seems to be that anyone who's been around for 300 years must be in a position to take full advantage of the miracle of compound interest.)"[4]

So that's the solution—since vampires live for so long, the money simply accumulates over time. But is it really that simple? For the rest of this chapter, we'll investigate what economists know about the relationship between time and investing to see if vampires could actually get that rich—and whether there's hope for us, too.

THE BEST PART ABOUT LIVING FOREVER

Depending on your age, the first vampire you encountered may have been the Count. Not Count Dracula or Count Orlok, but Count von Count, the mathematics-loving vampire of *Sesame Street*. We can use the Count to develop an understanding of how compound interest works. When the Count counts 1 . . . 2 . . . 3 . . . 4 . . . (imagine this in your best Transylvanian accent), he is counting out a linear progression: each number is greater than the previous number by one. In other words, values increase by a constant *amount*. Let's see what that would mean for investing. Say that you put $100 in the bank and earned $20 of interest each year. Just like with the Count, your money would increase in a linear fashion $100 . . . $120 . . . $140 . . . $160. . . . Fortunately, bank accounts and other investments don't work like that; the interest you earn is not a constant amount but is instead determined as a *percentage* of the amount invested. Values increase at a constant *rate* instead of a constant *amount*. So instead of $20 of interest, you would be paid 20 percent of your principal as interest each year. After the first year you would have $120, just the same as with the linear progression. But after the second year you you'll end up with about $144. While you earn $20 in interest in the first year, you earn $24 of interest in the second year because the first year's interest *also* earns interest in the second year. Compounding is this process whereby interest earns interest. Instead of a linear progression, you end up with the *geometric* progression of $100 . . . $120 . . . $144 . . . $173. . . . As time goes on, the geometric progression gets further and further from the linear progression. Given enough time, compounding can produce dramatic results, and one thing vampires have is time.

Imagine that you are a vampire planning on hiding away and sleeping for one hundred years. You intend to put some money aside in various investments and let it grow while you sleep. How much should you expect to have when you awake?

This will depend, of course, on how much your investments earn. Unfortunately, most data on investing only goes back a short time; however, three economists at the London Business School (Elroy Dimson, Paul Marsh, and Mike Staunton) have gone back and calculated investment returns over a hundred-year period. The results are reported in the book *Triumph of the Optimists: 101 Years of Global Investment Returns.*[5] The authors examine investing returns from 1900 to 2000 for the following countries: Australia, Belgium, Canada, Denmark, France, Germany, Ireland, Italy, Japan, The Netherlands, South Africa, Spain, Sweden, Switzerland, the United Kingdom, and the United States. They find that the average annual return on investment in stocks ranged from 2.5 to 7.6 percent, with the return for the United States being 6.7 percent. We know that because of inflation, the value of money tends to fall over time. However, these numbers have been corrected for that and tell you what you would get after taking into account the effects of inflation.

The upshot is that if you invested your savings in U.S. stocks, and history repeated itself (which is not guaranteed, of course), you would expect to earn an average of 7 percent per year (rounding up the U.S. return for convenience). If you invested $10,000, earning 7 percent per year, how much would you have after one hundred years? The top line in figure 8.1 gives us the answer.If you invested just $10,000 and earned 7 percent per year for one hundred years, you would wake up to nearly $9,000,000! This is fantastic; no wonder the vampires are rich.

How much of that is due to compounding? To figure that out, let's imagine an alternate experiment. Assume that any interest you earned was taken out and put aside, so that your interest didn't earn any interest (in other words, no compounding). You would get $700 each year (7 percent of $10,000) for one hundred years, which would equal $80,000 (including your initial $10,000). Eighty thousand dollars versus $9,000,000 is a stunning difference (you can barely see the bottom line representing no compounding in figure 8.1) and is entirely due to interest earning interest and the power of time.

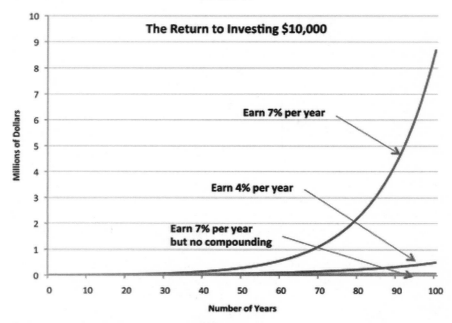

Figure 8.1.   The Return to Investing $10,000

Over long periods of time, it's even better to get lower rates of interest with compounding than higher rates without. Figure 8.2 focuses on the bottom two lines of the first chart. Earning 4 percent per year with compounding is still dramatically better than 7 percent without compounding.

But why stop at one hundred years? If it made sense to sleep one hundred years to get rich, maybe you should sleep another one hundred years to get even richer. At the end of two hundred years, you would have three hundred *billion* dollars. Now that's real money. However, you might be suspicious of this number; after all, while people don't last that long, families do, and money handed down generation by generation should accumulate in just the same way.

"BUT I HAVEN'T SPENT ANY MONEY! I WAS ALL DEAD AND FRUGAL."

Vampires are not the only ones that come back from the dead. At the end of the fifth season of *Buffy the Vampire Slayer*, Buffy dies (for the second time) but then is pulled back to the living at the start of the sixth season via an incantation performed by her witch friend Willow. Unfortunately, after her return to her home in Sunnydale, she finds herself with a flooded basement and no money to pay for repairs.[6] Her response is the title of this section, which reminds us that the waiting strategy only works if you don't use the

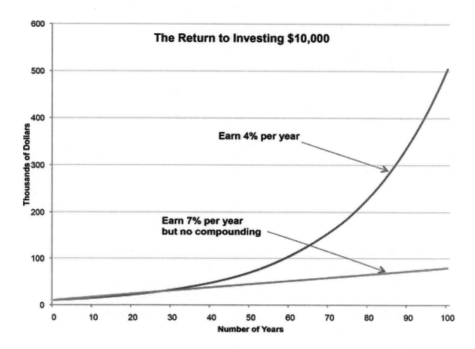

Figure 8.2. The Return to Investing $10,000

money in the meantime. Unfortunately for Buffy, even though she was dead, there were still expenses to be covered while she was gone.

This is why great fortunes are often not built up over time, but rather are spent down. The reality is people don't want to wait and so will pull out some of the interest in order to consume. It's a natural thing to do and even makes economic sense (maybe it's better to have some nice things now than to have nothing now and extravagantly great things in the distant future), but the more income is consumed, the closer the path of wealth shifts toward the no-compounding line. Modern vampires could only be fantastically rich if they spent most of the previous time being poor or were willing to sleep away the time in a crypt somewhere and not consume anything at all.

There are other problems with our waiting strategy. If we look at the first chart we see that the spectacular wealth comes only toward the end of the one hundred years. This is because a 7 percent return on a $1,000,000 investment provides significantly more dollars than a 7 percent return on a $150,000 investment, and it takes a lot of time to get to a million dollars. If you only had forty years to invest—which is a more human scale—a 7 percent return would only give you around $120,000. Still pretty good, but not vampire good.

Also, the 7 percent return is only an average. Investing in stocks can involve a lot of risk, so while in some years you might get better than 7 percent, in other years you might lose money. If you were not comfortable with that risk and wanted to invest in safer securities, you would get a lower average return. As you can see in figure 8.1, at a safer-but-smaller rate of 4 percent your wealth would grow much more slowly than with a 7 percent return. After one hundred years at 4 percent you would only end up with around $500,000. And if your investments were really conservative, let's say earning only 2 percent, you would only have around $72,000 at the end of one hundred years. Better than nothing, but why give up one hundred years of sucking blood for something that wouldn't even be a down payment on Lestat's penthouse?

So how long should a prudent vampire rest? It would depend, of course, on how much he would regret the bloodsucking he missed while sleeping and how much he would value the extra income when awake. However, if money spent in one year is just as good as money spent in another year, then why not sleep this year and have a little more money next year?[7] Taking this argument seriously, and treating vampires' lifetimes as literally infinite, then paradoxically he might as well sleep for an infinite amount of time—because there is an easy way to improve on any finite time spent sleeping. By resting an extra year, he could generate more wealth and would still have an infinite amount of time remaining to spend it! But more realistically, we don't know what kind of world there will be a thousand years from now, and a vampire who slept too many years might find himself so far out of touch with the world he returned to that he wouldn't know how to enjoy it.

Leaving these issues aside, one way to approach this question is to ask how much a patient vampire would need to accumulate before he could live indefinitely on just the interest. With a 7 percent rate of return, he could have a modest income of $50,000 per year from accumulated savings of about $714,000. But to have a more exciting income of $100,000 per year, he would need wealth of roughly $1.4 million. And if the interest rate were only 4 percent, he would need $2.5 million. The general rule is simple: take the desired income per year and divide by the rate of return. This works as long as his investments generate a constant return. Unfortunately, in the real world, returns are uncertain, and so the prudent vampire should have more wealth than needed in order to cover the bad times.

A similar calculation can be done for human investors, taking into account our finite lives and the fact that we cannot wait, sleeping, for as long as needed. The process requires three steps. First, determine how long the money needs to last after retirement. Second, use the assumed rate of return to determine how much money will be needed at retirement. And then third, determine how much must be saved before retirement to reach that amount. Because both the working and retired lives are finite, the math turns out to be more complicated than in the vampire example, but the principle is the same. And, as with the vampire example, it's the uncertainty that makes the calculation difficult. No one knows for sure what the world will bring in terms of investing returns and financial needs.

RIGHT PLACE, WRONG TIME

If you did invest in ways that promised 7 percent, and you didn't spend your earnings, it seems like you'd still have a good plan—you save for a long time and end up with a pile of cash. But is there anything else that could go wrong? Here's a hint: Look at the countries Dimson, Marsh, and Staunton studied; do you see what they have in common?

Before I answer, let me tell you another story from a lesser-known piece of vampire fiction. Baron Federov was a minor aristocrat in the court of Alexander I of Russia in the early 1800s. Known mostly for various bits of scandal related to the wife of a fellow noble, he lived a life of genteel poverty. However, his life radically changed one night when he was visited by Count Vardalok, who drank his blood and left him for dead. Accidentally, some of the Count's blood dripped down the baron's throat, and so Federov woke that night as a vampire. Now, the baron was a practical man and understood compound interest. Selling off what possessions he had, he invested in several promising Moscow properties and businesses, making a will that gave his assets to a "future descendant." He faked his own death as a human and then hid away in a crypt, confidently planning to return many years hence to claim his inheritance and live the rest of his time in prosperity.

In 1917 he awoke to claim his riches. Unfortunately for the baron, this also happened to be the time of the Russian Revolution, and he awoke not to the riches that compounding promised, but instead to see all his property taken away in the Communist revolution. Penniless, he wandered the streets and was staked the next night by a patrolling revolutionary guard.

Okay, that isn't a real story, but it illustrates an important point. It's said that history is written by the winners, and that's true of investing stories as well. Nobody is going to tell you about the money they lost playing the stock market. Because of that, you get a distorted idea about how likely it is for *you* to win. In the study that came up with our 7 percent average return, all the countries in the survey were winners. They were around in 1900 and they're around today. If they weren't, they couldn't be included in the study.

Economists have a name for this problem: *survivorship bias*.[8] Survivorship bias can cause you to misinterpret past performance and overestimate the returns you should get. It's important to look at the losers as much as the winners. However, people like winners, and so we only hear about the rich Mr. Cullen and not the unfortunate others such as our Baron Federov of

Russia, or Señor Gonzalez of Cuba, or the dread Guo Xiang of China, all of whom happened to be in the wrong country at the wrong time.

Because of survivorship bias, expecting a 7 percent return is probably optimistic. It also reminds us of the risks of investing in a single location. A solution to this problem is diversification—not putting all your eggs in the same basket. In other words, make sure that you have put your wealth in a number of different investments so that if one of them goes bad you will not go completely broke. Common investment advice is to diversify across a large number of stocks and bonds and also not to invest heavily in the same industry you work in. Recently we've seen the importance of this. Pity the poor Enron employees who had their savings in Enron stock. When they lost their jobs, they lost their retirement savings as well!

Of course, just investing in a number of different Russian properties wouldn't have saved Baron Federov. In order to really address this problem, the prudent vampire investor needs to make sure that his wealth is hidden around the world. It's tempting to try to predict which country will work out—or which country won't. Will China be the next great economic power or will it fall apart in internal dissention? Will Russia join the capitalist countries or fall back into an authoritarian regime? What about India or Indonesia? The right answer is that we don't know for sure, and so instead of trying to figure out the answer, we should spread our money across a number of different countries. Not surprisingly, Carlisle Cullen, being the wise investor, does exactly this. His wealth is described as "bloated accounts that existed all over the world."[9] Indeed, not only is the money spread around the world, the family even owns an island in the South Atlantic.

Fortunately, this is one piece of vampire investing advice that we can follow. The cost of investing internationally has fallen with the increased availability of low-expense mutual funds that invest in individual countries or parts of the world. Ironically, though, at the same time that it's become easier to invest internationally, we've also seen increasing globalization of the economy. Countries are more closely connected, so that when the economy of one country runs into trouble, the economies of other countries will suffer as well, reducing the benefits of diversifying internationally.

STATISTICS FOR VAMPIRES

When Buffy went off to college, she found that vampires were already there, occupying an abandoned fraternity house close to campus.[10] While the vampires could have used their proximity to the college as an opportunity to increase their education, mostly they just spent their time eating freshmen. However, as future investors, a class in statistics and probability would have done them some good, as probability is at the heart of diversification.

It would seem that vampires would have an extra advantage over human investors in that they can invest over a large number of years, allowing the good years and bad years to cancel out. In other words, diversifying across time. Unfortunately, it's not that simple.

To see why, we need to spend a little time studying how diversification works. A simple numerical example can provide some intuition, if not a thorough mathematical treatment. Imagine you made an investment that is equally likely to pay you $0 or $100. Now imagine cutting up the investment into one hundred little bets that pay $0 or $1, where the outcomes of the bets are unrelated. You could end up with one hundred wins or one hundred losses, but the chances of that happening are small. What you are more likely to get is something around $50. This is the standard story of diversification. What's driving this result is that some of the good and bad outcomes cancel out and the range of outcomes doesn't change; just like before, the most you could get is $100 and the least is $0.

But investing over time is different. Imagine that you make that $0-or-$100 bet every year. Instead of cutting the bet into smaller pieces, what happens is that the bets accumulate over time. This year you either get $0 or $100. Next year, you get another $0 or $100, so after two years you might end up with $0, $100, or $200. In the first year, the "middle" of the range (or "expected value") is $50, with the extremes being $50 higher or lower. In the second year, the middle outcome is $100, with the range of outcomes being $100 higher and lower. When you invest over time, you benefit from the good and bad individual bets canceling out (as in the previous example), but that doesn't outweigh the effect of the increase in the probability of outcomes far away from the average, so the variability of your final wealth increases over time. Although there's some good news in that the amount of added risk declines with each additional bet.[11]

To make matters worse, each additional year of investing isn't actually an additional bet; it's really a multiplication of all the previous bets. If you are reinvesting all your wealth each year (which is what you would need to do to get the returns we saw earlier), then one bad year at the end could change everything. If the stock market were down 30 percent in the year you decided to cash out, you wouldn't just lose 30 percent of one year's investment, you'd lose 30 percent of *all your wealth*. Imagine a poor vampire who chose to awake just after the stock market crash of the Great Depression. He'd probably be tempted to go right back to sleep.

There is one exception to this story that just might provide some protection to the long-term vampire investor. In the previous example, I assumed that the results from each bet were unrelated. If you won one bet, it didn't change the probability of winning the next. If we flip a coin and it comes up heads, we don't think it will change the probability of getting heads on the next flip. But imagine a different kind of coin where the outcome in the past affects the outcome in the future. For example, suppose getting heads on one flip made it more likely that the next flip would come up heads. Statisticians call this relationship a *positive* correlation. It is called positive because you are more likely to get the *same* result. If coming up heads made it more likely that the next flip would be *tails*, that would be *negative* correlation. There is some evidence that, over a long period of time, stock returns have a negative correlation. This means that if stocks grow faster than average for a period of time, then they'll grow slower than average, or even decline, for a while after that. This also holds for periods of stock declines; they are more likely to be followed by periods of above-average growth. Of course, this is only a tendency and is not guaranteed, nor do we know exactly when things change. But still, this statistical characteristic can be important for investors.

What it means is that if we invest for a large number of years, the uncertainty we face with stocks with respect to other investments will be reduced. Even if we see a decline in stocks, it may be reversed if we wait long enough (although the reverse is true, too—if we see a particularly good period of stock returns, we should expect slower growth after that). This is the logic behind Jeremy Seigel's *Stocks for the Long Run*, which argues that people with long investing horizons should be more aggressive about their investments. If you are retiring in five years you might want to be more conservative with your investments. However, if you are a vampire investor, when the market turns down, you can just wait it out. This is also the logic behind another, more speculative approach to investing that is of particular interest to immortals.

BLOOD IN THE STREETS

One of the reasons for negative correlation over time may be that investors are driven by their passions. If people are too optimistic about the future, this may cause prices of stocks and other investments to temporarily soar beyond what they are worth (this was dubbed "irrational exuberance" by former Federal Reserve chairman Alan Greenspan). On the other hand, when the economy is bad and people are pessimistic, they might be too pessimistic, and so investment bargains can be found.

This was best expressed by the financier Nathan Rothschild, who lived during the time of the Napoleonic wars. "The time to buy," said Rothschild, "is when blood is running in the streets." Now that is the kind of investing philosophy that a vampire could get behind!

Indeed, vampires would be well suited for this approach, because what it really requires is patience. It takes someone with a very long investment horizon to be able to wait for one of the occasional moments when an economy collapses and then be able to hold the investment until the economy recovers. Time allows flexibility, which your average human investor, saving for an investing goal ten years from now, may not have.

We all know the exploits of Abraham Lincoln in his fight against vampires in the American South during the U.S. Civil War.[12] However, for a vampire, the economic opportunities that the Civil War represented were at least as important as the political struggle. While the economic devastation in the South was dramatic, its reunification with the North implied that, in the long run, the South would be prosperous and grow. The economic significance of the burning of Atlanta was that real estate there would be *cheap*. A smart vampire, who carefully saved his money waiting for this moment, could purchase a substantial part of downtown Atlanta and find himself one hundred years later a very rich property magnate.

CAN WE BE VAMPIRE INVESTORS?

As we've seen, the formula offered by the *Wall Street Journal* at the start of this chapter, money plus time equals riches, is not so simple. Compounding can produce some amazing results, but not by itself. You need to get a high enough return on your investments, invest for a *long* time, resist pulling out money for present use, and avoid catastrophic risks (or take advantage of them, if you can).

Being a vampire does have its advantages when it comes to investing. However, we can get some perspective from Sookie Stackhouse: "We were in a service and delivery alley that ran behind all the stores in the little strip mall. There were several other cars parked back there, Eric's sporty red convertible among them. All the vehicles were high priced. You won't find a vampire in a Ford Fiesta."[13]

Even if time will not help us become as fantastically rich as Carlisle Cullen, time and careful management of risk can help us with more human investment goals such as buying houses, preparing for retirement, and avoiding Ford Fiestas. And who knows, if things do work out well for us, we can visit the bank and join the Count in counting up our money, $1,000,000 . . . $2,000,000 . . . $3,000,000. . . .

Chapter Nine

Zombification Insurance

Eleanor Brown and Robert Prag

Before becoming the first person to fly solo from England to North America, Beryl Markham scouted elephants in east Africa, where she once found herself cornered by an angry bull. Markham recalls facing the prospect of being soundly trampled, "a fate no more tragic than simple death, but infinitely less tidy."[1]

The circumstances of people's deaths can themselves be tragic, quite apart from the tragedy of death itself. Hamlet is not just moping because his father died: he's tormented by a fratricide he must avenge. Even while being stabbed, Julius Caesar especially laments being stabbed by Brutus, his friend. Among common folks, the death of an outcast, denied rituals to honor the dead, was tragic. To this day, many poor Americans pay two or three dollars a week for burial or "final expenses" insurance, a small life-insurance policy that covers the costs of a proper funeral.

With zombies among us, we face a new tragic circumstance surrounding death: beyond untidiness, death by zombie attack brings the unsettling prospect of becoming undead ourselves. Whatever improprieties we have allowed ourselves over the years, few of us have contemplated with relish the thought of remorselessly tearing others to shreds. Fewer still have contemplated doing so indiscriminately. We are appalled by the prospect of rising up as marauding zombies and will pay good money to ensure that we do not.

Who might offer services to address these fears? Burial insurance providers, adept at responding to clients' notions of dignified disposition after death, face incentives to expand their services to ensure that a corpse once reposed will continue to rest in peace, with no unseemly interlude of brains-seeking rampage. Medical insurers will have relevant areas of expertise as well. Entrenched insurance providers will face competition from new entrants with expertise not in insurance but in dealing with the zombie threat and specializing in the niche market of zombification insurance.

Anticipating that there will be no shortage of potential buyers and sellers, we explore the idea of zombification insurance. Because insurance markets, like certain corpses, have been known to go awry, and because this particular market has implications for public health and national security, it is worth anticipating the contours of its development. Are background conditions right for an insurance market to develop? What zombification insurance services will people be willing to pay for, and how do they align with the public interest?

A MARKET FOR ZOMBIFICATION INSURANCE?

Insurance rarely appears in tales of the zombie apocalypse. None of those people running screaming through the streets in *World War Z* are looking for their claims adjusters. The ravaged cities of *Return of the Living Dead* or *Resident Evil 3* do not call for insurance markets; they call for the military, or for Jill Valentine.

Insurance is at its most useful in a stable world sprinkled with small chances of isolated calamities that loom large for individuals—an expensive hospital stay or the death of a breadwinner—but not for whole populations. If everybody buys hospital insurance and only a few are hospitalized in any given year, nobody has to pay very much for hospital insurance, and nobody faces the bankrupting prospect of huge hospital bills. People don't have to worry about how they might pay a big bill; that risk has been transferred to the insurance provider. Insurance companies pool lots of relatively small premiums in order to make a few relatively large payouts. If the insurers can count on the proportion of the population being hospitalized to be pretty stable, or at least predictable, year to year, then they can charge premiums that allow them to pay the claims that arise. This is the genius of insurance: by bringing together lots of people with small chances of isolated calamities, total risk is reduced as some people's good luck offsets other people's bad luck.

In a full-blown zombie apocalypse, then, anybody who wants to run screaming through the streets in search of her claims adjuster should be heading for the courthouse where the insurers are filing their bankruptcy papers. Apocalypse is not the stuff of insurance markets, or at least not the simple, risk-pooling kind that depend on a lot of people having good luck while a few others are being eaten. When everyone has bad luck, insurance does not work.

To discuss zombification insurance, then, we must tear ourselves away from our movies and video games and plant ourselves firmly in the real world, in which zombies are unlikely to get out of control. Because of the widespread influence of the media's overheated imaginings and because scientific progress in understanding the mechanisms of infection and reanimation has been slow, we begin by stating clearly the mundane circumstances in which we expect the market for zombification insurance to develop. As with earlier scourges such as polio and tuberculosis, we imagine a world in which public health is attentive to the rare but serious outbreak; we assume the zombie population to be small, approximately stable, and beyond our powers of eradication.[2] We rely on *The Zombie Survival Guide*'s authoritative depiction of the process of viral infection, human death, and reanimation. In this view, an otherwise healthy but newly infected person has about twenty-one hours before losing a pulse and another three hours or so before reanimation. For persons who have purchased zombification insurance and survived a zombie encounter, this day of decline represents the first opportunity to collect on their insurance coverage.

THE SCOPE OF ZOMBIFICATION INSURANCE COVERAGE

Fearing our own reanimation as unlovely asocial people-munchers, what services might we seek? The movie *Fido* shows a funeral with separate caskets for head and body, rendering the reordered brain inert. This is a simple arrangement that scarcely calls for insurance beyond the sort of burial insurance we see today.[3]

Decapitation (or gunshot to the frontal lobe, etc.) is not a wholly attractive prospect, however. In many traditions, mourning a death involves a viewing of the body, and great care is taken to present the corpse in as attractive and lifelike a manner as possible. More generally, Americans are squeamish about bodily integrity; witness the fact that most of us have resisted public campaigns to register as organ donors. The incidence of needless decapitation, among, for example, newly deceased persons whose degree of exposure is unknown, could be reduced by holding the body in restraints for a day or two; corpses that do not reanimate could then safely be buried intact. Similarly straightforward diagnostic services exist for living persons who may have been infected but who are for the moment asymptomatic. *The Zombie Survival Guide* reports that swarming insects will not bite an infected person, for example, suggesting a quick, easy, low-cost test for infection. It may also prove to be true that dogs can be trained to reliably identify infection by sense of smell, as portrayed in *World War Z*.

One worrisome objection to prophylactic decapitation goes to the nature of death itself. Has an infected person died, leaving behind a personless corpse to reanimate as a soulless zombie? Or does the viral nature of the transmutation argue for a model of disease rather than death? And if a zombie is a diseased human who poses a threat to others, isn't quarantine a prescribed response? Americans are not at ease with suicide or euthanasia, and if the zombie in question was recently Grandma rather than an anonymous member of the horde surrounding your farmhouse, humane quarantine—especially if it is cheap or covered by insurance—may appeal to family and friends. Sensationalistic as media images of zombies have been, this human impulse toward quarantine has made it to the screen: Shaun shelters his zombified friend Ed, and the feuding Muldoons are religiously devoted to maintaining their zombified kinfolk.[4]

Loyalty and sentimentality have their limits, however, and considerations of public health and private burnout suggest that many people will demand quarantine services in the market rather than provide them at home. How humane, and how cheap, quarantine might be is a matter that markets will be quick to explore. Available evidence is consistent with the view that zombies, restrained from seeking flesh, do not suffer. Although the physiology remains mysterious, it is alleged that zombies need no external fuel sources; they do not experience starvation in the usual sense.[5] Quarantine services might resemble a lock-down variant of a Japanese business traveler's pod hotel, with drawer-like spaces stacked neatly and monitored electronically. Formerly favorite music, family photos, periodic gift baskets of stem-cell-cultured brain tissue: America's consumer culture, coupled with an all-too-human reluctance to say good-bye to a loved one, suggests that the zombie version of the nursing home is on the horizon.

By covering quarantine services, zombification insurance becomes less a variant of burial insurance and more similar to long-term care insurance. The expense of such services is likely to draw into the zombification insurance market many middle-class families whose budgets would allow them to pay for smaller services, such as diagnosis and prophylactic lobotomy, out of pocket, with no need for insurance. The importance to the insurance industry of being able to expand into the middle-class market through offering quarantine services may pose a serious challenge to government regulation. We return to this point later.

Some of us do not wish to become zombies, even if we might be successfully restrained from wreaking havoc and even if we might be warehoused with something approaching tender regard. The indignities of human aging offer ample vexation; the thought of succumbing to Alzheimer's terrifies; zombification is altogether a step too far. Especially for young survivors of zombie attack whose infection is untimely, there is powerful motive to wish for a third way between death and undead existence. Absent a cure, hope lies only in delay: in the first precious hours after a victim is infected and before the virus has shut down the body's normal human functioning, there is the possibility of cryogenic intervention. The still-functionally-human victim may be stored at low temperatures and maintained, waiting for the discovery of a way to destroy the virus. The cryonics industry in the United States is up and running, on the storage end if not yet the restoration end, the details of which are left to future invention. One cryonics firm recently reported that, employing the services of a private jet, scarcely more than seven hours elapsed between the death of its most recent patient and the beginning of the preservation procedure.[6] The time frame for cryonic intervention, then, is in keeping with the requirements of zombie attack victims who hope to suspend the process of zombification in anticipation of the eventual discovery of an antidote.[7]

Whole-body cryonic preservation is not cheap. An insurance policy offering this quarter-million-dollar service to zombie attack victims will be affordably priced only if the policy is purchased by many persons who in the end are not attacked.[8] While economies of scale and increased competition are likely to bring down the cost structure of this industry, it is too early to predict the size of the market for such high-end insurance coverage.

IS ZOMBIFICATION INSURANCE GOOD FOR SOCIETY?

From diagnosis to burial, warehousing, and low-temperature vitrification, there exists a range of services we can expect to see offered in a brisk market for zombification insurance. Economists generally view this sort of insurance market as improving people's well-being by making it easier for them to go about their lives. Small risks of large uninsured disasters leave people not knowing how much money to set aside for a rainy day; planning is much easier when one can make small, regular payments in exchange for a guarantee of large help should disaster strike. This is the fundamental way in which the availability of zombification insurance is expected to increase well-being.

A secondary way in which insurance affects well-being stems from people getting careless once they are insured. People often take precautions to reduce the chance of disaster striking. It is prudent, for example, to refrain from approaching unkempt persons with black teeth and rotting skin who shamble toward you mumbling something about brains, however much you'd like to offer them a shower and a meal. One downside to insurance markets is that by making personal calamities less dire, they may also make them more common and more expensive for society as a whole, because people relax and take less precaution. To some extent, insurance companies can guard against this, writing necessary precautions into the contracts they offer. Homes must have working smoke detectors in order to be insured against fires, for example, and drivers must be licensed in order to get auto insurance. But contracts are almost always incomplete—there are no rules about not leaving lit candles on the dining room table when you head for the bedroom or avoiding Los Angeles freeways at rush hour when the kids are fighting in the backseat and you've got a terrible headache and your GPS shows zombies wandering in the slow lane up ahead—and we take risks when insured that we just wouldn't take otherwise. And when disaster strikes and our home burns down or our car is in an accident, being insured gives us incentives to rebuild more lavishly or to fix smaller dents than we would have done if we were footing the bill. These behavioral responses to insurance go by the name *moral hazard*, and they will affect the net benefits economists see as arising from insurance markets.

In a world of zombie apocalypse, everything is on the line and nearly everyone is taking every precaution they can think of. But in orderly, everyday life, with more people drowning in swimming pools than dying from zombie attack, do we expect zombification insurance to cause less precaution? It is easy to imagine margins of behavior that might be affected. Consider a parent, one of whose children has been attacked. Will that parent offer more aid to the stricken child, seeking quarantine perhaps, when assured that if bitten the parent will be also be quarantined before causing harm to the other children? Or might someone who had been an advocate of gun control in the pre-zombie era respond to insurance coverage by deciding not to keep a gun in the house? Will we see an increase in the risky behavior of persons engaging in unprotected sex with people who have had contact with zombies or with zombies themselves? The costliness of these zombification-increasing behavioral responses remains an empirical question, but our intuitions say that they are small relative to the benefits of insurance.

More costly will be the demand for excessive remediation when an insured person suffers and survives a zombie attack. With insurance paying most of the bills, the stricken people will demand more and better services—better coffins, less deforming destruction of the frontal lobes, quarantine in a more comfortable facility, transportation by private jet to the cryonics lab—than they might if they were worrying about the bills they were leaving to their loved ones. Zombification insurance is in this regard a lot like medical insurance: more people get care, and the care gets more expensive, driving up expenditures in two ways at once.

A more perverse form of moral hazard may arise in the presence of insurance that offers cryonic services. Companies offering fire insurance are suspicious when a failing business burns down; could it be that the owners, well insured, purposely increased the chances of fire, preferring the payout to the business? Is there anyone who, possessed of zombification insurance, would analogously seek a zombie encounter?[9] It seems doubtful on the face of it, but the benefits of a policy offering cryonic services are, like the cash from the fire insurance settlement, ameliorative of more than the insured-against risk. Zombie attacks are rare relative to the diagnosis of inoperable medical conditions, making widely subscribed contracts promising cryonic preservation in the event of a zombie attack cheap relative to contracts promising cryonic intervention in the case of, say, stage four cancer. Insured persons who might value cryonic services for non-zombie-related reasons might be tempted to gain access through zombie attack.

This possibility would not be lost on insurance companies, who would have incentives to write contracts to avoid letting people with stage four cancer buy zombification insurance that included cryonic services.[10]

CORRECTIVE MORAL HAZARD

Zombification lies at the heart of a public-health priority; in the language of economists, it is a source of negative externalities. You may not want to die or become a zombie, and your aversion will lead you to take a certain amount of precaution as you go about your daily affairs. Your neighbors are similarly hopeful that you will not die and rise undead, but your degree of caution is not affected by their concern because there is no mechanism for your fellow citizens to bribe you into taking extra care. It is an extra public-health benefit of zombification insurance, then, that when insurance foots the bill you—and your neighbors—are suddenly much more willing, in cases of suspected infection, to seek immediate diagnosis and immediate restraint. In other settings, this behavioral response to being insured amounts to wasting resources by demanding too much care. In this setting, however, the public-health externality implies that we started with too little care, and the behavioral response is a corrective action at a societal level.

Another behavioral response to being insured might be seen in the occupations people are willing to enter. Occupational hazards are facts of life, and many of them are addressed through insurance markets. Some occupations endanger life and limb; many soldiers, firefighters, and police officers would be in different lines of work if they could not depend on life insurance policies, should disaster strike, to take care of their dependents. Hospital workers and first responders to scenes of medical emergency face a heightened risk of zombie attack on the job; uninsured risk can be expected to drive some workers into other, safer jobs, even though they would have been more productive in these medical fields. These medical jobs will become more attractive in the presence of well-functioning zombification insurance markets, and we expect that labor will be allocated more productively as a result. Moral hazard in occupational choice is once again a corrective response rather than a distortion.

The picture is considerably less rosy when we turn our attention to national security. The most serious public concern arising from a developed market for zombification insurance comes from the provision of quarantine services. The nursing home analogy goes only so far: a zombie quarantine facility is a store of lethal force.[11] Would we trust our government, and others, not to see zombies as low-rent, imprecisely aimed drone substitutes? Could terrorist groups, foreign governments, turncoat fanatics, or anomic computer hackers set loose our own zombies on our own soil? Zombies are not explicitly dealt with in the Geneva Conventions and their protocols.[12] Any international treaties surrounding the military use of zombie populations are likely to be opposed in the United States by an insurance industry eager to expand its zombification business. The industry has deep pockets: in the first half of 2010, at the height of the political battle over the estate tax, it spent $10,000,000 per month on lobbying activities.[13] Government decisions to prohibit the establishment of private quarantine facilities will be made more difficult by the presence of a zombification insurance industry that stands to profit from their existence.

REGULATION OF ZOMBIE INSURANCE MARKETS

People fear death in all its forms. Death by zombie is a lot like being stomped to death by an elephant: no more tragic than simple death, but markedly less tidy. Rising up undead in the wake of a zombie attack, however, is a tragedy in its own right, one people will pay to avoid. We have identified a range of services to address the needs of zombie attack victims, some of them expensive enough to warrant the emergence of a robust market for zombification insurance. We have discussed the mechanisms through which we expect this insurance to enhance the well-being of both insurance customers and society at large.

Fruitful areas for further research include interactions between the private market for zombification insurance, the scope of public zombification insurance, and the public-health consequences of leaving substantial populations uninsured. Poor Americans will rely on state-run Medicaid programs for their zombification insurance coverage, and these programs will vary, both in the proportions of the population insured and the range of benefits offered, from state to state. Variations in the severity of zombie outbreaks across more and less broadly insured parts of the country could provide data that would allow us to estimate the public-health benefits of zombification insurance. We suspect the results will provide a gory answer to the question of why some small-government-leaning parts of the country are referred to as red states.

We urge the public and its elected officials to take seriously the likely development of privately owned zombie quarantine facilities as the increasing availability of insurance increases the demand for their services. Such facilities may require levels of regulatory oversight generally applied to arsenals or nuclear waste sites, given the lethal potential of their inhabitants. Despite the clear benefits of zombification insurance, an underregulated market for zombie quarantine facilities, encouraged by an insurance industry that stands to profit from it, might provide the crack in our public-health defenses that leads from a contained and stable coexistence to a real zombie apocalypse.

Chapter Ten

Monsters of Capital

Vampires, Zombies, and Consumerism

Lorna Piatti-Farnell

The Gothic world of the undead and the materially bound discourse of economics are intrinsically linked. Although, at first glance, the two could seem far apart, they connect through the use of imagery and metaphor. In *Capital*, his famous work of political economy, Karl Marx often uses Gothic terminology to discuss the workings of capitalism. Marx is particularly fond of employing metaphors of the undead to explain the nature of capitalist economies, and in this group, vampires and zombies are privileged creatures. Marx likens the capitalist to a vampire on several occasions, the idea of "draining workers" being unavoidable: "Capital is dead labour which, vampire-like, lives only by sucking living labour, and lives the more, the more labour it sucks."[1] And while the power and control of the capitalist are identified with the vampire, the factory workers—alienated and exploited—find symbolic representation as zombies: the unfair division of labor, Marx contends, converts "the worker into a living appendage of the machine."[2] The politics of consumer capitalism seem to aptly mesh with undead folklore to generate a conceptual association between acquisition and satisfaction, production and desire. Although *Capital* was first published 1867, the conceptualization of labor, economic gain, and commodities in Marx's text draws attention to the important connections between representation, identity, and consumerism that are still pertinent to the economic context of the modern day.

Implicit in Marx's perspective is a critique of consumerism: that our consumption choices may not reflect our own needs, but the needs of the system. Stuart and Elizabeth Ewen have long claimed that consumerism "puts leisure, beauty, and pleasure in the reach of all," so that the logic of consumption is "embroiled in our intimacies," it is "the insatiable urge for new things."[3] Yet, not all forms of consumerism are alike. While the nature of open markets provides buyers with an array of desirable commodities, services, and purchasable "experiences," price still remains an important definitive characteristic in the capitalist game.[4] So, just as not all products are alike, neither are all consumers. On the one hand, we have the small circle of the upper classes, the consumer elite, who can indulge in acquiring objects that can signal the owner's high social status. These are the practitioners of what I like to call "high consumerism," a way of buying and displaying that is beyond both the financial and the social capabilities of the masses. On the other hand, we also find various instances of "low consumerism," a phenomenon that is not only more economically accessible, but also connected to mass production. This engagement with consumerism is mostly associated with the working and middle classes, where quantity and common "branding" become important cogs in the system of social identification.[5]

Taking the conceptual associations between monstrosity, commodities, and social status as a point of departure, this chapter discusses the role of zombies and vampires as two different critiques of contemporary consumerism. To say that vampires and zombies act as metaphors for consumerism is, of course, not new. Academic scholarship and populist views alike have been keen to link both undead creatures to critiques of consumer capitalism, probably a legacy of Marx's own metaphorical use of them in his works. On the one hand, we have vampires, often portrayed as rich and surrounded by beautiful, expensive objects; on the other, we have zombies, undead creatures often depicted as dispossessed and detached, who are forever cursed to wear the literal and figurative rags of their former human lives. My perspective, however, places an emphasis on behavioral psychology and synthesizes a number of socioeconomic perspectives in order to uncover how the monsters of fiction are distorted, Gothicized images of the consumerist "monsters" who shape the real world. Focusing on the ways in which the two types of undead are portrayed in contemporary narratives—ranging from literary fiction to film and television—my analysis aims to show how these fantastical consumer "monsters" reflect cultural anxieties and desires.[6]

IMMORTAL LUXURIES

The term "luxury" provides a common ground for the modern experience of the vampire. Even traditional literary vampires were known to enjoy the experience of lavish surroundings. Count Dracula himself lived in castle that, although left to ruin and decay for the most part, still communicated the former grandeur of the vampire's aristocratic status. Joseph Sheridan Le Fanu's *Carmilla* (1872) preferred to hunt young ladies from the upper-class layers of society and to dwell in sumptuous surroundings; similarly, Varney the vampire—in James Malcolm Rymer's novel of the same name (1847)—showed a distinct interest in luxury living, and his actions were often motivated by monetary concerns. While the association between vampires and aristocratic luxury was common in nineteenth-century narratives, it was the twentieth century that successfully showed the vampire as a creature attuned to the workings of consumerism, a "new monster" who enjoyed the finest things in life and whose bloody appetites were often likened, metaphorically speaking, to the vampiric nature of capitalism. Marx's famous definition of capitalism as a vampire-like parasite naturally provided an important jumping-off point for critics and fictional writers alike in constructing the vampire's connection to lavishness, wealth, and surplus value. And, in the past forty years, vampires truly have become creatures of affluence and taste, accustomed to the aesthetic properties of expensive commodities.[7]

In Anne Rice's *Vampire Chronicles* (1976–2003), vampires are often described as sophisticated creatures with an aristocratic taste for extravagance and indulgence, perennially interested in acquiring wealth. The vampire Lestat—arguably the central character in the long-running series—is portrayed as loving expensive objects and opulent living; spanning over two centuries, Lestat's life is characterized mainly by his predatory, bloodthirsty endeavors, on the one hand, and his consumerist, luxury-obsessed habits, on the other. Acquiring a large fortune that will allow him an aristocratic lifestyle is seemingly the main reason that moves Lestat to approach, and later turn into a vampire, Louis de Pointe du Lac, the narrator of the now famous novel *Interview with the Vampire* (1976). In *The Vampire Lestat* (1985), Lestat's consumer propensities become even more obvious as the vampire is transformed into a rock star, a figure in itself intrinsically connected to the world of ostentatious display and consumption. We are told on a number of occasions that he loves "luxurious things" and that all his possessions speak of the remarkable individual he truly is. Lestat's luxury living indicates an emphasis on the symbolic nature of possession. The dynamics at work here are reminiscent of Jean Baudrillard's theory of *sign value*, a term denoting the value afforded to an object because of the social prestige that it imparts on its possessor rather than the utilitarian value that would be provided by its primary use.[8] Far from being an "aristocrat" in the ancient, European sense, Lestat enjoys the lavish lifestyle of the socioeconomic "1 percent" by being both the producer (in the form of his music) and consumer of expensive commodities—designer cars, clothes, and houses—in the sign value–obsessed context of the 1980s.

A similar instance of luxury-living, brand-obsessed vampires can be found in Whitley Strieber's *The Hunger* (1981), where yuppie vampires—including the truly irresistible Miriam Blaylock—commonly enjoy the extravagance of consumerism, where designer labels become almost an extension of the vampire itself. Miriam's consumerist tendencies are further amplified in the film adaptation of the novel directed by Tony Scott in 1983. Here, the visual medium of film proves very efficient in communicating vividly the capitalism inherent in the vampire's existence and the high-consumer habits that define the creature at an economic level. Designer brands are everywhere, and the unmistakable logos of Dior and Chanel announce the vampire's presence in a way that is perhaps even more eloquent than fangs and blood. In these 1980s examples, vampires are trendy, consumer-obsessed personifications of the age and pointedly "indict the yuppie consumerism encouraged by American economic politics of the time."[9] The rampant consumerism of characters such as Lestat and Miriam sets them apart from the common human not only in social and evolutionary terms, but also in economic terms, highlighting the vampire as a figure of distinction—to use a term favored by Pierre Bourdieu—within the wider landscape of consumer and popular culture.

While both Lestat in the *Vampire Chronicles* and Miriam in *The Hunger* may pretend to "live" a normal life with their human acquaintances, their consumer habits and true way of life remove them from the everyday socioeconomic context and place them in the sphere of *conspicuous consumption*. This term, coined in 1899 by economist Thorstein Veblen, is useful in identifying the yuppie vampires as belonging to a higher order of consumer, an upper-class group for whom the acquisition of expensive goods is part of the display of their social status. Conspicuous consumption is the spending of money and the acquisition of luxury goods in order to display economic power. That economic power translates into higher social status for the conspicuous consumer, whose public display of wealth makes him the source of not only envy, but also desire.[10] Luxury, therefore, equals prestige. Although Veblen's understanding of conspicuous consumption was based on his analysis of nineteenth-century socioeconomics, the term still has relevance in the late twentieth century and, arguably, the twenty-first, where significant material improvements—including the increasing disposable income of the larger middle-class group of the Western world—have allowed extravagant items to become a sign of prestige. This is particularly pertinent in view of the development of brand-extended, "masstige" versions of everyday luxury that are now within the reach of many.[11]

In our contemporary twenty-first century, the vampire's lavish consumption has become the order of the day. Far from simply being an extravagant occurrence, consumerism in the vampire's life is not only unavoidable, but to be expected. The media-rich environment of the post-2000 era has truly made a virtue of portraying vampires as incredibly wealthy. Across the representational spectrum, vampires are creatures of means, surrounded by expensive commodities and living in luxury. Although, when it comes to the vampire's possessions, different and disparate examples can be found (and it would be unwise to generalize), it is reasonable to suggest that vampires are "upper class" in their tendencies. [12] The list of rich, consumerist vampires in contemporary media is long and plentiful; examples range from the extravagant specimens in *True Blood*—a television series adapted from Charlaine Harris's well-known *Sookie Stackhouse* novels (2001–2003)—to the sexy, trendy vamps in L. J. Smith's *The Vampire Diaries*, both in their ongoing literary and televised incarnations. On the silver screen, vampires are portrayed as rich and powerful in the *Blade* trilogy (1998–2004), the *Underworld* film series (2003–2012), and Timur Bekmambetov's *Abraham Lincoln: Vampire Hunter* (2012), based on the 2010 novel of the same name. The connection between high consumerism and vampires is so well established that Rob Latham has gone as far as labeling the creature as the "exalted representative" of economic "difference" and perpetual "accumulation." The vampire, Latham suggests, is an "insatiable consumer." [13]

Where mainstream examples are concerned, however, the high-consumerist existence of vampires is nowhere more obvious than in the popular and truly unavoidable *Twilight* saga. The vampires in this storyline—both in their original incarnations in Stephenie Meyer's novels and in their cinematic adaptations—are portrayed as the ultimate creatures of affluence. From the aristocratic creatures of Europe to the nouveau riche families of the New World, vampires are depicted as having an immense wealth at their disposal, evidently granted to them by their long-existing, often centennial status. Winning in popularity and attention is the Cullen family—captained by the youthful-looking Edward—a group of blood-bonded vampires who fill the protagonist role in the series. The Cullens live in a large mansion with high ceilings and wooden floors; the mansion, however, is not their only foray into real estate, as we are told they own luxury properties all over the world. They drive expensive cars and wear the latest designer clothes. The visual advantages of the cinematic medium make the Cullens' wealth even more explicit in the film adaptation, where the brands are granted more attention, and Edward Cullen is seen driving a Volvo XC60, a custom-made car sold only in Europe. The European nature of the car here loudly communicates its status as a luxury item for the American audience. The Cullens' wealth has been depicted as so immense that *Forbes* magazine ranked Carlisle Cullen— the patriarch of the family—as the richest (fictional) man of the year in 2010, the second richest in 2011, and the third richest in 2012, his accumulated fortune amounting to $36.3 billion. [14] An impressive figure for a three-hundred-year-old vampire who pretends to be a human doctor at the local hospital in the small American town of Forks, Washington.

The custom-designed nature of the Cullens' houses, cars, and even clothing removes them from the reach of the middle classes who, even with substantial disposable income, cannot hope to match the uncountable wealth of the vampires, whose designer luxury is customized, personalized, overexpensive, and, therefore, unattainable. Mark Tungate contends that luxury itself is inseparable from notions of "authenticity" and "engaging experiences" that, in turn, are intrinsically connected to the "consumer sensibilities" of our contemporary moment.[15] One might be tempted here to see the contemporary vampires' engagement with luxury commodities as a form of rat race, a status competition that forces them to continually search for better things, better objects, better representations of themselves in the world of commodities. This would place the vampires within the framework of Robert Frank's theory of unsustainable accumulation. Frank describes an "expenditure cascade" in which the effects of status-seeking economic behavior ripple through all layers of the economic scale, causing the system to rely on untenable competitive consumption.[16] Status is seen in a negative light by Frank, who perceives it as the main cause of excessive and potentially self-destructive behavior in society.

In this light, the vampires' overly active, status-driven consumer tendencies could be perceived as unsustainable, their unrestricted nature posing an untenable aim for the wider economic framework. And yet, contemporary twenty-first-century vampires—the Cullens in particular, but also examples from *True Blood* and *The Vampire Diaries*—seem to take their wealth for granted; these vampires have moved on from the money-driven, trademark-obsessed behavior of their ancestors. The Cullens' accumulation may be conspicuous in that it displays status, but that social visibility is only evident through the eyes of others. It is not portrayed as a "negative" trait: it is aspirational for those who look upon it and yet conspicuously unmentioned by the vampires themselves. In this sense, the Cullens' affluence does not "cascade"—to use the term favored by Frank—through the economic structure, but relies on a seemingly self-regenerating, nucleus-based system whose source, like that of the vampire itself, is left unchallenged.

The Cullens' lavish, taken-for-granted lifestyle—in its obvious divergence from the realistically achievable—is symptomatic of a socioeconomic framework that not only distinguishes individuals in terms of ownership, but showcases a new category of consumer: the consumer whose prestige is beyond simply being "upper class," but is in fact "without class." It is the economy of the inaccessible, the exclusive domain of an elite whose luxury does not simply lie in owning and flaunting expensive brands—as it would still have done in the late twentieth century—but in accessing a category of branding that goes, paradoxically, beyond the brand. While brands may now be within the reach of the masses, the personalization of the Cullens' objects places their activities within the postmodern realm of experience, where the real luxury is not simply to be found in possessing, but also in familiarizing the excessive.

UNDEAD COMMODITIES

While the high consumerism of vampires is indulged in numerous contemporary representations, the zombies' narrative of low consumerism is also clearly addressed by examples in popular culture. Evocative links between consumer capitalism and the "zombification" of everyday modern life are clearly made in George A. Romero's 'Dead' series. The series quickly gained popularity with audiences, and Romero is regarded as a very influential figure in establishing the view of the zombie we still hold today. Romero's work can be credited with distancing the zombie from its folkloristic origin as a magically commanded, soulless individual and transforming into a walking, rotting corpse obsessed with consuming human flesh. And even though variations on the theme have been produced over the years—from *28 Days Later* (2002) and *World War Z* (2013) to television's *The Walking Dead*—the impact of the Romeroesque, corpse-like creatures changed things forever in the zombie landscape.

Romero's innovation within "zombie lore" also allows the zombie to act as a contemporary critique of consumer capitalism.[17] The unavoidable connection between zombie behavior and shopping mania is particularly evident in *Dawn of the Dead* (1978). Set in a suburban shopping mall, the film offers a not-so-veiled critique of the consumer-obsessed culture that has become a distinctive characteristic of Western life. *Dawn of the Dead* shows the zombies drawn to the mall, the former "wonderland of consumption,"[18] where the location recalls faint human memories of material pleasure that they cannot help but covet. In true Romero style, the zombies shuffle through the mall's darkened interior and roam its halls in search of something they cannot find, animated—or, perhaps, reanimated?—by the call of the popular shopping location. The value of the mall as not only a capitalist center but also a social venue is difficult to ignore. In the movie, the character Steve gives a clear explanation of why the zombies are drawn to the location: "It's a kind of instinct, a memory [of] what they used to do. This was an important place in their lives." The zombies in *Dawn of the Dead* are drawn back to the mall by what Matt Bailey calls "a deeply embedded sense of place."[19] Deprived of their lives, the zombies seek solace and a sense of connection in a location that, when they still breathed, represented the height of social interaction and the center of their desire-filled consumer existence.

The certainty offered by the mall—at least, to its zombie inhabitants—is counteracted by the consumption-deprived wider context of the film. The United States—and, it is suggested, most of the Western world—has descended into anarchy. Zombies have overtaken the country and destroyed everyday life as it was known. All that remains of the America that was—with all its political, cultural, and social power—are the historical signs of its world dominance: in *Dawn of the Dead*, the shopping mall functions as a monument to the consumer culture that collapsed.[20] The suburban nature of the mall is placed in stark contrast to the decayed nature of the cities. When civilization was at its peak, the mall was a representation of convenience, cleanliness, and comfort, a core of shopping dreams that made life easy and carefree for the willing consumer. After the zombie apocalypse, the mall continues to exercise its appeal. Overtaken by dead creatures, the shopping center provides a destination for the roaming, stumbling zombies—evocative, heedless creatures that are all too apt to mirror the nature of the mindless consumer.

This object-based sense of zombie identification is not an exclusive characteristic of Romero's films, but it has set a representational mold that is visible in the behavior of zombies in recent films. A good example is *Warm Bodies* (2013), directed by Jonathan Levine. The movie—which acts, among other things, as a contemporary adaptation of *Romeo and Juliet*, focusing on the unlikely romance between a zombie boy and a human girl—continues to portray the zombie as an undead creature, detached from the world, whose only interest seemingly lies in eating flesh. A note of consciousness comes from the narrative voice of the main zombie character, R, who roams the halls of an abandoned airport, together with a horde of shuffling zombie companions. R comments on how his existence as a corpse disconnects him from the world, as he is "unable to say much of anything."

In *Zombie Economics*, an important text centered on behavioral economics, John Quiggin pointedly argues that "every sustained period of growth in the history of capitalism has led to the proclamation of a new era."[21] This new era is often the culmination of the most distinctive features of capitalism and mirrors the context in which it thrives. *Warm Bodies* suggests that the new era of contemporary consumer capitalism is, somewhat uncannily, the "zombie era." At the height of its development, high-tech consumer capitalism could only collapse into an era of stillness and stagnation, where the common consumers—driven by their desire to own expensive gadgets and to be in charge of their own means of communication—could also lose sight of themselves and therefore cause the capitalist system to implode into an aimless scheme. An evocative symbolization of this process appears when R imagines what it was like "before," when people could actually communicate and enjoy each other's company. As the zombies shuffle around, the surroundings are quickly replaced by an image of the time "before." Ironically, people are portrayed as busily walking around, not making any kind of contact with their fellow man. Every individual is engrossed in some sort of technological device; smartphones rule the scene, and no one attempts to make any form of conversation with others. The critique of contemporary society offered by Levine is not subtle but still has visual power: people are "zombified" by technology, their relationship with objects of desire—not to mention, of course, the communication network, which is, in itself, a powerful consumer presence—detaches them from any form of interpersonal relationship. In the paradoxically disconnected world of the consumer network, the only certainty that remains is that of the commodity, the signified presence that speaks loudly of the value of the individual in contemporary economies. The clear suggestion in the movie is that, at some point, these certainties collapsed, as did the assurance of consumer capitalism. The "zombified consumer" led the way to the actual zombie, a creature of lost consciousness and economic passivity. In this sense, *Warm Bodies* provides a view of the zombie that is not only reminiscent of the Romeroesque tradition, but also offers an even clearer and more explicit critique of the impact of consumer capitalism in a time of globalized, networked existence.

Although the zombies in *Warm Bodies* maintain their basic characteristics and seemingly human form, they are unable to function as humans. The only hint of what they used to be is their clothing, a powerful representational commodity that allows R to engage in a guessing game, uncovering the presence of "a janitor," "a personal trainer," and "the rich son" of a powerful CEO. Although metaphorically stripped bare of their identities, the zombies are still catalogued by their clothes, powerful communicative mediums that maintain their function in the zombie world, just as they did before the wider civilization collapsed. The zombies' old and ragged clothes expose how, as Michel de Certeau would put it, the everyday use of commodities makes explicit the existing "models of action" that continuously determine the choices of the consumer.[22] Even in the zombie world, clothing functions as an agent of social practice, and an economic identification that is proper to both the personal and collective everyday.

The signified importance of objects—particularly conceived as commodities—is made ever more explicit in the film when R is revealed to be a collector of mementos from the time "before." R has commandeered an abandoned plane and filled it with masses of knickknacks—from snow globes to old vinyl records and Blu-ray discs of old zombie movies. Although R has not technically purchased the objects, he is still animated by a sense of acquisition and possession that highlights his behavior as low consumerist. He enjoys his time surrounded by these commodities, as they give him a sense of the self he has lost: to put it simply, these consumable objects give R a sense of identity. It is not by chance that his bonding with the human girl Julie begins through these desirable objects, as though to say that, while unable to establish a connection—in the interpersonal sense—the two find a way of relating through the social meaning imbedded in commodities. This way of dealing with commodities is reminiscent of what Grant McCracken calls *possession rituals*. According to McCracken, through the collecting, comparing, and flaunting of objects, individuals are able to express themselves within the bounds of social experience.[23] In this framework, R's collection and flaunting of desirable objects allow him to extract the meaningful properties that have been invested in the consumer goods.[24] Even in the postapocalyptic wasteland of zombification, commodities continue to exercise their appeal for those who do not have upward mobility on the socioeconomic scale.

The continuing impact of commodities in *Warm Bodies* suggests that the zombies are still subject to forms of what is commonly known as *social programming*. In behavioral psychology, this term refers to the set of rules and regulations that each individual learns and conforms to in order to fit in society. Learning these rules—so as to become a functioning part of society—is known as the "socialization process," a careful shaping of individual sensibilities and behaviors that, as Mihaly Csikszentmihalyi argues, aims to produce "responsible citizens."[25] People become passive entities and therefore tend to accept the social framing of particular situations, ones that dictate how they should act, what they should like, and what goals (if any) they should pursue.

Social programming has a particular bearing on the economic behavior of the individual within society. The socialization of the individual, within the everyday framework of late capitalism, prescribes that people will be driven to crave and possess endless amounts of commodities in order to feel satisfied and fulfilled. Csikszentmihalyi suggests that economic forces, such as manufacturers, merchants, and advertisers, "program" individuals into spending their earnings on commodities with an idealized consumer value. And although the messages of social adjustment can be very different, Csikszentmihalyi goes on to say, the outcome is always the same: they make people "dependent on a social system" that "exploits" their energies "for its own purposes."[26] Gratification becomes inextricably interlinked with commodities, and this makes people vulnerable to a form of existence that pivots on the endless consumption of goods.

The promise of happiness, however, can never be fulfilled; commodities, it soon becomes obvious, can scarcely satisfy the emotional needs of the individual. Therefore, in both the psychological and economic sense, socially programmed people are left forever wanting, forever unfilled, forever unhappy. They are but passive shells, low consumers of capitalist desires: they are, to put it simply, socioeconomic zombies. The effects of social framing, in the economic and emotional sense, are metaphorically uncovered not only in *Warm Bodies*, but also in earlier examples such as *Dawn of the Dead*, where zombies continue to live their passive, socially programmed existence, one that demands their constant engagement with commodities in search of a sense of happiness and fulfillment that, sadly, can never be achieved.

In *Warm Bodies*, the zombies' drone-like, passive role in the consumer cycle is exposed when, recalling the historically consumerist zombies of *Dawn of the Dead*, R continues to perform the low consumer role, collecting commodities even if little satisfaction can be obtained from it. R's actions are

closely reminiscent of Csikszentmihalyi's view of the fully programmed individual, who desires "only the rewards" that society has agreed "he should
long for."[27] It is clear that a certain element of nostalgia for life moves R's
activities, and there is no denying that the film takes a more positive stance
on his retro commodities than it does on the high-class amenities of the
humans, who live a detached and unachievable existence in the zombie-free
safe havens. Nonetheless, R's desirable objects and his obsession with collecting and comparing highlight his place on the consumer ladder: the zombie is at the bottom of the consumer scale, the wishful thinker of the economy, plagued by a social emptiness that no object—as fanciful as it might
be—will ever be able to fill.

BOTTOM-FEEDERS AND TOP-FEEDERS

As economic frameworks are uncovered through the powerful and evocative
metaphor of the Gothic undead, the wealth of vampires emerges in stark
contrast to the zombies' possession deficiencies, a commercial tragedy of
richness versus scarcity. Operating on two different levels of both economy
and sociality, zombies and vampires function as apt metaphors for consumer
relations in our world. Their behavior resonates so vividly with the Western
context—deeply animated by commercialization—that it is easy to imagine
zombies and vampires as real creatures. This conclusion is tied to visualizing
vampires and zombies as exaggerations of certain types of existence in the
real world. Vampires represent the elite upper classes, their high consumerism visible in their luxury, custom-made items. By contrast, zombies exemplify the working and middle classes, obsessed with being surrounded by
objects and zones of consumption, and blissfully unaware of the effects that
such behavior entails. Subjected as they are to the capitalist culture industry,
the consumer activities of the undead derive "from the collective uncon-
scious" to expose and shape the inner workings "of mass-consumption."[28]
Zombies and vampires, therefore, emerge as apt mediums for uncovering the
reality of consumer economies in the our contemporary world.

Chapter Eleven

Trading with the Undead

A Study in Specialization and Comparative Advantage

Darwyyn Deyo and David T. Mitchell

Could the living and the undead trade with each other, or would they just kill each other instead? What sort of trade could occur between the living and the undead? Fortunately, there are hundreds of examples in fiction of trade between the living and the undead. In *Shaun of the Dead*, the zombies work at shopping centers and compete in Japanese game shows. In *Buffy the Vampire Slayer*, Spike helps humans in exchange for their assistance or just for cold hard cash.[1] In *Harry Potter*, lonely ghosts trade information to the living willing to befriend them. Obviously, there are many significant differences between the living and the undead—and that is exactly why both groups stand to benefit greatly from voluntary exchange.

Things that are difficult for the living come naturally to the undead. Ghosts have information from the past and the ability to go places where the living can't, so they could easily look for bombs or survivors of mine accidents. Imagine vampires working as surgeons, special ops soldiers, or moneylenders. Zombies could take over dangerous or monotonous jobs. Although we think of humans and the undead as adversaries, they could instead easily engage in commerce that benefits both sides.

Some might worry that the undead are simply too dangerous and hostile to engage in trade, yet we regularly benefit from trade with dangerous and potentially adversarial partners. The United States traded with the Soviet Union even while fighting proxy wars and threatening to annihilate each other with nuclear weapons. We can even gain from trade when our trading partners are more productive than us across the board. It turns out that trade with the undead makes sense even if vampires are better (or zombies are worse) than humans—at everything.

The main argument for trading with other people, other countries, and even other creatures is that we all have different abilities and strengths, and we should play to those strengths. Trade raises the relative incomes of both parties to the transaction. Just as it is advantageous for someone who is good at one task, say sewing, to specialize and trade with someone who is good at another task, such as farming, it is also advantageous for countries to specialize and trade with each other. For example, the United States specializes in the production of aircraft engines while China specializes in the manufacture of children's toys. The United States trades aircraft engines for toys and China trades toys for aircraft engines. Even though the trade does not occur directly (it happens indirectly through the medium of money), both countries end up better off than if each country had tried to produce both aircraft engines and toys by itself. And for the very same reasons, humans and the undead could both benefit dramatically from ceasing to fight each other—and starting to trade instead.

THE WORKING DEAD

The benefits of trade are huge. We trade so that we don't have to do everything. Most people don't grow their own food, don't make their own clothes, and don't live in a homemade house built with homemade tools. Instead, we specialize in activities we are individually good at (such as teaching economics, pumping gas, doctoring, or taking blood donations) and we trade away the product of our goods and services (usually in the form of money) to farmers, clothing manufacturers, and home builders for their goods and services. And we all have a much higher standard of living as a result.[2]

Specialization isn't just useful for the sake of specialization. It also gives us more time for other things. If vampires don't make their own coffins, they can spend more time collecting blood. If zombies purchase brains from the MegaMart, they don't have to spend all day wandering around haphazardly, saying "brains" until they stumble upon a living person. Working as hall monitors and buying brains from the MegaMart could also let zombies avoid shotgun blasts from the living, focus on doing their jobs, and maybe have a hobby or two.

If you want to specialize and then gain from trade, you need two conditions. First, others must value the good or service you provide. Trade doesn't work if nobody wants to buy your zombie-vampire romance novel. Second, you must value the goods and services that others produce. It is pretty easy for most living humans to know what they can do and what they want (it comes naturally to us), so let's examine what the undead can do. Then we will consider what the undead want so we can imagine potentially beneficial trades.

Trade with Vampires

Vampires' unique abilities create tremendous opportunities for trade. The obvious thing that vampires could offer is voluntary eternal life (in an undead murderous sort of way). In the BBC television series *Being Human*, one vampire points out that if he went up to the children's ward of the hospital, every parent would agree to any terms in order to grant their children immortality.[3] In *True Blood*, some humans buy vampire blood since, as it turns out, vampires are excellent hallucinogen manufacturers. Since vampires live forever, they also make excellent financiers. They can maximize profits over very long time horizons without having to worry about myopic stock markets. Similarly, vampires would be supremely good at collecting debts. Their superhuman abilities would also make them excel in a broad range of professions from special ops soldiers to surgeons.

But what do vampires want? Some humans do sell their blood to vampires, as they do in the young adult series *Blood Coven*. Of course vampires are very interested in procuring blood, but why assume that vampires only want one thing? You want more than one thing, don't you? Vampires want nice places to stay. Someone has to run the mansion or castle and keep the lights on. They need to pay for electricity and for someone to guard them during the daytime. Maybe vampires occasionally stay up all night surfing the web and shopping on Etsy. Maybe they want a fast car or a new Harley. Just like humans, vampires need money for these things.

Trade with Ghosts

There is little doubt that ghosts could provide all manner of services to the living. We don't know what his compensation is, but in *Harry Potter*, Professor Binns has been teaching the History of Magic class for approximately forever. He died in his staff chair and his ghost got up to teach class. Ghosts have certain advantages when it comes to detective work, such as the ability to talk to the dead, natural stealth, and the capacity to get into blocked spaces. Further, ghosts face no risk associated with these activities, so they could charge less for these activities than vampires or zombies and still make huge profits.

But what would ghosts want in exchange? Ghosts have many needs. They sometimes want physical things brought to them; this is especially true in worlds where they can't leave the places where they died. The ghost in *Being Human* faces this problem, and in *Dead Like Me* some souls are forced to stay with their bodies. The ghost in the novel *Stonewords: A Ghost Story* also has severe limitations on how far she can travel and thus needs help from the living.

Ghosts also want to communicate through mediums with those who are unable to converse with the dead, as in the movie *Ghost*. Ghosts often get lonely because they are trapped or because their circle of friends is necessarily small. As a result, sometimes ghosts will trade information for simple conversation or for help finding their way to the other side. Harry Potter, for example, trades listening for information. He learns from the Grey Lady (who turns out to be the daughter of a founder, Rowena Ravenclaw) where Voldemort's last Horcrux is hidden. Using the same strategy, Harry Potter learns a lot from Nearly Headless Nick about how death works and how becoming a ghost works. On the other hand, since Ron Weasley doesn't pay attention to Nearly Headless Nick, Nick ignores him in turn—an excellent example of how the failure to trade is a disadvantage.

Trade with Zombies

From pop culture, we've seen that zombies have some skills that they can use to produce goods and services. We've seen zombies working in *Shaun of the Dead*. The Heart and Stroke Foundation of Canada hired zombies to dance and teach in a public service announcement on CPR. It is easy to imagine zombie soldiers; they might not be smart, but they are fearless. Working with biohazards from toxic chemicals to sewage treatment would be no problem for zombies, whose health might even improve in such conditions. And who would be better for setting up bases on the moon and Mars than the undead?

If you saw the movie *World War Z*, you might have thought that there were potentially endless opportunities to get the mindless zombies to do work. In *World War Z* the zombies have superhuman strength as well as jumping and climbing abilities and thus would be fantastic for a variety of jobs. You might not let zombies babysit, but they don't eat trees. Why couldn't zombies rush into national forests as fire jumpers? Zombies could also be used for carrying and moving things. Zombies might not be master masons, but they could carry enough stone to remake the Pyramids. They might also be great at crime and trauma scene cleanup.[4] As described in Wes Craven's *The Serpent and the Rainbow*, getting free work was the original reason for Haitian voodoo priests to create zombies. These priests compelled their zombies, but we could be more enlightened and trade with them instead.

Of course, zombie abilities and desires depend heavily on which universe they inhabit. In *Day of the Dead*, some zombies remember parts of their past lives and even display some human emotion, which could make them easier to trade with. In the Charlaine Harris world (the *Sookie Stackhouse* novels and the *True Blood* television show) as well as in Terry Pratchett's Discworld novels, zombies are not mindless killers. The zombies are differently-abled humans who happen to be dead. Because these zombies retain their reason and do not have an all-consuming preference for homicide, their economic activity is not so different from that of the living. It would be easy to trade with zombies like these. In the movie *Warm Bodies*, zombies think and even love, at least until they become "bonies." They also appear to enjoy classic rock albums and other memorabilia from their previous lives. *Shaun of the Dead* offers a middle ground where zombies are slow-moving dimwitted creatures who do, however, have interests other than eating brains: they like to play video games. These zombies are perhaps the most interesting case for trade with the undead.

Of course, some zombies are too stupid to trade. But that doesn't mean that they can't be made useful. It could, however, mean that we trade not with zombies but with zombie handlers. Just as animals can be motivated by skilled trainers to perform useful tasks, perhaps zombies could too. We might see zombie wranglers appear—people who develop specialized skills to deal with the dangers presented by zombies and to motivate zombies to operate productively. These zombie wranglers would catch zombies and put them to work. Being a zombie wrangler is dangerous. But, if zombie wrangling becomes a family business and a zombie bites your boy, you haven't lost a son—you've gained an asset.

One added bonus to trading with zombies is that zombies are the ultimate carbon offset. They don't use fossil fuels. Talk about recycling! Although we can imagine clothing zombies in nanofibers and harvesting energy from zombie movements, those are technically not examples of trade. For trade to occur, we need to offer them something in return. Do they want video games like in *Shaun of the Dead*—maybe with really big buttons on the controllers because zombies have clumsy fingers? Or do zombies just want brains from our slaughterhouses? Next time you hear about the destruction of animals with mad cow disease, just think of the happiness those cow brains would have brought some poor zombie toiling away in a menial job at the mall.

NUMERICAL EXAMPLES OF TRADE WITH THE UNDEAD

In order to see clearly why trade makes everyone better off, imagine a very simple economy with two goods and two beings. There is one human doctor and one vampire. The two goods are blood collection and healing. The doctor would be interested in healing people because that is what doctors do. Doctors already draw human blood for testing, and hospitals keep blood stores on hand for use in emergencies. The vampire is, of course, interested in drawing blood as a food source. In many universes, including *The Vampire Diaries* and *True Blood*, vampire blood has healing properties. Why would a vampire heal someone? One reason is that the vampire might want to trade, or she could just be the sort of sadistic killer that takes pleasure in getting her victims up to full strength before she sucks the life out of them. [5]

As shown in table 11.1, the vampire can collect one hundred units of blood or heal two patients each week. The doctor can collect twenty units of blood or heal ten patients each week.

Table 11.1.   Potential Output of Blood Collected or Patients Healed

(per week)	Blood	Healing
Vampire	100 units	2 patients
Human Doctor	20 units	10 patients

If both the human and the vampire fend for themselves and spend half their time collecting blood and half their time healing people, they can produce the following:

- The vampire will collect 50 units of blood and heal 1 patient.
- The doctor will collect 10 units of blood and heal 5 patients.
- The total production is 60 units of blood and 6 patients healed.

However, if the human doctor focused only on blood collection while the vampire focused only on healing, then total production would be one hundred units of blood collected and ten patients healed. That's forty more units of blood and four more patients healed for the two beings to share through trade.

Without adding any extra labor, through specialization and trade the doctor and vampire have produced more. By trading with each other, they can make sure that *both* parties have more of *both* goods than they would have had if they hadn't specialized.

If the vampire wants to heal one patient, she can do it herself by *not* collecting fifty units of blood—or she could instead trade with the human. The human can heal one more patient by not collecting two units of blood, which is a much smaller sacrifice. This works because the human and the vampire have different *opportunity costs*; that is, they give up different amounts.[6] What the human gives up in order to heal someone is different from what the vampire gives up in order to heal someone. This is what creates the opportunity for mutually beneficial trade between them.

In the previous example, it was easy to see that vampires were better at drawing blood and humans were better at healing. After all, humans could draw more blood than vampires and vampires could heal more than humans. But what if one being is better at both tasks? In many literary worlds, vampires have many strengths and few weaknesses. In these worlds vampires are faster, stronger, smarter, and have a wide range of supernatural abilities. Often vampires can hear the thoughts of the living, which they rationally use to their advantage. In a situation like that, a skeptic might wonder how humans could beneficially trade with vampires. Aren't we just asking to be their larder?

Sometimes one party is better at producing both goods. Nevertheless, mutually beneficial trade is still possible. The classical economist David Ricardo was the first person to fully explain the concept of *comparative advantage*. When two people (living or undead) are obviously good at different things, it is easy to see that it makes sense for them to trade. But Ricardo, whose work focused not on trade between the living and the undead, but on trade between nations, discovered that both parties benefit from trade *even when one side is more productive at everything.*

For example, suppose that the United States is not only better than China at making aircraft engines, but also at making toys. Even if China is worse at both things, it (and the United States) is still better off specializing and trading.

What matters here is that the *degree* of superiority will always be greater for some products than for others. Imagine a simple world where there are only two jobs. The first job is a vintner at a winery; vampires with their supernatural abilities are the very best at this. Not only does their super speed allow them to stomp grapes at a high speed, but they are experienced winemakers, having learned the job back in their native Romania.

Vampires average one thousand barrels per day of grapes picked, crushed, and stored. Humans can only produce fifty barrels of grapes, so humans are only one-twentieth as good at winemaking.

The other job available is mortician. An average human can embalm two bodies per day. Vampires are also far more efficient than the average human mortician. A vampire could embalm twenty bodies per day.

Table 11.2. Potential Output of Embalming or Wine Making

(per day)	Embalming	Wine making
Human	2 bodies	50 barrels
Vampire	20 bodies	1,000 barrels

In table 11.2 we see that the vampire is much better than the human at both things. But the vampire is not *equally* better. She is twenty times better at wine making but only ten times better at embalming. This gives us a good clue as to what her comparative advantage will be. When a vampire spends a day working as a mortician, she isn't spending the day as a vintner, so her *opportunity cost* for being a mortician is very high. Since the vampire gives up less to be a vintner than she gives up to be a mortician, she works as a vintner. Meanwhile, the human specializes in being a mortician.

Suppose the human chooses to spend more time embalming and less time making wine. He embalms two bodies, which means he has to give up making fifty barrels of wine. Meanwhile, the vampire reduces her embalming by two bodies, which frees up enough time (one-tenth of her day) for her to make one hundred more barrels of wine. The end result? The same number of bodies get embalmed, while the amount of wine increases by fifty barrels. The human could trade the vampire the two additional bodies he embalmed for twenty-five of the extra barrels of wine, and both sides would be better off as a result.

Because it is so costly for the vampire to be a mortician, the human has a *comparative advantage* in being a mortician even though the vampire has the *absolute advantage* in both. Even though the vampire is better at both occupations, she can benefit from trading with the living. The human can benefit from trading with the vampire as well, just as China would benefit from trade with the United States even if the United States were better at manufacturing both aircraft and toys.

THE DANGER OF THE DEAD: BUG OR FEATURE?

One fear is that if we try to trade with the undead, they will just kill us instead. Not every vampire would be willing to trade with humans, particularly for blood. In most worlds, vampires are faster and stronger than humans and could theoretically force humans to feed vampires against their will. There are, however, humans who are faster and stronger than other humans, and yet the majority of humans find it more to their advantage to trade with each other. Vampires who have seen other vampires killed may even have an incentive to collaborate with humans in order to limit the damage caused by voracious vampires or to prevent human retribution. As Spike tells Buffy in the television series *Buffy the Vampire Slayer*:

> Spike: I want to save the world.
> Buffy: You do remember that you're a vampire, right?
> Spike: We like to talk big. Vampires do. "I'm going to destroy the world." That's just tough guy talk. Strutting around with your friends over a pint of blood. The truth is, I like this world. You've got . . . dog racing, Manchester United. And you've got people, billions of people walking around like Happy Meals with legs. It's all right here. But then someone comes along with a vision, with a real . . . passion for destruction. Angel could pull it off. Goodbye, Piccadilly. Farewell, Leicester bloody Square. You know what I'm saying?[7]

If Spike is right, then there is every reason to think vampires will choose trade over violence, at least much of the time.

But it's not as obvious that zombies will eschew violence; some types of zombies may not even be capable of restraining themselves. In Charlie Huston's *Joe Pitt*, Richard Kadrey's *Sandman Slim*, and Peter Clines's *Ex* novels (and many, many more), zombies are thoroughly mindless, unrelenting killers. Their very horror derives from the fact that we cannot reason with them and certainly cannot trade with them. These zombies do not want to eat cow brains, nor are they willing to work minimum-wage jobs so they can play video games in their spare time. They want to kill. In *Return of the Living Dead* the dead can think, speak, use technology, organize collective action, and so on, but they must consume the brains of the living or endure the pain of being dead. They seem to have no qualms about killing to reduce that pain. Moreover, they have no desires other than reducing their pain by eating the brains of the living. In this case, there really isn't any opportunity for trading with someone whose only desire is to crack your skull and slurp the still-pulsing brain from your noggin. "Tina, it was wrong of you to lock me up. I had to hurt myself to get out. But I forgive you darlin' and I know you're here, because I can smell your brains."[8]

Despite the risks, we can expect that people would still rationally trade with the undead. After all, people do lots of risky things when the benefits outweigh the costs. They drive cars. They work in dangerous jobs like coal mining. They join the army. People also often trade with dangerous groups. There is trade with and between criminal gangs. Engaging in trade could actually reduce the risks of interacting with the undead, because then the undead would at least have a nonviolent means of supporting themselves. Besides, as international relations experts have often observed, "If goods don't cross borders, armies will."[9] Since countries engaged in trade with each other rarely go to war, perhaps we could extend this lesson to the living and the undead.

TRADE WITH THE UNDEAD: WINNERS AND LOSERS

Not everyone will be happy about trade with the undead. The net benefits for society as a whole will be positive, because most of us will enjoy the benefits of freer trade in terms of goods and services at lower prices. But some people will inevitably lose out, at least in the short term. Human phlebotomists (people who draw blood samples for a living) might not be as good as vampire phlebotomists when it comes to drawing blood. Hospitals and blood banks, as well as their customers, will love the extra efficiency that vampires bring, but human phlebotomists may have to do something else.

The human phlebotomists will have to work in their second-best jobs instead of phlebotomy. Sometimes your second-best job is much worse than your best job. Phlebotomists will have the same problem that American textile workers had in the 1980s, when trade opened up with cheaper foreign countries. Everyone but textile workers loved the lower prices for clothing. The textile workers were forced to find something else to do to make a living. Eventually places like South Carolina moved from producing textiles to producing cars, but it was a painful process for some. When a country suddenly engages in free trade, either because it has a new trading partner or because it got rid of existing trade impediments, some people will have to change jobs.

In Anne Rice's *Interview with a Vampire*, there are both powerful vampires and much less powerful revenants. Revenants are like vampires without all of the sexy powers. When the traditional and more advanced vampires come to an area, we can predict that revenants would suddenly have to retool their work. They will have to take on some other profession.

Changing jobs can be costly and painful. Before vampires come to a town, revenants are the powerful undead that make the villagers fearful (for example, in a Halloween haunted house). After the vampires come, the villagers are able to get a better-quality scare for a much lower price, but the revenants have to get new jobs. The revenants may be forced into low-paying, backbreaking jobs such as being Amazon distribution center workers, network operations center administrators, or Walmart stockers. Not only will the revenants make less money, but their self-worth may plummet.

We could worry about the distributional effects of trading with vampires, and surely some people will argue that we should ban such trade. Certainly the revenants would make this argument. But workers can and do move from one industry to another. When we think of people losing their jobs to the undead, we need to remember that those workers will eventually change professions. And the benefits from trade are large. When goods and services get cheaper because the undead can do some of them more efficiently, the living will have more wealth to spend on other goods and services. Trying to preserve all existing jobs is a recipe for a stagnant standard of living.

For a real-life example, when President George W. Bush turned down the benefits of free trade and imposed a tariff on steel, steelworkers rejoiced but auto workers suffered. When the tariff was reduced, the auto workers and consumers benefited more than the steelworkers lost. With free trade, not everyone gains, but the total gains to an economy exceed the total losses. Even the people who temporarily lose their jobs will benefit from the lower prices that come with more efficient production. When we start trading with a new group, some people will be sad (the steelworkers or human phlebotomists), but consumers and other professions will rejoice (auto workers or medical patients). The people who lose their jobs to vampires will eventually find different jobs. Moreover, we could create programs to help people deal with the temporary costs of switching professions.

FORCE AND FREE WILL: THE IMPORTANCE OF VOLUNTARISM

Like animal rights activists opposing the use of animals, some people may oppose trade with the undead not because of their concern for the humans, but because of their concern for the undead. They might contend that the undead, especially zombies, are exploited by trade. The problem with this argument is that we wouldn't expect people (including the undead) to voluntarily specialize and trade if it didn't make them better off. You wouldn't trade with someone if the price were so high that you could make the good yourself for less.[10]

When each person is analyzing his own gains from trade and voluntarily trading, we don't expect to see people exploited. We might see people get bad bargains, but the bad bargains still must be better than the alternative of no bargain or the best alternative bargain available. That's what economists Benjamin Powell and Paul Krugman found about sweatshops.[11] Separately, both economists found that sweatshop workers in poor countries earn much less than workers in richer countries, but more than they would earn in other jobs within their own countries. Sweatshop workers stay at the sweatshop because it is rationally their best opportunity, even if the opportunity isn't that great. Depriving workers of their best option would make them worse off.

Therefore, if both the undead and the living are capable of rational thought, the undead and living will only agree to trade if the trade is mutually beneficial. The basis of comparative advantage is that each person (dead or alive) gives up something in exchange for something else. With vampires, ghosts, and other thinking beings, this doesn't pose a problem. Zombies, however, might not be rational—they might be too stupid to be rational and too easily tricked. Getting zombies to work for free without their consent isn't a mutually beneficial exchange. It's just good business—and good for the environment. But if there is no free will, you can't assume that trade is beneficial to both parties. Nevertheless, it's still possible that both sides might benefit, just as with humans and their pets. Voluntarism may require free will, but gains from comparative advantage do not.

In *True Blood* as well as *Being Human*, vampires can use a type of mind control known as glamouring. In *The Vampire Diaries*, it's called compulsion. Bram Stoker's Dracula seems to have this ability, too. If vampires are able to use mind control, then it is much less clear that there are gains from trading with them; they might glamour humans into accepting poor trades.[12] In deciding what to force us to do, vampires will still want to focus on their comparative advantage and have us focus on our comparative advantage, but then we can't expect to get anything in return for our work. When it comes to the problem that vampires might refuse to trade and just take without our consent, we have to listen to the advice of Buffy Summers on how to deal with an unpleasant member of the undead: "Oh come on! Stake through the heart. A little sunlight. It's like falling off a log."[13]

THE QUICK AND THE DEAD: VIVE LA DIFFÉRENCE!

The undead have such different abilities from humans that we can expect the gains from trade between the living and the undead to be huge. The living will be very good at things the undead aren't good at all, and vice versa. Even if the living are better than the undead at everything, the undead can still do the things that they are less bad at. And if *they* are better than us at everything, *we* can still do the things that we are less bad at. Trading with the undead will involve some element of danger, but it also promises substantial benefits. It's so beneficial that we should jump at the chance to do it.

After all, who is the vampire or zombie going to kill first? The person he depends on for trade, or the person who refuses to trade with him at all?

Chapter Twelve

Buy or Bite?

Enrique Guerra-Pujol

I think I am on the side of the vampires, or at least some of them.
—Donna Haraway, neofeminist Marxist, *Modest_Witness*
@ Second_Millennium. FemaleMan Meets_OncoMouse (1997)[1]

Are vampires "bad"? Are they inherently evil or unethical creatures? From the sinister Count Dracula in Bram Stoker's cult-classic novel *Dracula* to the cunning Lestat in *Interview with the Vampire*, from the hideous Master in the popular *Buffy the Vampire Slayer* TV show to the outlaw vampire Skinner Sweet in the American Vampire comic book series, most members of the vampire race resort to coercion, compulsion, and confiscation to get what they want the most—blood. But why? Why are vampires such parasitic predators? Maybe we are asking the wrong question. Maybe we should be asking, Why don't vampires offer to buy our blood instead of taking it by force? In short, why don't more vampires *buy* instead of *bite*?

BLACK MARKETS 101: FORCE AND FANGS

Simply stated, my thesis is that a large fraction of vampire violence is the result of *legal failure*: the lack of a legal market for the purchase and sale of blood. But first things first. What is a market, and why does the lack of a legal market tend to produce so much violence?

From an economic perspective, a "market" is not a physical place or space, like the mall or a used-car lot. A market is just a collection of willing buyers and willing sellers of a given product or service. Buyers comprise the demand side of the market, while sellers comprise the supply side, and the resulting price and quantity produced are, in turn, a function of supply and demand.[2] So, why is there is no market in blood?

Consider vampires. These nocturnal creatures are in the business of bloodsucking, plain and simple. Vampires lust after human blood because without it, they cannot survive. Bloodsucking is thus a necessary and unavoidable by-product of a vampire's physiology, a matter of life or death. Not surprisingly, vampires are portrayed in fiction and folklore as predatory bloodsuckers and dangerous villains, and traditional vampire tales like *Dracula*, *Interview with the Vampire*, and *Buffy the Vampire Slayer* all contribute to this image of vampires as cunning, crafty, and violent creatures. But how could it be otherwise? For in the absence of a legal market for blood, vampires typically must prey on innocent victims and suck their blood without consent.[3]

Furthermore, these violent examples from the vampire world teach us a general lesson about the intimate relation between black markets and violence. In general, when the legal status of markets is uncertain or when markets are banned by law, we should expect illegal or "black" markets to emerge to fill the void. In addition, one should also expect the level of violence to increase as suppliers compete with each other to corner this lucrative market, just as violent drug cartels fight over the spoils of the illegal drug market. Vampire violence is really no different in this respect, for in the absence of a legal market in blood, vampires have no choice but to resort to deception, predation, and other coercive tactics to obtain fresh supplies of blood. When we outlaw a product, whether it be drugs or blood, demand for that product does not simply vanish or go away. Instead, it goes underground; that is, the product moves into the black market, where anyone who wants it can get it.[4] Consider, for example, the supply and demand for drugs in prisons—the authorities are still unable to keep illegal drugs out of the hands of their prisoners!

Moreover, when legal uncertainty reigns or when a product is banned or made illegal, the law of the gun replaces the law on the books, for law-abiding sellers will exit the market, to be replaced by sellers who are willing to risk breaking the law to make a buck. And when lawbreakers, in turn, "crowd out" law abiders, such lawbreakers are more likely to resort to violence to maintain their profits and enforce their agreements. If a buyer reneges on a contract for cocaine, for example, the seller has to take matters into his own hands because he can't sue to enforce his contracts. In the worst-case scenario, when sales of a given good are illegal, both buyer and seller are not only "criminals" in the eyes of the law, they are both witnesses to a crime. And in some cases, a criminal buyer or a criminal seller would prefer not to leave any witnesses behind. This is why so many big-time drug transactions are so tense and often go wrong—because black-market agreements are enforced by force or fangs, not law.

LET THE BLOOD FLOW: THE CASE FOR MARKETS

Legal markets, by contrast, create incentives for converting mutual conflict into joint cooperation, for converting coercive *bites* into voluntary *buys*. Instead of stalking or hunting their hapless victims, vampires would have the option of bargaining with them on a voluntary and consensual basis—buying their supplies of blood instead of taking them by force. Moreover, markets are an especially effective way of allocating blood because blood is a renewable resource, so in theory there is plenty of blood to go around for everyone.[5]

But why would vampires and vampire victims ever agree to trade or bargain with one another? Consider first the demand side of the market. As long as there are vampires and other bloodsucking creatures, the demand for human blood will not go away, and if vampires can't buy what they need, then they must steal it. This is precisely what we observe in the vampire world. But if there were a competitive market in blood, vampires could openly and freely buy their needed supplies of blood for a price. Instead of resorting to parasitism or predation or other violent tactics, vampires could become peaceful and productive members of society. These nocturnal creatures would have an incentive to sell their labor and creative talents in return for wages or other forms of income. In sum, with markets, vampires would have a meaningful choice: they could *buy* instead of *bite*.

But, on the demand side, why would a vampire ever agree to pay for blood when he or she could take it for free? Put crudely, what's in it for the vampires? To begin with, one must concede that a legal market in blood will not eliminate all vampire violence, just as a legal market in used cars does not eliminate car theft. But a legal market changes the incentives of vampires in a visible and dramatic way, for the price of a pint of blood will now include the peace of mind that comes with a lawful transaction. By buying blood on a voluntary and consensual basis, vampires will substantially reduce the risk of retaliation by vampire slayers.

Put another way, the act of taking someone's blood by force is not "free" because such coercive transfers create a risk of retaliation. Indeed, this is precisely the reason why we have vampire slayers. (As an aside, one of the most remarkable aspects of the vampire world is the wide variety of vampire-slayer types, ranging from Professor Abraham Van Helsing in Victorian England in the classic vampire novel *Dracula* to high school cheerleader Buffy Summers in contemporary Sunnydale, California; from the Great Emancipator in the 2012 film *Abraham Lincoln: Vampire Hunter* to the femme fatale Agent BloodRayne, one of the characters in the vampire video game *BloodRayne*.) But despite the surprising diversity of slayer types in the vampire world—medical doctors, high school students, U.S. presidents, and femmes fatales—all such vampire hunters share an important feature: their function is to punish vampires in order to prevent them from taking blood by force. Legal markets would reduce a vampire's risk of such lethal punishment.

Now consider the supply side of the market. Since sales on legal markets are by definition voluntary, no one would be compelled or forced to sell his or her blood or to bargain with vampires. So, even if most humans are unwilling to trade with vampires on moral or repugnance grounds, other persons with different moral values or different levels of repugnance might be willing to step in and sell their blood to vampires for a profit. Still other persons might find secure alternative sources of blood supplies or invest in research to discover new ways of harvesting artificial or synthetic blood. These "vampire entrepreneurs" would respond to the demand for blood, providing vampires with a safe and stable supply.

In addition, with legal markets in blood, we can expect markets for premium blood and other "specialty bloods" to arise—for example, perhaps some vampires would be willing to pay a premium for rare AB+ blood, while others would prefer "intoxicated blood," or blood with high levels of alcohol content. Markets not only expand the possibilities for trade, they also cultivate our imaginations and create the conditions for human and vampire creativity to flourish.

The bottom line is that legal markets convert conflict into cooperation because *both* sides in a market exchange are able to benefit when they are able to freely trade and bargain with each other on a voluntary and consensual basis. Put another way, markets produce positive-sum games in which both sides are able to win; in the words of economist Murray Rothbard, "Trade, or exchange, is engaged in precisely because both parties benefit; if they did not expect to gain, they would not agree to the exchange."[6] In addition, if there was a legal market in blood, there would be less violence in the vampire world, because such markets reduce the need for violence. If you doubt the truth of this proposition, consider the black market for illegal drugs and then ask yourself: why aren't violent cartels also fighting over the tobacco and liquor trades?

LEGALSCLEROSIS: WHAT'S BLOCKING THE BLOODSTREAM?

Thus far, we have seen that when there are no legal or economic barriers to trade, people with conflicting interests, even vampires and vampire slayers, will have a powerful incentive to trade—to negotiate mutually beneficial bargains—instead of resorting to violence or coercion. So, why do we rarely observe such voluntary and consensual bargains in the vampire world?

In two words, the answer is legal failure—the longstanding legal prohibition against trading in human organs and tissues and the resulting legal uncertainty regarding the legality of trade in blood.

Broadly speaking, there are three types of legal failure or regulatory impediments to trade—in brief, a legal failure occurs (1) when the law fails to define or enforce property rights in a contested resource; (2) when the law criminalizes, prohibits, or otherwise impedes trade in a given good or service; or (3) when the law itself is either uncertain or unclear about what transactions or activities are legal. Textbook examples of the first type of legal failure (lack of well-defined property rights) are common-pool resources such as ocean fisheries, public roads, and waterways.[7] Examples of the second type of legal failure (prohibition), by contrast, are draconian drug laws that make it illegal to buy or sell certain drugs and laws prohibiting prostitution, while a good illustration of the third type of legal failure (legal uncertainty) is the longstanding uncertainty regarding the legality of the purchase and sale of blood. From an economic perspective, such legal uncertainty is undesirable because it makes the outcomes of legal cases difficult to predict and hence prevents buyers and sellers from planning their transactions in the shadow of the law or settling their disputes peacefully out of court.[8]

We label these three types of legal barriers to trade as "legal failures" because such legal impediments prevent mutually beneficial and voluntary bargains from taking place.[9] Some economists, however, confuse these legal failures with so-called market failures, or situations where markets on their own fail to produce efficient outcomes.[10] Air pollution, texting while driving, and business monopolies are textbook examples of market failures. Vampire violence, however, is not the result of a market failure, for in this case there is no legal market!

Let us now return to our original question: why are there so few examples of voluntary trade in the vampire world? The reason is not economic, since it makes rational sense for vampires and humans to trade with each other. In addition, the reason is not the lack of well-defined property rights. In the case of blood, the legal assignment of property rights to blood is clear: you own your own blood.[11] No, the problem here is a combination of prohibition and legal uncertainty about whether you are allowed to buy or sell rights to blood. The World Health Organization encourages all countries to adopt a "100% unpaid, voluntary blood donation policy."[12] Many countries—such as the United Kingdom—have explicitly banned blood sales.[13] In the United States, whole-blood sales are not *explicitly* banned, but they exist under the shadow of a broad legal prohibition on the sale of human body parts.[14]

So, why doesn't the legal system remove this uncertainty and openly allow the sale and purchase of blood? By all accounts, the answer is political: vampires have no voice in human politics or in the legal system, while many well-organized interest groups are opposed to the "commodification" of blood for ideological or moral reasons.[15]

Consider the anti-commodification arguments from one of the leading critics of markets in blood, British philosopher Richard Titmuss. In his influential and oft-cited book *The Gift Relationship: From Human Blood to Social Policy*,[16] Professor Titmuss advances three main arguments in favor of a nonmarket or altruistic system of blood donations.[17] In summary, Titmuss argues that markets in blood would result in blood shortages by crowding out altruistic donations of blood, would produce lower-quality blood by attracting unscrupulous and unhealthy sellers, and would end up exploiting the poorest and most vulnerable members of society. Let us now consider the merits of each of these standard anti-commodification arguments in turn.

The Crowding-Out Argument

Do markets in blood end up reducing the supply of blood by crowding out altruistic donations, as Titmuss alleges?[18] In a recent report in the journal *Science*, a group of researchers tested a wide variety of in-kind incentive-based blood programs, ranging from coupons and lottery tickets to a paid day off work, and after careful evaluation of these various systems concluded that economic incentives increased blood donations in every case.[19] So why should altruism work any better in the vampire world? For a bloodthirsty vampire in desperate need of blood, one would expect a market system to generate the greatest and most reliable quantity of blood. Why? Because, simply put, it stands to reason that in the aggregate, people will be willing to offer more blood when they are paid to do so than when their only option is to offer it for free. Of course, anyone who still wanted to give their blood away for free would remain free to do so.

The Quality Argument

Of course, *quantity* is not the only goal of a blood supply system; *quality* is also a goal. But is "paid blood" really any less safe than "volunteer blood," as Titmuss and other critics of markets in blood allege?[20] In place of idle speculation or moral philosophizing, researchers who have reviewed the evidence relating to safety have found no significant effect on blood quality when economic rewards are provided to motivate blood donations.[21] In fact, one could argue that suppliers would have strong incentives to screen and certify the quality of their blood supplies under a market system, since vampires would presumably be willing to pay more for safe or screened blood, or in the alternative, the law could regulate the quality of blood through labeling and safety regulations, as it currently does for most other food and drug products. Also, it is worth noting that the quality of human blood may not matter that much to vampires, for to the extent that vampires are less prone to blood-borne diseases, vampires would provide a ready-made market for sick people who otherwise would not be able to sell their blood. [22]

The Exploitation Argument

Critics of "paid blood" or blood markets also argue that the "commodification" of blood would end up exploiting the poor. [23] But consider the exploitation that already exists under the current system of nonmarket donations. Under the current system, blood donation centers like the Red Cross are allowed to sell their blood supplies to local hospitals to cover their operating expenses, while individual blood donors receive no compensation for their donations. [24] So, which system is more exploitative?

The vampire world poses the problem of exploitation in even more stark terms. Currently, most vampires must resort to violence to obtain fresh supplies of blood, taking what they need by force from their human victims. Moreover, without markets, vampires are more likely to prey on the poor and disadvantaged—people who tend to live in areas with higher crime rates and less police protection. With a legal market in blood, by contrast, vampires and humans could bargain and cooperate with one another on a voluntary and consensual basis. The author thus leaves it to the reader to decide which system produces more exploitation.

In any case, whether one uses the label "exploitation" or not to describe a voluntary and consensual market transaction, one thing is for sure: the existence of a legal market actually gives people (including vampires) more choices than they had before (without a legal market). When there is a legal market, no one is compelled to sell his or her blood. We humans will sell our blood to vampires only if we think that such sales will make us better off. Otherwise, we will continue not selling our blood. [25]

A SANGUINE FUTURE

To reduce violence in the vampire world, we should consider legalizing trade in blood, thus allowing vampires and humans to make and enforce voluntary contracts for the purchase and sale of blood. In the absence of such a legal market in blood, vampires have no other choice but to take their blood supplies through force. Legal markets, however, convert mutual conflict into joint cooperation—with legalized markets in blood, in short, vampires and humans would have incentives to trade with one another. Vampires could "come out of their coffins," so to speak, and vampire slayers could lay down their stakes. Vampires are not inherently bad. If they had a meaningful choice, more vampires would *buy*, not *bite*.

Chapter Thirteen

To Shoot or to Stake, That Is the Question

The Market for Anti-Vampire Weapons

Charlotte Weil and Sébastien Lecou

During a cold night, a man is slowly walking in the quiet streets of a small town. Suddenly, a vampire emerges from the dark and jumps in front of him. Our hero quickly plunges his hand under his coat to reach for a stake that will soon pierce the heart of the creature. . . . This small scene has been seen in hundreds of movies and at first glance does not seem to require any further explanation. But wait a minute. . . . Where did the stake come from? Did the man whittle it himself? Or did he buy it, and if so, at what price? And why did the man use a stake and not, say, a sophisticated handgun firing silver-infused exploding bullets? Does he simply prefer the more traditional killing method? Or was it because of the price difference between the different weapons? And if so, what's behind the price difference? This chapter proposes to answer some of these questions by applying the tools of *industrial organization* to the market for anti-vampire weapons.

Industrial organization is the branch of economics that studies the structure of firms, markets, and industries.[1] The realism of the theory has been helpful in understanding the behavior of firms and has also shaped public policies—for example, in antitrust or regulatory issues. The tools provided by this theory have been applied to a wide variety of issues, from the Japanese beer industry[2] to the use of sweet potato in Asian food[3] to waiting times in the fast-food drive-through industry.[4] Surprisingly, the theory of industrial organization has never been applied to the market for anti-vampire weapons, and this chapter proposes to fill that void.

This chapter will first focus on the manufacturers of anti-vampire weapons and describe the supply side of our subject. We will then concentrate on the demand side, with an emphasis on the demand for weapons by vampire hunters. The chapter will conclude by applying our analysis to a proposed merger between two weapon manufacturers.

WHEN THE INVISIBLE HAND WIELDS A STAKE: THE SUPPLY OF ANTI-VAMPIRE WEAPONS

A wide variety of instruments can be used against vampires: among others, stakes, sunlight, silver, garlic, holy water, a crucifix. . . . But we will simplify the analysis and narrow our study to two kinds of weapons: stakes and firearms.

Staking through the heart is traditionally the preferred method for destroying a vampire. Most cultures and popular sources refer to the necessity of using wooden stakes; some suggest that the wood should be from a particular tree, like ash or hawthorn. Silver stakes have also sometimes been considered a legitimate way to kill vampires.

If staking is traditionally the most common killing method, the use of firearms is more and more prevalent. Once again, different materials can be used for the fabrication of bullets, and while silver and wooden bullets are the most common, some manufacturers have been more innovative. The sixth season of the TV show *True Blood* has, for example, introduced the use of upgraded silver bullets with a compartment filled with ultraviolet-radiating fluid inside their shells. These bullets take advantage of the weaknesses of vampires to both silver and sunlight.

One of our objectives in this chapter will be to assess the extent of the *market power* enjoyed by the different weapon manufacturers. A firm possesses some degree of market power when it can profitably set a price higher than its costs. It is easy to understand that this ability to set high prices will depend upon the intensity of competition in the market; the more competitive the market is, the lower the prices will be. One useful concept for determining the market power that a firm will enjoy is that of the *barrier to entry*. A barrier to entry refers to any obstacle that could make it difficult for a new firm to enter in a market, therefore decreasing the competitive intensity and increasing the prices. A useful example for discussing the different drivers of market power is the iPhone, which is frequently considered to be one of the products with the highest margin of price over cost.[5]

Several factors allow Apple to set prices significantly above its costs without losing too much market share to its competitors. First, entry into the smartphone market is difficult and requires large investments in research and development. Second, entry into the market is restricted by intellectual property and the existence of a large number of patents. Finally, Apple has developed a brand loyalty so that consumers willingly accept higher prices for Apple-branded products. Although brand loyalty can be a powerful driver of market power, we do not possess enough information on the brand loyalty that will develop on the anti-vampire weapons market, and we will therefore concentrate our analysis on the barriers to entry implied by technological properties of the market and intellectual property. The manufacturing of stakes, and particularly of wooden stakes, is unlikely to present high barriers to entry. There is no need for huge amounts of physical capital to enter the market, because access to the primary resource (wood) is easy, and there is no particular complexity in the production process. The ease of entering the market can be demonstrated by the example of vampire slayers who are able to make their own stakes, like Kendra's Mr. Pointy on *Buffy the Vampire Slayer*. *Buffy* also presents several instances of improvised fabrication of wooden stakes. Buffy has dispatched vampires by driving various pieces of wood into their hearts, including a mop handle, a drumstick, a pool cue, a pencil, and even a ceramic unicorn with a wooden horn.[6] Manufacturers will therefore also easily enter the market, and it is likely that the market for stakes (and more particularly wooden stakes) will feature many active firms competing with each other. And even if one among them managed to monopolize the market, the self-production by vampire slayers themselves would limit the market power of this company.

By contrast, the manufacturing of anti-vampire firearms is likely to present some substantial barriers to entry. The manufacturing of firearms requires a significant amount of physical capital and is more complex to set up. It is possible to develop a better understanding of the competitive conditions that would emerge on this market by observing the characteristics of the market for standard firearms in the United States today.[7] Studies show that some segments of the market are very concentrated, with the top two brands of shotguns (O. F. Mossberg/Maverick and Remington Arms) holding more than 90 percent of the shotgun market, and the top four producers of revolvers (Smith & Wesson, Ruger, Colt's Manufacturing, and Freedom Arms) also holding more than 90 percent of the market. Although the market is concentrated, it nonetheless exhibits a competitive fringe, with more than two thousand manufacturers active during the period 1986–2010. We should expect this tendency toward concentration to be exacerbated in the market for anti-vampire firearms. Indeed, the technology is likely to be more complex, and fewer manufacturers will have the skills necessary to develop accurate weapons. First, concerning firearms using silver bullets, several studies[8] show that because silver is not as dense as lead, the accuracy of silver bullets can suffer. Firearm and silver-bullet producers will thus have to develop more sophisticated techniques compared to regular firearms and will have to invest in research and development in order to correct this problem. Moreover, the production process will also be more complex, since lead melts at 621 degrees Fahrenheit while silver melts at 1,761 degrees Fahrenheit, and will therefore require better furnace techniques.[9]

The production of useful firearms using wooden bullets will also prove challenging, since wooden bullets in regular rifles are usually only lethal at a twenty-five-meter range. Once more, important spending on research and development will be necessary to develop efficient firearms using wooden bullets.[10] Note that the market will also exhibit sunk costs, meaning costs that cannot be recovered if the firm decides to leave the market. For example, if a firm has invested in research and development or an assembly line in order to market a bullet that radiates ultraviolet light, it is unlikely that the assets developed by the firm could be used for other purposes than vampire hunting. Sunk costs therefore increase the risk incurred by a firm entering the market and can also deter entry.

Historically, the most common and forbidding entry barriers have often been imposed by government actions through the granting of monopoly rights. In the market for vampire-killing tools, the government could, for example, protect innovative firms that developed efficient firearms using silver or wooden bullets by granting them patents to prevent other firms from producing the same output without permission.

The foregoing supply-side analysis might seem sufficient to conclude our analysis of the market power of manufacturers of anti-vampire weapons. The stake market will exhibit intense competition, meaning that stake manufacturers are unlikely to possess any significant market power and will therefore set low prices. In contrast, a monopoly (protected by a patent) selling rifles using wooden or silver bullets will possess significant market power and will set high prices. However, notice that when we say that the manufacturer of firearms using wooden bullets has a monopoly on its market, we implicitly define the market where this firm is active as the market for firearms using wooden bullets. Is this true? Or does this manufacturer actually operate within a wider market, for example, the market for anti-vampire firearms, where the firm competes with manufacturers of rifles using silver bullets? Or does the firm actually operate in an even wider market, the market for all anti-vampire weapons, where it also faces intense competition from stake producers? We see that, depending on the definition of the market, a manufacturer may appear to be confronted by very different levels of competition. This definition of the "relevant market" is a central problem in many antitrust cases and often settles the issue of the case. For example, in 2007, the Federal Trade Commission tried to block the merger between Whole Foods and Wild Oats, two grocery chains specializing in natural and organic food.[11] The court stated that if the relevant market was the "premium natural and organic supermarkets," there could be little doubt that the acquisition of the second-largest firm by the largest firm in the market would tend to harm competition.

If, on the other hand, the defendants were operating within the larger market of "supermarkets," in which the two merging firms possessed a very small market share, the proposed merger would not tend to harm competition. The same issue arose in 1997 in a proposed merger between Office Depot and Staples; the merger did not appear anticompetitive when the market was defined as that of "superstores" or "office-supply stores" but did appear anticompetitive when it was defined as "office-supply superstores."[12] However, the definition of the relevant market is not arbitrary. Product A is said to be part of the same relevant market as product B *if* a 5 to 10 percent price increase for product A leads a significant proportion of consumers to switch from product A to product B, so that this price increase isn't profitable. In order to analyze the relevant markets for anti-vampire weapons, we therefore have to study the *demand* from vampire hunters.

BUFFY GOES TO WALMART: THE DEMAND FOR ANTI-VAMPIRE WEAPONS

Most users and buyers of anti-vampire weapons are "vampire hunters" or "vampire slayers." These individuals have developed knowledge of vampires and their weaknesses and have developed the necessary skills to fight them. One influential vampire hunter was Professor Van Helsing, a character in Bram Stoker's *Dracula*. In this chapter, we will focus on more modern vampire hunters representative of today's market. One example of a modern vampire hunter is Buffy Summers; another is Blade, who features in the Marvel comics and movies of the same name. Jason Stackhouse, from the *True Blood* TV show, is not a formally trained vampire hunter but has developed such skills as an autodidact. Vampire hunters can rely on very different arsenals of weapons. The choice of a particular weapon will depend upon two main factors: the weaknesses exhibited by the vampire (toward silver or wood) and the skills of the vampire hunter himself.

Silver and Wood: The Weaknesses of the Vampire

The first decision for the vampire hunter is choosing between a weapon made of wood and a weapon made of silver. The choice will be driven by the weaknesses presented by the hunted vampire (note that we suppose that a vampire hunter specializes in the hunting of a specific race of vampire that inhabits his or her community). If the vampire only exhibits a weakness to wood, the hunter will choose a wooden weapon; if the vampire only presents a weakness to silver, the hunter will choose a weapon made of silver. If the vampire presents a weakness to both types of material, the hunter will be indifferent and will simply choose her preferred weapon or the less expensive one.

An analysis of vampire traits in folklore and fiction[13] based on a study of a hundred species of vampires shows that 70 percent of species present a weakness only to wood, while 28 percent of vampire species present a weakness to both wood and silver. A fact that will later prove useful is that only two kinds of vampires (described in the book *The Strain* and *Vampire Academy*[14]) present a weakness to silver and not to wood, whereas a majority of vampires present a weakness only to wood and not to silver.

The Skills of the Vampire Hunter: Choosing between Stakes and Firearms

Most vampires have enhanced physical abilities. For example, we have found[15] that more than 80 percent of vampire species present enhanced speed. Very often, the rapidity of a vampire will make it impossible for a normal human to kill this vampire at short range using only a stake. In this situation, a normal human being will have to use a firearm in order to kill the vampire. This is well illustrated by *True Blood*, where firearms are by far the favorite weapons used by humans to hunt vampires.

However, some vampire hunters possess superhuman senses and have received training that allows them to fight vampires at short range using stakes. For example, the opening of *Buffy the Vampire Slayer* states that she is the Chosen One, possessing the strength and skills to fight vampires. Such vampire hunters will have the option of choosing between firearms and stakes according to their preferences and their skills. The following dialogue from *Buffy the Vampire Slayer* is in that regard very telling.

> Member of the Initiative: We use the latest in scientific technology and state-of-the-art weaponry, and you, if I understand correctly, poke them with a sharp stick.
> Buffy: Oh, it's more effective than it sounds.[16]

We should remind the reader that the Initiative is a secret government agency tasked with the capture and study of demons. Its members are soldiers who do not possess the supernatural skills of Buffy and thus have to resort to firearms. But, as pointed out by Buffy, the use of stakes can be highly efficient in the hands of a properly trained slayer. Blade represents another type of vampire hunter who can use stakes but, unlike Buffy, also chooses to rely intensively on firearms.

It will prove useful later to consider a simplified categorization of vampire hunters: Buffy types who rely on stakes, Jason Stackhouse types who can only use firearms, and Blade types who can use both types of weapon.

IMPLICATIONS FOR DEFINING THE RELEVANT MARKET

There are two important questions to consider. First, are weapons firing silver bullets on the same market as weapons firing wooden bullets? Second, are firearms on the same market as stakes?

Silver Bullets versus Wooden Bullets

There are two ways to address the issue of substitution between firearms using silver bullets and firearms using wooden bullets. The first is to ask whether an increase in the price of silver-based firearms will lead silver-based firearms consumers to use wood-based firearms. We think that this will be the case. Indeed, we have seen that there are almost no vampires that can be killed by silver bullets but not by wooden bullets. Therefore, there is no captive demand for firearms using silver bullets, and vampire hunters will be able to switch to wooden bullets if the price of firearms using silver bullets increases. We therefore find that wood-based firearms are indeed in the same relevant market as silver-based firearms.

The other way to address the issue is to ask whether an increase in the price of wood-based firearms will lead a large number of vampire hunters using wooden bullets to switch to silver-based firearms. Here, the answer is surprisingly negative. Indeed, as we have seen, there exist a large number of vampires that can only be killed by wood and that present no weaknesses to silver. The manufacturer of firearms using wooden bullets may therefore be able to increase the price of its product, and many hunters will not be able to switch to silver bullets. It may seem surprising and even contradictory that firearms using wooden bullets *are* part of the same relevant market as firearms using silver bullets, but that firearms using silver bullets are *not* part of the same relevant market as firearms using wooden bullets. But this situation, even if uncommon, has already been observed in other real-world cases. It has for example been noted that consumers in the United States may like Korean noodles, but Korean consumers may not be willing to purchase American noodles. On that basis, Korean noodles could be a substitute to American ones for all consumers, while American noodles would only be an imperfect substitute for Korean consumers. [17]

We conclude that weapons firing wooden bullets will be able to exert intense competitive pressure on weapons firing silver bullets, but the reverse will not be true. Manufacturers of weapons firing wooden bullets could therefore enjoy some market power. However, this will only be true if manufacturers of wood-based firearms are not in the same market as *stake* manufacturers.

Wooden-Bullet Firearms versus Wooden Stakes

Here, we wonder if vampire hunters who usually buy firearms that fire wooden bullets would be able to switch to wooden stakes in the event of an increase in the price of the firearms. In order to answer this question, it is useful to refer to our segmentation of vampire hunters between Buffy types (using stakes), Jason Stackhouse types (using firearms), and Blade types (using either stakes or firearms). Since the Buffy types do not usually buy firearms, they are not relevant for this analysis. Jason Stackhouse types will not be able to switch to stakes in the event of an increase in the price of firearms and are thus captive to the firearms manufacturer. However, we should not conclude too quickly that firearms manufacturers could increase their prices without being constrained by the existence of stake manufacturers. The features of our case are actually very close to those exhibited in a famous real-world antitrust case judged in the European Union.[18] In the United Brands case, the court wondered if bananas could be part of the same relevant market as other fruits. The court said that because of the physical characteristics of bananas (seedlessness, easy handling, softness), the very young and the very old (basically toothless people) could not substitute away from bananas, and other fruits could therefore not be part of the same relevant market. But this reasoning was flawed. Indeed, it is not necessary for all consumers to switch away from bananas in order to widen the relevant market. It is only necessary that a number of consumers (people with teeth) would consider other fruits as substitutes, a sufficient number to render a price increase for bananas unprofitable. This kind of mistake in antitrust cases has henceforward been known as the "toothless fallacy." It would certainly be ironic to fall for this "toothless fallacy" in a study dealing with vampires. In our context, the Stackhouse types play the role of the toothless, who cannot switch to another product. However, if Blade types are numerous enough compared to Stackhouse types, a price increase for firearms will lead a large number of hunters to switch to stakes. Wooden stakes will therefore be in competition with firearms firing wooden bullets, and firearms manufacturers will therefore not be able to enjoy strong market power.

APPLICATION: A PROPOSED MERGER BETWEEN FIREARMS PRODUCERS

The implications of the analysis above can be illustrated through the pending antitrust case described below:

Transylvanian Trade Commission
PRESS RELEASE
Castelul Bran, 500007 Braşov, +40 268 72-4 79-8
For immediate release: October 1, 2014

Opening of an inquiry concerning the merger between "Deadwood Inc." and "TRANS-SILVERNIA CORP."

The Transylvanian Trade Commission (TTC) is currently investigating the proposed merger between "Deadwood Inc." and "Trans-Silvernia Corp." Deadwood Inc. is a manufacturer possessing a patent on the production of firearms that fire wooden bullets. Trans-Silvernia Corp. possesses a patent for the production of firearms that fire silver bullets and sells a large selection of anti-vampire weapons made of silver, from stakes to firearms. Deadwood is renowned for the quality of its manufacturing and the solidity of its weapons, while Trans-Silvernia has developed a solid know-how in the production of high-precision firearms. A market study commissioned by the TTC has found that despite a long tradition of stake hunting, the younger vampire hunters that represent an important proportion of slayers in the country seem to rely predominantly on the use of firearms.

How should the Transylvanian Trade Commission respond to the proposed merger? We have seen that firearms using silver bullets do not exert an important competitive pressure on the segment of the market of firearms using wooden bullets. But the wooden-bullet market does exert intense competitive pressure on the silver-bullet market. By suppressing this competitive pressure, the merger would risk leading to a sharp price increase in the price of silver-based firearms. Moreover, stakes are not a good substitute for firearms using silver bullets for Stackhouse types, who apparently constitute a large proportion of the Transylvanian population and cannot therefore prevent a price increase for silver firearms. The proposed merger might therefore at first glance seem anticompetitive.

However, the merger could also bring some benefits. One could imagine that the new entity could develop a firearm capable of shooting both silver and wooden bullets. The new company could also develop a new weapon that would combine the know-how of the two companies in accuracy and solidity. Finally, firearms using wooden and silver bullets are likely to use similar components and could share the same production process. The new firm could therefore realize important savings from economies of scale (that is, cost savings that result from mass production) and from integrating the production of the two kinds of firearms. It is possible that these different positive effects of the merger would counterbalance the negative ones so that consumers would benefit from it. However, the realization of these efficiencies is uncertain, while the negative effect of the merger on the intensity of competition is a certainty. There is therefore some doubt about the impact that the merger will have on consumers. One possibility to make sure that the merger will benefit vampire hunters would be to make the approval conditional on the merged firm licensing its patent on firearms using wooden bullets. Indeed, the patent seems to be the main barrier to entry into the market. By licensing the patent, the merged firm would allow the emergence of a competitor that would constrain the price of both the silver-based and wood-based firearms.

This proposed merger is just one instance where our framework can be used. The functional definition of markets, and more generally the tools developed by industrial organization theory, could also be applied to a diverse set of issues dealing with anti-vampire weapons. To name just a few, future work could concentrate on collusive behaviors between the manufacturers of firearms using wooden bullets, mergers between firearms manufacturers and synthetic blood companies, bundling of different types of firearms, the impact of market power on the quality of the weapons, discriminatory pricing according to the type of vampire hunter, incentives to innovate on the anti-vampire weapons markets, and more. Such developments are left for future research.

Chapter Fourteen

Taxation of the Undead

Nonsentient Entities

Joseph Mandarino

> In this world nothing can be said to be certain, except death and taxes.
>
> —Benjamin Franklin

If Ben Franklin was right, then after a zombie apocalypse, the field of taxation will take its rightful place as the preeminent endeavor of what remains of humanity. This chapter addresses the taxation of the undead, joining a growing body of undead taxation scholarship. [1]

The undead can generally be divided into nonsentient entities (zombies) and sentient entities (vampires). This bifurcation is critical because entities in the first category are appropriately treated as property under existing tax rules, while entities in the second category would likely be treated as taxpayers. This chapter focuses primarily on nonsentient entities. I will leave the treatment of undead taxpayers for a future volume.

First, I will consider important transition rules for the undead as property. Second, I will examine the concept of cost recovery as it applies to undead property. Finally, I will analyze tax issues raised by the commercial sale of the undead. As we shall see, tax rules can have a significant impact on economic incentives, especially when it comes to maximizing the value of the newly undead.

TRANSITION ISSUES

Tax Status of the Nonsentient Undead

I will first consider at greater length whether a nonsentient entity should be treated as property rather than as a taxpayer. This makes intuitive sense because the literature suggests that zombies are not capable of thought and can be analogized to wild animals (albeit ones that only eat brains). It thus seems appropriate to treat zombies the same way animals are treated for tax purposes—as property.

A rule that treated zombies as taxpayers would create unwise incentives. For example, low-income individuals are eligible for tax credits in some instances (e.g., the earned-income tax credit). If zombies were treated as taxpayers instead of property, then an unscrupulous person could corral several hundred zombies and file for these credits on their behalf. A similarly motivated person might form a partnership with a large group of zombies and have it absorb the taxable income from the partnership's investments. While many doctrines under current tax law would mitigate the effectiveness of such strategies, the temptation of a ready army of nonsentient taxpayers susceptible to manipulation could pose significant risk to the tax system. Incentives for such bad conduct can be eliminated if zombies are treated for tax purposes as property and not as taxpayers.

Tax Attributes of Zombies

I next consider what should happen to a person's tax attributes after conversion to zombie status. A person's tax attributes are her tax credits, deductions, or liabilities at a given time. Although salaried employees will generally not have material tax attributes, entrepreneurs often have extensive inventories. For example, a real estate developer may amass enormous tax losses over a multiple-year period before recognizing a profit and absorbing those losses. Thus, a developer who dies before the end of such a cycle will have an extremely valuable inventory of tax losses—valuable because they can be used to reduce tax liabilities.

Under the current rule, tax attributes disappear upon death. If the same rule applied when a person became a zombie, then both death and zombification would result in parallel tax treatment. However, if a different rule applied to a person who became a zombie, then different incentives might be created. Suppose that we adopt a rule that permits tax attributes to be inherited if a person becomes a zombie. In that case, there would be a strong incentive to convert a terminally ill person (willingly or not) into a zombie so that her heirs could acquire her tax attributes.

Moreover, such a rule would also increase the windfall that unscrupulous heirs would reap if they murdered a wealthy relative (without getting caught). Not only would such heirs obtain the deceased's tangible property, but, if they were careful to convert their target into a zombie while committing the murder, they would also obtain a tax windfall.

Given these incentives, it makes more sense for death and zombification to be treated identically, at least as to the issue of tax attributes. Tax attributes should expire upon zombification.

Estate Planning for Zombies

Generally, transfers of a taxpayer's assets during her life or at the time of death are subject to taxes, typically measured by the value of the assets transferred. In the case of the federal system, these taxes are generally triggered by the death of the taxpayer. If a taxpayer is converted into an undead entity, then technically there is no event of death and the tax would never be due. However, I assume that conversion to zombie status would be treated as "death" for estate- and gift-tax purposes.

Generally, the value of an estate is determined as of the date of a person's death. However, if a person converts to zombie status, is the person's estate increased by the value of the zombie she has become? As the zombie literature makes clear, with the right safeguards zombies can be used as a source of labor. See, for example, *Plague of the Zombies* (1966) and *Fido* (2006). Indeed, the Haitian origins of the zombie myth are inextricably linked with slavery.[2]

An important disclaimer must be made at this point. This article considers the use of zombies as unpaid labor, analogous to work animals. Ethically, such use of zombies may be tolerated because, although human in form, zombies lack sentience. Conversely, it can be argued that zombification is the result of a traumatic event, and a zombie is no different than an individual who suffers brain damage in a car accident. Society generally does not sanction the use of brain-damaged individuals as slave labor, and the same concerns might be raised against the enslavement of zombies. This article takes no position either way, but considers the possibility solely because it is mentioned in the literature of the undead.

Given the possible commercial value of a zombie, tax authorities hungry for tax revenue to rebuild society after the zombie apocalypse could take the position that estate tax is owed on the value of the zombie that the deceased converts into. The net effect of this would be to place a burden on the estates (and thus the heirs) of people who become zombies. This would incentivize certain actions. For example, in *Shaun of the Dead* (2004), the penultimate scene features Shaun and Liz prepared for a seemingly doomed standoff against a horde of undead. Faced with such low odds of survival and, given the adding-insult-to-injury aspect of inflicting a higher estate-tax liability on their next of kin if they did not survive, it would appear more logical for them to commit suicide than to risk becoming zombies. However, this would have been a disastrous choice given how the scene ends. In such situations, the estate-tax burden would incentivize suicide rather than fighting to the last breath.

In the *Walking Dead* universe, Rick Grimes's band of survivors develops a pact that if any member turns into a zombie, the others will inflict the type of brain injury necessary to end that status. Assuming that this is generally a beneficial result (fewer zombies), the estate-tax burden discussed above would create a conflicting incentive. Because the survivors wait until a person becomes a zombie before acting, this type of pact would result in greater estate-tax liability than would be the case if traumatic brain injury were inflicted before death. As a result, survivors would be incentivized to kill community members earlier to reduce their expected tax liability. Thus, humans who sustained life-threatening wounds might be culled preemptively, even though they might have survived.

Assuming that a *Walking Dead*–type pact is beneficial (i.e., it's best to inflict a traumatic brain injury only *after* it is clear that a person has become a zombie), the ideal rule would be to exclude the value of a person's own zombie from that person's estate.

However, after the zombie crisis subsides and order is restored, the benefit of zombie labor may be viewed as more important than eliminating zombies. In that case, a rule including the value of a person's zombie self in that person's estate would incentivize the estate's heirs to preserve such a zombie and sell it in order to offset the increased estate tax. Moreover, if this rule were adopted after safeguards were put in place to keep humans safe from zombies, then the risk of suicide or of preemptively killing the wounded would be minimized. Thus, the appropriate estate-tax rule will depend on whether society is in the midst of the apocalypse or has managed to survive it.

Restoration of the Undead

A relatively new theme in the literature of the undead is that such an entity may "return" or be cured of zombie-ism. Should such a person be deemed a continuation of her former human self or a "new" person? In part this will depend on the nature of the restoration.

In *Warm Bodies* (2013), the zombie protagonist R develops sentience and, eventually, becomes human. Notably, R has no recollection of his own past life. In contrast, the zombie protagonist in *In the Flesh* (2013) regains sentience, including memories of his past life and his zombie life but appears to remain undead (for example, he does not eat).

In the former case, the person is fully restored to human status, so it would make sense to confer on him all the attributes of such status, including treating such a person as a taxpayer rather than as property. However, because all connection to his past human life has been lost, it may make sense to treat him as a new person. Under this approach, he would not reacquire the tax attributes of his former self that expired on his death.

Unfortunately, this approach could provide a perverse incentive to a tax debtor, particularly if the chance of converting back to human status was relatively high. For example, assume that a failed businessman owed millions of dollars to the IRS and was broke, destitute, and depressed. Under such circumstances, the idea of starting over, free of any debts and obligations, might be appealing. Thus, our businessman might have a strong incentive to intentionally convert to zombie status and then back to human. However, this problem will probably be a minor one if the restored individuals genuinely have no memory of their past lives, because in that case a temporary zombification is functionally equivalent to death.

In the case of a restoration in which the entity retains his zombie status, the person is still undead but is clearly sentient. This chapter assumes that sentient people, whether dead or undead, should be treated as taxpayers, and that the nonsentient undead should be treated as property. Accordingly, it would seem appropriate to treat such a being as a taxpayer. However, if such a being were permitted to "start over" with respect to his or her human tax attributes, then there would be an even stronger incentive to escape a tax liability by intentionally becoming a zombie and then undergoing *In the Flesh*–type drug therapy to regain sentience. Because such an entity would retain all of his or her memories, there would be greater reason for our failed businessman to subject himself to this gauntlet to avoid paying a tax liability.

COST RECOVERY OF UNDEAD ASSETS

Let us assume that, with appropriate security precautions, nonsentient undead beings could be used as a source of labor, just as work animals are. If such entities can be reliably used in commerce, then it would follow that they will be sold and purchased, just like any other property. Such transactions raise several important tax issues.

One of the key tax-policy issues in connection with property is the concept of cost recovery. There are many forms of cost recovery, such as expensing, depreciation, amortization, and capitalization, but the concept is best illustrated with an example.

Assume a coal company pays a worker $100 to mine coal for a year. The worker mines a quantity of coal that the company sells for $300. To simplify the example, assume that there are no other expenses of production. Most people would agree that the coal company has income of $200. That is, it has revenue of $300 and expenses of $100, so net profit is $200. Now assume that the coal company instead purchases a mining machine. Assume that the machine costs $500, will last five years, and during that time will mine a quantity of coal that is sold for $1,500. Furthermore, assume the coal is mined at the rate of $300 per year. In the aggregate, the coal company will earn $1,000 over five years from using the mining machine, or $200 of income on average per year. As noted, the coal company could also earn $200 in one year from using human labor. Thus, at first glance it appears that the machine would not produce any more income for the coal company than a human worker but would entail a significantly higher up-front cost (i.e., $500 upon purchase, versus $100 per year to the human worker). This would create a mild incentive to use labor instead of the machine.

This decision may change, however, depending on whether the tax rules are designed to incentivize purchases of this type of machinery. For example, one approach, called expensing, would permit the coal company to deduct the entire cost of the mining machine in the year it is purchased. That would not change the pretax economics; the coal company would still have the burden of the large up-front cost and would only earn $200 of profit per year. However, it would significantly affect the company's tax bill. In the first year, the coal company would have a tax loss ($300 of coal revenue against $500 of expense, for a net tax loss of $200). This would eliminate any tax on the mine in that year and, if the coal company had other mines, could be used to offset taxes on other mines. Assuming a 40 percent tax rate, the mine would go from paying $80 of tax in the first year when using human labor ($200 profit × 40 percent tax rate) to having a tax benefit—that is, a reduction in taxes—of $80 ($200 tax loss × 40 percent tax rate) in the first year using the machine. That swing of $160 could more than make up for the up-front cost of the machine. Thus, cost-recovery rules embedded in the tax code can incentivize purchases and decisions that may not be economical on a pretax basis.

In a world where zombies are a viable alternative to human laborers, the cost-recovery regime could be critical. In the prior example, replace "machine" with "zombie" and it becomes clear that a cost-recovery rule that permits expensing of zombies will incentivize the use of the undead as labor.

Assume, instead, that it is beneficial to discourage the use of zombie labor. The government might believe that it is better that all zombies be hunted (this might particularly be the case before order is restored) or might not want humans to lose jobs to the undead (because, after all, the government is elected by humans). In either case, a cost-recovery rule that defers the timing of deductions for zombies, rather than allowing the zombie's price to be deducted in the first year, will discourage the use of zombies as labor.

Arguably the least attractive cost-recovery rule, from an economic perspective, is capitalization. Under capitalization, no deduction is permitted for the cost of any item until it is sold or becomes unusable. Continuing the foregoing example, assume the coal company can hire a human at $100 per year for five years or buy a zombie for $500, which will last approximately five years. To simplify things, assume the zombie completely withers away at the end of the fifth year.

With respect to the human worker, the coal company would be entitled to a $100 deduction each year for five years. In contrast, if the coal company buys a zombie, it will not be entitled to any deductions until the end of year five, when it will be able to take a $500 deduction. Although both choices produce the same nominal amount of deductions, the time value of money must be considered. Because money now is worth more than money later, the present value of a series of $100 deductions for five years is greater than the present value of a deduction of $500 five years from now. Thus, all other factors being equal, the coal company would have an incentive to use human labor if it were forced to capitalize the cost of a zombie.

Notwithstanding the foregoing point, the effect of cost-recovery rules on behavior is mitigated in part by their complexity (as, unfortunately, the above discussion may demonstrate). Indeed, the complexity of tax rules can often dim the economic signals they are intended to send. For that reason, such incentives are often best understood and utilized by larger taxpayers with finance departments. In our example, the coal company is apt to be able to decipher the relevant tax rules and quantify the benefit of, say, an expensing regime for zombies. Conversely, these signals might be lost on the owner of a small family farm who is considering whether to buy a zombie or continue to use human migrant workers.

COMMERCIAL TRANSFERS OF UNDEAD PROPERTY

Now we turn to the taxation of general commerce in undead property. How should the tax authorities treat sales of zombies from one owner to another? And how should they treat entrepreneurs whose business involves capturing zombies for commercial use?

Specific decisions on whether to permit zombie hunters (not killers) to deduct the costs of supplies will affect whether, and how many, people follow this line of work. For example, assume that Huey captures a zombie and sells it to Dewey. Huey expends $10 on supplies to capture the zombie and sells it to Dewey for $100. Huey will earn $90 in income from this transaction ($100 sales proceeds minus $10 in expenses). If the tax rules permitted Huey to deduct his supplies—which, judging from depictions of zombie hunters in the literature, would include nets, ropes, cattle prods, shovels for digging pits, and leather outerwear—Huey's taxable income would also be $90. Conversely, if Huey could not deduct the cost of his supplies, his taxable income would be distorted and he would, effectively, be subject to a higher marginal tax rate than otherwise. If the government wished to discourage zombie hunting, perhaps because zombie killing is preferred, it could eliminate the deduction for supplies. This would make other lines of work more remunerative on an after-tax basis. But if the government wished to encourage zombie hunting, or at least treat it equally with other lines of business, then deduction of zombie-hunting supplies should be permitted.

Besides taxing income, most governments also tax the transfer of property. Transfer taxes can pose an obstacle to the flourishing of commerce if not designed carefully. Specifically, in the absence of certain exceptions, transfer taxes can be applied repeatedly on back-to-back transfers. Such *iterative application* (as it is called) can make even a nominal transfer tax a significant burden.

Suppose that Huey is a resident of Ohio and hunts zombies exclusively in that state. Assume also that the sale and physical transfer of the zombie to Dewey occurs in Ohio. In the absence of other rules, the sale described here would be subject to Ohio sales tax. But now suppose that Dewey is a broker and travels throughout the hinterland buying zombies that he intends to sell at the Zombie Exchange in Chicago, Illinois. Accordingly, a transfer tax would be imposed on the purchase of the zombies in Ohio and again when they are sold at the exchange in Chicago.

This repeated application of transfer taxes would discourage the business model described above. Instead, in order to reduce their taxes, buyers would be motivated to travel into potentially dangerous zombie lands and purchase captured zombies directly from hunters like Huey. This would make it difficult for both sides to achieve the optimal sales price that a free and open auction can provide.

Thankfully, most regimes that impose transfer taxes also provide an exemption for brokers like Dewey. Under the "sale-for-resale" rule, a transaction generally is not liable for sales tax if the purchaser acquires the property and plans to sell the property subsequently. This would permit Dewey to specialize in buying zombies from hunters in potentially unsafe areas and selling the zombies at a public auction, thereby providing the widest selection to potential buyers.

Assume now that Dewey takes a zombie acquired from Huey, along with any other zombies he has purchased on his travels, and returns to Chicago. Suppose that Dewey sells Huey's zombie, along with others, to Louie, the owner of an electronics factory in the southern part of Illinois. Assume also that Louie plans to use the zombie to work in the factory and does not plan on reselling the zombie. In that case, the sale-for-resale doctrine would no longer apply, and it would appear that Dewey would have to collect sales tax on the sale to Louie.

However, note that the zombie will be used to produce electronics, such as MP3 players. If MP3 players are subject to a transfer tax when sold, and if the cost of the zombie is reflected in that sales price, then the goods will be subject to multiple transfer taxes—once on inputs such as Huey's zombie and again on the MP3 players when they are sold.

Many transfer-tax regimes have an exception for supplies or component parts. The economic rationale for this exception is that supplies and components will ultimately be converted into a finished product that will itself be taxable. In the absence of such an exception, the final product would really bear double taxation. Unfortunately, because the main source of transfer taxes in the United States is the states themselves, there is little uniformity in rules. States that have transfer-tax regimes that avoid iterative tax burdens will attract more inputs than otherwise.

For example, assume that in Illinois there is no supply exception, and thus Louie is required to pay a transfer tax on the zombie originally captured by Huey in Ohio. In contrast, assume that a bidder from a chemical plant in Indiana is also present at Dewey's auction, and that Indiana does have a supply exception, such that no transfer tax would be due on the purchase of the same zombie. In that case, Louie's bid would be lower than the Indiana bid, because Louie would have to factor in paying a sales tax if his bid was successful. The bidder from Indiana could bid more because she would not be liable for any transfer taxes. As a result, some zombies might end up in the chemical plant even though they would be more productive assets in the electronics factory.

As this discussion makes clear, the application of disparate rules in each state may hinder the operation of markets. The ideal policy goal is that a transfer of taxable property should be subject to only one tax levy. A uniform transfer-tax regime that embodied rules to eliminate cumulative tax burdens would help markets operate in the most efficient fashion, allocating zombies to their best possible uses.

OPTIMAL TAX POLICY FOR A POST-INVASION WORLD

As the earlier discussion attempts to make clear, the treatment of zombies as property raises a host of tax issues. A critical step in the process of designing rules to tax zombies is to decide on the ultimate policy goal. If it is beneficial to eliminate zombies, then the tax rules can be set up to burden the accumulation or ownership of the undead. Conversely, if zombies can be used as labor, and if a flourishing market in captured zombies is desired, tax rules can be set to advance such goals. Although the atavistic reaction of society to a zombie epidemic is likely to be to kill all of them before they kill us, we hope that policy makers will take a longer view. Provided appropriate safeguards can be taken, the undead represent a significant economic resource, and appropriate tax rules can help to fully realize this value.

Part IV

The Dead Body Politic

For the first century after Adam Smith's *An Inquiry into the Nature and Causes of the Wealth of Nations* was published in 1776, the discipline he helped found wasn't called economics. It was called *political economy*.

The entanglement of economics and politics is inevitable. Virtually all economic activity takes place within a context created, in part, by legal and political institutions. And when government is not involved, private mechanisms of governance emerge to fill the gaps. In this section, our contributors bring the theory of political economy to bear on the world of the undead.

From the perspective of vampires, human beings are just a food supply—one that could be hunted to extinction if the hunters aren't careful. Glen Whitman addresses this looming "tragedy of the blood commons" and considers how the vampire community might address it, whether through government policy or other means.

Zombies are arguably not that different from other invasive species that societies have had to cope with, from Asian carp in North America to cane toads in Australia. Michael O'Hara uses the tools of resource economics to analyze which public policies would be best suited to addressing the threat of a zombie invasion, with some surprising conclusions inspired by the popularity of zombie video games.

A common theme in stories of the zombie apocalypse is the collapse of law and order. What happens to the rules of property and contract when ravenous corpses roam the landscape? Brian Hollar tackles the question of law in a post-apocalyptic world. Although enforcement of legal rules will inevitably be difficult after the collapse, Hollar says, the economic principles that should guide us in choosing the best legal rules will remain intact.

Another common theme in undead fiction is the total incompetence and lack of preparedness on the part of government. Is that realistic? Ilya Somin says that, sadly, the answer is often yes. Voters often have very poor incentives to become informed about undead threats (and other issues), which means vote-seeking politicians have poor incentives to adopt smart policies to address them.

But maybe that's okay, because politics might actually work better with vampires in charge. Fabien Medvecky, observing that vampires are highly political creatures, ponders what policies a vampire secretary of the treasury might support. The long-term perspective that comes with immortality could result in different, and possibly better, policies in such areas as climate change and Social Security.

Last, A. L. Phillips, M. C. Phillips, and G. M. Phillips suggest that the undead have *already* taken an active role in American politics, especially at the local level. Using data on the "graveyard vote" across the fifty states, the Phillipses perform a statistical test to determine where the undead reside in the greatest numbers and also which amenities—both natural and man-made—seem to attract them.

—GW & JD

Chapter Fifteen

Tragedy of the Blood Commons

The Case for Privatizing the Humans

Glen Whitman

"Gentlemen, we are starving. Our latest statistics show that less than five percent of the human population remains."

"What we're talking about is the extinction of the human race—"

"—what we're talking about is only having enough blood to sustain our population until the end of the month."

—Daybreakers (2010)

The film *Daybreakers* offers a cautionary tale for vampires: a dark future in which vampires have hunted humans to the brink of extinction. Despite getting many details of our physiology and culture wrong, the movie depicts a starvation scenario that is no idle fantasy. At present, humans are plentiful and vampires relatively rare—but that pleasant situation may not last forever. The rising vampire population, together with declining human birthrates in developed countries, could eventually turn human blood into a scarce resource. We need to think seriously about how to manage our food supply before it's too late.

Our dilemma is hardly unique. Humans, too, have faced situations in which valuable economic resources have been devastated by excessive consumption—for instance, fish in the international oceans, elephants in Africa, and buffalo on the nineteenth-century American plains. In most of these cases, the culprit was not simple greed or gluttony; if that were true, then wheat and cattle would also have been harvested and slaughtered into extinction. Instead, the problem arises from poor incentives to manage resources that are openly available to everyone.

Human economists have given this problem a simple name: *the tragedy of the commons*. And economic theory and practice have shown that, under the right circumstances, it has a simple solution: *private property rights*.

Put simply, vampires may someday need to privatize the humans.

TWO PARABLES OF THE BLOOD COMMONS

To understand the perverse incentives that accompany open-access resources (also known as common-pool resources or "commons" for short), it's useful to consider a short parable.

The vampire Reynaldo has trapped a young human woman in a dark alleyway. Just as Reynaldo is preparing to sink his fangs into her flesh and suck her dry, his keen hearing picks up something unusual . . . *a second heartbeat*. The woman is pregnant!

Reynaldo pauses for a moment, deciding what to do. Maybe he should let her go. If he does, then the woman will eventually give birth. At some later date, Reynaldo thinks to himself, he can trap her again, drain her, and still have her offspring left for dessert. And being immortal, Reynaldo isn't so impatient that he couldn't wait a while longer. Resisting his bloodlust for now seems like the rational thing to do.

And yet . . . if Reynaldo lets this woman escape, who's to say it will be Reynaldo who gets to drink her later? There are plenty of other vampires out there, all of whom would happily take this woman's lifeblood, and her child's, too. If there are just nine other vampires out there, Reynaldo thinks to himself, then he has only a one in ten chance of being the lucky one. So it's one meal for sure now, versus a 10 percent chance of two meals later. Reynaldo frowns as he does the math. . . .

And plunges his teeth deep into the young woman's neck.

Reynaldo's choice is not unusual; humans face similar choices on a regular basis. Take ivory hunters in Africa. Despite an international ban on the ivory trade, hunting elephants for tusks to sell on the black market remains a lucrative business. Think about the incentives of an ivory hunter with a vulnerable baby elephant in the crosshairs of his gun. He can kill the elephant now, claiming its tiny tusks as his reward. Or he can let it escape, in which case it will grow up, grow much larger tusks, and possibly give birth to more baby elephants. But if he lets it go, the odds are very low that he personally will reap the gains; after all, there are *lots* of other hunters out there. And so, like Reynaldo, our hunter faces a choice: a sure prize now or a small share of a larger prize later. The rational response? Bang!

It might seem like the problem arises from the hunter's lack of certainty: the present gains are guaranteed, while the future gains are risky. But the real problem isn't the risk; it's the *sharing*. Even if Reynaldo were guaranteed a

10 percent share of the young woman and her child's blood, he would still prefer to have 100 percent of a victim now. Likewise for the ivory hunter. The gain from allowing the human or elephant population to grow is not enough to overcome the loss from having to share.

To drive home the point, let's consider a second parable—one that uses game theory to show how multiple parties interact. Suppose that two vampire clans, Matador and Slaughter, feed on the same human population. The two clans have already fed just enough to sustain themselves, and there are one hundred humans left. Each clan must decide whether to eat forty more humans now or wait until next year. We'll call these two options "drain" and "abstain," respectively. After this year's hunting is done, the remaining human population will increase by 50 percent (an unrealistically high rate of reproduction, but it will make the math easier). In the following year, each clan will claim one-half of the humans for themselves.

Here are the relevant calculations:

- If both clans choose to drain, they will each get 40 humans immediately. In addition, the remaining population of 20 will grow to 30, of which each clan will take half, or 15. Each clan therefore gets 55 humans total.
- If both clans choose to abstain, they will both get nothing immediately. Then the population will grow to 150, of which each clan will take half, or 75.
- If one clan drains while the other abstains, then one clan gets 40 humans now and the other zero. The population falls to 60, then grows to 90, of which each clan gets half, or 45. Therefore, the clan that drained gets 85 total, and the clan that abstained gets 45 total.

These results are summarized in figure 15.1. The Matador clan's choices and rewards are in bold; the Slaughter clan's choices and rewards are in italics.

		Slaughter Clan's Choice	
		Drain	*Abstain*
Matador Clan's Choice	**Drain**	**55**, *55*	**85**, *45*
	Abstain	**45**, *85*	**75**, *75*

Figure 15.1.

Suppose the Matador clan's leaders believe that the Slaughter clan plans to drain. Then Matador must choose between fifty-five humans (from draining) and forty-five (from abstaining), as shown in the table. Because fifty-five is better than forty-five, Matador's best response is to drain as well.

But what if the Matador clan's leaders believe the Slaughter clan plans to abstain? In that case, Matador must choose between eighty-five humans (from draining) and seventy-five humans (from abstaining). Because eighty-five is better than seventy-five, Matador's best response is still to drain.

In short, Matador's best option is to drain *no matter what the other clan plans to do*. This is known as having a *dominant strategy*.

And what about the Slaughter clan? Their situation is exactly symmetrical, so the Slaughter clan also has a dominant strategy: drain. We can therefore predict that both clans will drain, and they will get fifty-five humans each.

But couldn't they have done better? If they had both abstained, they would have gotten seventy-five humans each. That would seem to be the rational solution—and yet the incentives work against it. Suppose that the elders of the two clans have a summit meeting. They solemnly promise to abstain this year for everyone's benefit. Then the Matador elders return home and decide whether to keep their promise. If they truly believe the Slaughters will keep their word, then the Matadors are faced with a choice between fifty-five humans from draining and forty-five from abstaining. We've done this math already. The Matadors will drain—and they should expect the Slaughters to do the same.

Obviously, I've made a few assumptions to simplify the story. But it turns out those assumptions don't change anything fundamental. We could have a smaller growth rate of the human population, or more than two clans, or a game that plays out over many years instead of just two, or more choices for how many humans to harvest each year. These alternate assumptions would change the numbers, of course. But for a wide range of assumptions, the same essential result would still occur.

The basic structure of the drain/abstain game is identical to the prisoners' dilemma—probably the most famous game in all of game theory. In that game, two prisoners must choose whether to confess to the authorities or stay quiet. And even though they'd both be better off if they stayed quiet, each one individually has a strong incentive to confess. This outcome depends, of course, on the particular set of punishments set up by the authorities. [1]

The prisoners' dilemma is justly famous because it shows how individually rational behavior can lead to a socially undesirable outcome. The drain/abstain game is another example of the same principle. Even though both vampire clans would be better off if they restrained themselves, their incentives lead them to consume too many humans.

A TRAGEDY FOR BOTH PREDATOR AND PREY

In 1968, ecologist Garrett Hardin coined the term "tragedy of the commons" to describe situations in which shared resources are consumed to the point of destruction.[2] But the phenomenon he described was hardly new.[3] Whenever a renewable resource (that is, a resource with some capacity to replenish itself) is available for use by multiple parties, there is potential for overuse. It doesn't always happen immediately, because the number of users might initially be small relative to the size of the resource—as is currently the case with vampires relative to humans. But as the demand for the resource grows, as Hardin says, "the inherent logic of the commons remorselessly generates tragedy."[4]

Possibly the best-known example to American history students is the near eradication of the American buffalo during the nineteenth century.[5] At one time, only the American Indians wanted buffalo. But as the European population of North America grew, so did the demand for buffalo furs and hides. By the late 1800s, the American buffalo had been hunted almost to extinction.

A modern-day tragedy of the commons is happening right now in the international oceans. For many decades, ocean fishing has been increasing in intensity—and the result has been a dramatic collapse in ocean fish populations. Some popular species have been fished nearly to extinction. According to one study, industrial fishing has reduced the number of large ocean fish to 10 percent of its preindustrial level.[6]

It would be easy to conclude that the problem is simply too much demand; people are just eating too much fish. But that conclusion is defied by other species whose population is not endangered, despite massive demand. Chickens and cows, which are raised and slaughtered for consumption, are in no danger of extinction. In fact, American buffalo are no longer endangered, either—and they, too, are now deliberately raised for commercial purposes. The key question is how vampires can make humans less like fish, and more like chickens and cows.

So what makes the difference? Why do some species' populations grow in response to higher demand, while others collapse? To put it simply, the rules are different. Good and bad incentives arise from the rules of the social game, also known as *institutions*.

Ocean fisheries are usually treated as *common property*. They are typically open to large numbers of fishermen and fishing companies, who try to catch as many fish as they can each season. Nobody has an incentive to conserve the fish, because the gains from doing so will be shared by all the other fishermen—regardless of whether they also choose to conserve. Nobody has an incentive to do things that could improve the fish population, such as spreading fish food in the ocean, for the very same reason: whoever does it will carry the entire cost while getting only a fraction of the benefits.

Cattle, on the other hand, are owned privately. A farmer who feeds his cattle, encourages them to breed, and allows them to procreate before slaughter will reap all the gains from doing so. None of those gains spills over to neighboring farmers, whose own cattle will thrive (or not) based on their own choices.

The same logic applies to the harvesting of humans by vampires. At present, humans are mostly treated as common property, leading to the unfortunate results described in our two parables. But what if the rules were different? Imagine what would happen if the vampire Reynaldo owned his pregnant victim. He would know that, if he waited for her to give birth, he would have two victims instead of one. Suddenly conservation makes sense.

Similarly, imagine what would happen if the Matador and Slaughter clans privatized the human population. Each clan would have a private herd of fifty humans. Each clan could drain forty humans now and fifteen more later, for a total of fifty-five; or they could abstain and have seventy-five humans later. They will naturally choose the latter. Each clan's ownership of its own human herd avoids the sharing problem, thereby giving the clan an incentive to leave more humans alive to procreate.

Simply put, the institution of private property is a solution to the tragedy of the commons. Private property faces a single party—the owner—with both the costs *and* benefits of consumption. As a result, the owner has good reason to maximize the resource's value rather than consuming it to the point of destruction.

Private property isn't the *only* means of solving the tragedy of the commons. Nobel Prize–winning economist Elinor Ostrom has shown that communities often develop their own customary methods of managing shared resources.[7] However, such solutions tend to be most effective with relatively small, homogeneous groups. Moreover, these groups typically have the ability to exclude outsiders. The same *principle of exclusion* lies at the heart of private property.

PRIVATIZATION: A MATTER OF TIME

The proposal to privatize the humans might seem premature. After all, the human population is currently growing and seems to face no danger of extinction. But this pleasant state of affairs won't last forever. The real question is not *whether* to privatize, but *when*.

Economic reasoning provides an answer: privatization should occur when the benefits of having private property exceed the costs of enforcing it. To have private property, we need a means of determining initial ownership, monitoring violations of property rules, and punishing violators. To justify privatization, these costs must be small enough compared to the advantages.

To illustrate, look again at the story of the Matador and Slaughter clans. With humans as communal property, each clan reaps only fifty-five humans each, whereas with humans treated as private property, they would reap seventy-five each. Thus, each clan stands to gain twenty humans from privatization. Is that worth doing? If enforcement of property rights were free, the answer would obviously be yes.

But what if enforcement is costly—in terms of dollars, effort, or blood? For simplicity, let's put everything in dollar terms, and suppose that vampires value humans at $1,000 apiece. The gain from privatization is therefore $20,000 per clan. If it costs $30,000 per clan to establish and enforce private property rights, it's just not worth it. Better to stick with communal property . . . for now.

But what happens when conditions change? As the vampire population increases and humans become relatively more scarce, the value of those twenty humans will begin to rise. If the value of humans reaches $2,000 apiece, the gain from privatization reaches $40,000 per clan—easily enough to justify the $30,000 enforcement price tag. In short, rising demand for a resource can make privatization the better option.

Alternatively, suppose the value of humans remains the same, but new technology makes enforcement cheaper. For instance, computerized record keeping could simplify the process of monitoring ownership, or GPS tracking could make it easier to locate missing humans. If the enforcement cost drops to (say) $15,000 per clan, then privatization suddenly makes sense.

Economist Harold Demsetz argues that changing economic conditions have, in fact, driven historical shifts from communal to private property. He offers the fascinating example of the hunting customs of the Montagne Indians of Quebec.[8] Sometime in the late 1600s to early 1700s, the Montagnes stopped treating their hunting trails and beaver lodges as communal property, and they shifted to *exclusive* hunting territories and *privately owned* beaver lodges—which they marked with family crests and patrolled to protect from poachers. Why the shift? Because a dramatic expansion of the European fur trade had boosted the intensity of hunting and thus the value of pelts. To avoid a tragedy of the commons, privatization suddenly made economic sense.

Terry Anderson and Donald Leal offer an example of how a new technology can lower the cost of privatization: grazing lands in the American West.[9] For much of the 1800s, ranchers grazed their cattle on communal grazing lands. Cattlemen often tried to establish private land rights, but wood was too scarce on the American plains to use for fencing, and the cattle themselves were not disposed to respect invisible boundaries. But that all changed with the introduction of barbed wire in 1870s, which provided a cheap means of fencing off large swaths of land. Privatization quickly ensued.

In thinking about how to privatize the humans, we need to be creative. Privatized humans would not necessarily have to be raised on farms or in factories. Heavy-handed methods like these, when tried in the past, have fomented rebellion in the human population, making them very costly to enforce. Humans, like fish, are what economists call a *fugitive resource*: they are difficult to corral and contain. This is why most fish haven't yet been effectively privatized. [10] But with humans, a smart approach could enable us to privatize them without their knowledge.

If we owned humans as families, for instance, then our claims to humans could "piggyback" on the extensive birth and death records kept by human governments. Innocuous RFID chips, embedded without their knowledge, could permit us to track our humans without restricting their movement. Computerized clearinghouses, similar to those used in financial markets, could ease the exchange of humans migrating between cities. In short, "free-range humans" might be preferable for both the vampire owners and the humans themselves.

HOW TO PRIVATIZE THE HUMANS

Property rights do not appear out of thin air. They must be created and enforced by someone. But whom?

The obvious answer is government. Human governments have usually taken on the duty of enforcing property rules, and there are several good reasons why. At least ideally, governments can provide an independent and neutral arbiter of disputes. If the state has established police forces and courts of law for other purposes, the added cost of having them enforce a new kind of property is relatively low. And perhaps most important, governments have the power to collect taxes to fund the system. If property-rights enforcement were funded by voluntary contributions, then many people might choose to "free ride" on the contributions of others.

But reliable and competent governments do not always exist—and this is a particular problem for vampires, a notoriously individualistic species that often resists the control of any outside authority. Nevertheless, we have sometimes managed to create effective governments—a fact reflected in some of the fiction about our kind. In the *True Blood* HBO television series, based on the books by Charlaine Harris, the Vampire Authority acts as a "shadow government" for vampires around the world, appointing sheriffs, magistrates, and other officials to enforce its edicts. Similarly, the Blade comic universe—which inspired the Blade film series—reveals the existence of the Vampire Nation, a governing body formed by a coalition of vampire clans. And we all know that vampires and humans have occasionally formed secret ruling coalitions, the USSR being the most infamous example. When vampire governments exist, they could take on the job of enforcing property in humans.

If a vampire government exists, one natural question is why it couldn't manage the food supply directly rather than enforcing private property rights. Couldn't the government simply command us all to drain fewer humans? The short answer is that governments just aren't very good at resource management. A government agency would have to track each and every vampire's consumption in order to identify those who drank too much. And without ownership, no vampire would have any incentive to report on other vampires who violated the rules. If you saw another vampire draining a random human, how would you know whether he was within his monthly quota? Private property, on the other hand, gives owners a strong incentive to track and report violations. Government authorities only need to act when a dispute arises.

Furthermore, private property encourages owners to make better choices based on local conditions. Vampires who own especially prolific humans will harvest more often, while vampires who own less prolific humans will find it wise to harvest less often. Vampire owners might also possess better knowledge of which humans are criminals or other unproductive members of society, and thus preferable for harvesting. A central authority is less likely to possess and use this kind of "local knowledge."[11] So it makes sense for governments to facilitate decentralized ownership instead.

But what if no vampire government exists? Although government can ease the establishment of property rights, it is not strictly necessary. Indeed, some customary systems of property rights have arisen not just without government, but in opposition to the government's official rules.[12] In many instances, property rights have been enforced by mutual aid societies—such as miners' organizations and claim associations on the American frontier, whose members pledged to defend each other's property claims in return for help in protecting their own.[13] In southern Italy, the Mafia seems to have emerged as a private enforcer of contracts and property rights in the absence of effective government.[14] The powerful clans, families, and houses of the vampire world could perform a similar function with respect to ownership of humans.

The biggest danger is that vampire clans, while successfully solving their *internal* tragedy of the commons, will fail to respect other clans' claims. But this problem need not be insurmountable. Respect for private property can emerge from the willingness of each clan to use violence in defense of its own claims—along with a realization, on the part of all clans, that provoking a war would do far more damage than it's worth.[15]

Absent a vampire government, private property in humans will most likely emerge first in existing vampire communities that are foresighted enough to see the coming crisis. Clans will establish their own internal rules for limiting consumption of their own human stocks. Meanwhile, they will aggressively defend their humans from predation by renegade vampires and other clans. Some clans will make common cause, forming larger associations for mutual support and protection of each others' claims. Over time, privatization of the humans can be expected to happen spontaneously and "from the bottom up."

But if this process is to happen peacefully, a cultural change may also be required. We must abandon the belief that all humans are simply ours for the taking and set aside our hostility to vampires who claim exclusive rights in specific human communities. While these vampires' claims might initially appear selfish, in fact they may provide the basis for a superior way of managing the blood supply. The survival of our race depends on it.

Chapter Sixteen

Zombies As an Invasive Species

A Resource Economics Perspective

Michael E. O'Hara

Zombies are fundamentally an economic problem. They spread quickly, disrupt economic systems, cause environmental damage, and lead to losses in human welfare. The zombie problem, therefore, requires an economic solution. In many ways, zombies are not unlike other invasive species that natural-resource economists have studied, such as kudzu in the American South, zebra mussels in the rivers and lakes of North America and Europe, or Asian carp currently spreading through the Mississippi and into the Great Lakes. Zombies can be treated as an invasive species and dealt with using the policy tools developed by resource economists.

The fact that zombies fit standard definitions of invasive species cannot be disputed. The Global Invasive Species Program (GISP) states that "biological invasion occurs when a species enters a new environment, establishes itself there and begins to change the populations of species that existed there before, as well as disturbing the balance of plant and animal communities."[1] In the case of a zombie invasion, this change of the existing population of species is quite literal. The invading species, the zombies, propagate by changing the resident human (and, in some cases, other animal) species into zombies.

Not all alien species become invasive. The Convention on Biological Diversity defines an invasive alien species as an "alien species whose introduction and spread threatens ecosystems, habitats or species with socio-cultural, economic and/or environmental harm, and/or harm to human health."[2] The GISP lists a set of characteristics that determines the propensity of a species to become invasive. These include:

- A capacity for rapid growth (and so expansion);
- A capacity to disperse widely;
- Large reproductive capacity—either by producing many offspring or by nurturing fewer progeny but with great efficiency;
- Broad environmental tolerance—being able to withstand a wide range of habitat pressures;
- Effective competition with local species—for food, space, light, water, resting, and nesting requirements.[3]

The zombie population certainly possesses all of these characteristics. Indeed, zombies might be considered the perfect invasive species. For comparison, a popular rule of thumb on invasive alien species says that about one in ten alien species introduced will become established in the new environment, and one in ten of those will become invasive, implying a 1 percent chance of an introduced species becoming invasive.[4] More recent research suggests that for vertebrate animals introduced into favorable habitats, the probability is closer to 25 percent.[5] But these numbers do not apply to the undead. For zombies, the number is essentially 100 percent. Introduced to a new environment, a zombie will always "survive," since it is not alive when introduced. The fact that it is already dead gives it almost complete environmental tolerance. It does not require food, shelter, water, or any of the other basic needs of other species. Once established, zombies have the capacity to spread over a large area in a very short time. The more modern, "fast" zombies, such as those depicted in *Zombieland* or *World War Z*, can often move much more quickly than normal living humans, but even the traditional slow-moving zombies seen in the Romero films never suffer from fatigue and can disperse widely in a surprisingly short time.

Zombies reproduce themselves by killing and turning human beings, which a single zombie can do theoretically without limit. There is no minimum sustainable breeding population as there is for other species. Only one zombie is needed to sustain a population—sometimes not even that, as long as the original cause of the corpse reanimation remains. Although zombies do not need to eat to survive, they do have a great hunger and compete for food with other species. In effect, zombies eat and reproduce in the same act, since feeding on a victim generally transforms that victim into another zombie.

The closest, though certainly not perfect, known parallel to the zombie invasion can be found in the spread of feral hogs in an increasing number of states in the United States. Like zombies, wild hogs start out as a domesticated and economically productive species. But once exposed to the wild, hogs quickly transform into a different version of themselves, becoming very aggressive and even changing their physical characteristics. They are extremely destructive of the habitats of other species, multiply very quickly, and are effective carriers of disease. Unlike zombies, they are not undead, and their bite cannot change another creature into a wild hog, but they offer the closest comparison available to us for analyzing the effects of policy intervention. Studying efforts to control the costs of feral hogs can inform our economic analysis of zombies.

THE ECONOMIC APPROACH TO INVASIVE SPECIES

The basis of the economic approach to invasive species is comparing the cost of damage caused by an invasion of a given species to the cost of measures taken to avoid that damage. This would be easy enough if these costs were known for certain, but generally this is not the case. A common way economists make such comparisons under uncertainty is the concept of *expected value*, which is defined as the probability of a given event occurring multiplied by the value (either cost or benefit) of the event, should it occur. Using this method of analysis, the expected value of the damage caused by a zombie invasion (EVZ) is the probability of invasion times the damage caused by an invasion if it occurs, or

$$EVZ = p(invasion) \times D(invasion)$$

For example, if the probability of a zombie invasion is 1 percent (or 0.01) and the damage caused by it would be $1 billion, then the expected value of the damage is $(0.01) \times (1,000,000,000) = \$10$ million.

An economic policy can reduce the expected damage of a zombie invasion either by reducing the probability of invasion (p) or by reducing the cost of the damage should it occur (D). Policy options can broadly be classified into three categories: prevention, control, and adaptation.

Prevention

If a measure could be taken to prevent this expected damage entirely, the expected value of the damage avoided ($p \times D$) becomes the benefit of the prevention measure. Subtracting from this the cost (c) of the proposed prevention measure gives us the expected net benefit (ENB) of undertaking that measure.

$$ENB(prevention) = p(invasion) \times D(invasion) - c(prevention)$$

If the costs of the prevention measures are higher than the expected value of the damages they prevent, then the expected net benefit is negative, which means we are better off living with the risk of damage caused by the invasion than undertaking the prevention measures. In the example above, if the cost of the prevention measure were greater than $10 million, then we would be better off taking our chances.

To decide whether prevention measures are worthwhile, we need to understand the different pathways by which the invasive species might enter the new environment. We also need to consider the likelihood of the species entering through any given pathway and the costs of closing the pathway. The source of the feral hog problem is easy to trace back to the escape of animals from containment on hunting preserves or, on occasion, farms. Feral hogs, like zombies, do not respect property lines. In the case of zombies, however, there are many possible pathways for invasion.

In most cases, the zombie invasion begins with a virus (e.g., *Resident Evil, Zombieland, The Zombie Autopsies, World War Z*). In some cases, where corporations such as Umbrella are performing research that carries an inherent risk of zombie contamination, a possible policy approach could be the issuance of assurance bonds of the type that has been investigated in other environmental contexts.[6] In principle, a corporation or government agency undertaking research with zombie risk could be required to purchase a bond in an amount designed to cover the costs of remediation should a zombie virus contamination occur. The money would be kept in an interest-bearing account and would be refundable, in whole or in part, if the company could demonstrate that their activity had not caused and would not cause a zombie outbreak, or if they could show that the potential costs had been miscalculated. Since this puts the external cost of a zombie invasion back on the company conducting the risky activity, it provides an incentive for them to take every safety precaution to avoid an outbreak and covers the cost should it occur. Although the costs of a zombie outbreak are largely un-known, since the burden of proof is on the corporation or agency to prove that they should be refunded, they would have an incentive to conduct very careful research into the risks and potential costs of their activities.[7]

While a "zombie bond" may have attractive features as a policy tool, it is unlikely to be an effective tool for prevention of a zombie outbreak. Most corporations or government agencies that undertake research on zombie risk do so in secret, and their activities only come to light once the outbreak has begun. This means that enforcement of a mandatory zombie bond policy would at best be a very costly venture and most likely would be entirely infeasible. However, these bonds can serve a different purpose, as will be discussed later.

Even if the risk of a zombie virus from corporate research could be minimized, this is by no means the only potential pathway for invasion. In other cases, it may be toxic waste (*Return of the Living Dead*) or the inges-tion of an unintentional chemical mixture confused with a recreational drug (*Zombies! Zombies! Zombies! Strippers vs. Zombies*)[8] that sparks the out-break. The source may even come from outer space, either unintentionally

(*Night of the Living Dead*) or intentionally (*Plan 9 from Outer Space*). In some cases, the source of the issue may be completely beyond comprehension (the entire *Trancers* saga). There are almost certainly many other possible channels yet unknown.

Although a zombie invasion through some channel is, at this point, a near certainty, each of these possible individual pathways is certainly a low-probability event, with probability likely far less than the 1 percent example used earlier, and steps taken to prevent invasion through any given channel are very likely to be both costly and unnecessary. This means that, while certain risk-reduction steps might be economically beneficial, prevention of the zombie apocalypse is likely to be cost prohibitive.

Control

Once an invasion has been established, policy makers face a set of options involving combinations of control and adaptation measures, ranging from complete eradication of the invasive species to pure adaptation with no control measures.

With many invasive species, complete eradication is extremely difficult once the species has established itself. This is currently debated regarding feral hogs, with some states, such as New York, still hopeful that eradication is possible, and others, such as Texas, accepting this as an infeasible option. This may be true of zombies for the same reasons discussed earlier regarding prevention measures. Eradication would require eliminating every single zombie as well as closing off the source of the invasion. This is the strategy adopted in *World War Z* (the book version). The feasibility of such an effort depends on how far the invasion has spread at the point when it is discovered.

Adaptation

Even if total eradication were possible, it is not necessarily clear that it would be desirable. Part of the difficulty of addressing the feral hog issue is that some people, such as farmers, consider the species to be a pest, while others, most notably hunters, see them as a benefit.[9] A central component of New York's feral hog eradication plan is a policy of "killing, but not hunting" the species. This means that if a feral hog is seen on one's property, it should be killed on sight, but organized hunting efforts should not be directed at the species. The motivation behind this policy is that when hunting efforts are concentrated on feral hog populations, this tends to drive the animals into other areas seeking refuge and so spreads the invasion more quickly than it might have spread without the hunting pressure. But some states have actively recruited hunters to assist in the control of feral hogs by encouraging hunting at any time, without need of a permit, and the state of Texas has even gone as far as to allow hunting from a helicopter.[10] This moves policy into the area of adaptation, since the benefits the hogs provide as a recreational hunting species as well as a tasty food source partially offset the costs they impose in ecosystem damage.

While zombies will never be much desired as table fare, they could provide economic benefits as a recreational hunting species. There is no danger of this spreading the invasion, since, by their nature, zombies are drawn toward hunters rather than away. Thus, hunting pressure will tend to concentrate them in an area and keep them from spreading. The demand for the thrill of zombie hunting is well documented by the popularity of games such as *Resident Evil* and *Left 4 Dead*. The same characteristics that make zombies an invasive species par excellence also make them a unique sport-hunting species. They require none of the basic needs of most species. They do not need to be fed or provided with shelter, making them very low cost to keep in a maintained hunting-preserve environment. They can withstand a wide variety of environmental conditions, allowing hunting to be conducted in any season or weather. In fact, their popularity as a sport species might in itself lead to their extinction.

But we also have the option of maintaining zombie hunting as a sustainable recreational sport. Zombies have the unique attribute of not dying, so unlike any other hunting species, they could be reused in multiple hunts. This is, of course, subject to the caveat that damage to the brain will deactivate a zombie permanently. But this could be avoided in a sport context by sheltering the head of the zombie with a helmet in order to slow the loss of stock. Perhaps higher-paying clients could purchase a head-shot permit, allowing the true "kill," while bargain permits would allow shooting at the zombies without a terminal blow. This would allow the sport to be available to a wider range of social classes in the population, so that zombie hunting might be enjoyed by all.

A complicating factor of a zombie invasion is that they are us. With feral hogs, for example, allowing the species to breed in captivity and maintain a stable population can be achieved without loss of human life. In the case of zombies, if we speak of maintaining some population for commercial purposes, we are implicitly allowing some harvest of humans for replenishing the population of zombies. In the wild, zombies will propagate themselves, but it is difficult to imagine that even the most ardent environmentalist would defend free-range zombies as an option. Zombies must be prevented from escape just like hogs. Here is where the "zombie bond" discussed earlier might be a useful tool, even if it would not prevent the original outbreak. A hunting preserve that desired to keep a zombie population could be required to post a zombie bond in order to provide an incentive for them to prevent escape, as well as to cover the costs should an escape occur. This would be easier than monitoring corporations at the prevention stage, since at this point there would be actual zombies present, which would be difficult to hide for any length of time.

But if the zombies are contained in sport preserves, how would we replenish the species in order to provide a sustainable harvest? One possibility might be provided by differences in risk preference among hunters. While most would avoid the risk of becoming zombies themselves, some hunters might actually enjoy the thrill of the risk and be willing to pay extra (and sign the appropriate waivers) to hunt in conditions where they are at risk of exposure, much in the same way that big-game hunters might pay top dollar for an African safari. Possibly this could be a way of allocating terminal head-shot permits: only those hunters who risk conversion into zombies would earn the right to permanently kill zombies. Some of these hunters would be exposed and so provide some turnover to the stock, though how quickly this would replenish the population depends on how many risk lovers there are among the zombie-hunting population.

Another possibility is to provide economic incentives for people to donate themselves to the cause after their death, as some people now donate organs. Benefits could be provided to those who sign donor cards for their corpses to be used for zombie hunting after they pass on. One can easily imagine a certain group that might enjoy the thought that they will live on in some sense after their deaths, especially as monsters. Immortality is, after all, achieved in many different ways.

ZOMBIES AS AN ECONOMICALLY VALUABLE SPECIES

A zombie invasion at some point seems inevitable, and while some specific preventive measures are likely worth taking, prevention of the invasion itself is very likely to be economically unjustified. A more balanced approach seems prudent, involving a combination of control and adaptation. Containment could be achieved within licensed hunting preserves that are required to post zombie bonds in order to provide them with incentives to prevent escape and to cover the costs of remediation measures in the case that escape does happen. In this way, zombies can provide an economic benefit as a hunting species that will to some extent offset the costs they entail and perhaps even turn the zombie apocalypse into an economic benefit.

Of course, once we accept the idea that zombies can be an economically valuable species, we cannot avoid the question of whether certain members of society might be more valuable as zombies than as living humans. It is not the intention of this author to make such value judgments, and, in any case, such questions fall outside the scope of this chapter. For now, it must suffice to trust that the free market is a remarkably efficient means of allocating resources to their highest-valued uses and leave it at that.

Chapter Seventeen

Post-Apocalyptic Law

What Would the Reasonable Man Do in a World Gone Mad?

Brian Hollar

In the world of *The Walking Dead*, nearly all social order has collapsed as most of the world finds itself overrun by zombies. Of course, the zombies pose a serious threat to the survivors—but as the show demonstrates, an even greater threat is often posed by the other survivors. Nobody expects the living dead to follow rules of good behavior, but desperate and opportunistic humans may also break the rules, to the great detriment of their fellow humans. With no existing government or law enforcement, survivors find themselves left in a world where people frequently kill, rob, kidnap, and harm other survivors. This lawless scenario brings up questions of how the law might evolve, if law would still exist, and how the law might be administered in a zombie apocalypse. This chapter attempts to use some basic economics to answer each of these questions.

FINDING LAW IN A LAWLESS WORLD

Economics contributes to our understanding of the law by suggesting that many doctrines of common law have an underlying economic logic. Common law is law made by the accumulation of judicial decisions over time that serve as precedents (case law) for future legal cases, rather than through statutes passed by the legislature.[1] Traditional legal theories developed with a focus on concepts of justice, retribution, and rights. In contrast, economic analysis of the law differentiates itself by focusing on cost-benefit analysis of various legal rules. Economists theorize that legal rules that generate more social benefits than social costs tend to persist over time, while legal rules with costs that outweigh benefits eventually get challenged in courts, overturned by judges, and replaced by more efficient rules. Economic analysis of the law also assumes that individuals behave rationally toward incentives created by the law, weighing costs and benefits of their behavior against the penalties and rewards incentivized by legal rules. Any changes in the law typically change the strength of these incentives, leading to predictable changes in behavior of some individuals within society. As these incentives get stronger or weaker, they cause more or fewer people respectively to engage in the associated behavior. Using this framework of economic analysis, we will explore what changes in laws and legal incentives might occur in a zombie-filled world.

One of the biggest challenges facing post-apocalyptic survivors will be the difficulty of enforcing laws. With no local or central government and decaying social order, courts and law-enforcement agencies will no longer exist. Until survivors develop some type of functioning judiciary and police force, law enforcement will be an incredibly challenging issue to resolve. But legal rules will inevitably get enforced in other ways—whether through self-defense, personal ethics, or ad hoc "frontier-style" justice. And once communities start to form (such as the town of Woodbury in *The Walking Dead*), formal courts and police forces will likely develop as well. For the remainder of this chapter, I will assume some type of enforcement mechanism exists and use economics to focus on what legal rules "should be."

TORT LAW: DOING WRONG WHEN NOTHING IS RIGHT

A troubling scene occurs in a third-season episode of *The Walking Dead*, when the group comes upon a small cabin as they are fleeing from zombies and takes refuge within.[2] To their surprise, there is a lone hermit inside who appears to be insane. After being disarmed, the hermit begins to make a lot of noise, attracting a large group of zombies to the cabin. The hermit continues to act irrationally and lunges toward the door to let the zombies in. One of the characters kills the hermit by stabbing him through the heart with her samurai sword just before he gets to the door. The group then throws the hermit's body outside to distract the zombies as they make their escape safely through the cabin's back door.

Does the group have the legal right to barge into the hermit's cabin while being chased by zombies? Does the hermit have the right to defend himself? Does the hermit have the right to force them to leave his cabin with hungry zombies outside? Does the group have the right to disarm the hermit? Does the group cause a wrongful death when they kill the hermit?

The answers to many of these questions can be found in the law of torts. Tort law is the branch of civil law that deals with wrongful acts. It sets rules for what duty of care an individual owes to strangers and what liability is incurred when these duties are violated. Tort law includes rules of negligence, intentional harm, product liability, defamation, trespass, and privacy.

One of the most frequently encountered concepts in tort law is the "reasonable person" (or, historically, the "reasonable man") standard. In a variety of circumstances, legal rules require that judges or juries consider how a reasonable person would have acted in a similar situation in order to determine if the defendant's actions were appropriate under the law. For example, if a defendant claims to have killed someone in self-defense, the jury must decide if a reasonable person would have feared for his or her life in this situation. If they find the defendant acted the way a reasonable person would have behaved, then the defendant is not liable for damages. Economist and legal scholar Richard Posner famously argued that the reasonable person standard involves an implicit cost-benefit analysis, weighing the costs of taking care against the likelihood of harm and magnitude of damage. This is perhaps best summarized by Judge Learned Hand in a simple equation, $B < P \times L$, where B is the burden of taking care, P is the probability of harm if the harm occurs, and L is the magnitude of harm if the harm occurs.[3] This relationship has come to be known as the Hand formula and is used to perform a cost-benefit analysis in determining when it is cost-effective for individuals to take care in their actions. The basic principle for this analysis is that you owe a duty of care when your cost of taking care (B) is less than the expected costs ($P \times L$) to others of your not taking care. If the costs of your taking care are greater than the likely costs to others, you do not owe a duty of care to another individual.

While the reasonable person standard is not precise, its lack of specificity is one of its most attractive characteristics. By being flexible in its application, it allows the standard to persist over time, even as the world around this standard changes. Since juries are made up of people from the surrounding society, their perspectives on how a reasonable person would calculate the costs and benefits of his actions change as their culture, technology, prosperity, security, and physical circumstances change.

By continuing to use the reasonable person standard, most existing tort law would continue to be applicable in the zombie-infested world. What would change is the cost-benefit analysis of how a reasonable person would behave. In a world full of zombies, alternatives of action are often limited due to a scarcity of resources and a lack of time as a horde of hungry zombies is about to bear down on you. Since few survivors remain and interaction between humans is limited, the likelihood of most actions harming another living person is also greatly reduced.

For example, it is not reasonable for someone in my home city of Arlington, Virginia, to simply break into a store late at night because she is feeling hungry. A reasonable person would instead wait until morning for the store to open to buy the food. However, it would be reasonable for a hunter lost in the woods to break into a cabin to get food to stay alive. A reasonable person would prioritize keeping himself fed in order to survive over protecting a window if he were uncertain when (or if) his next meal might come. In this case, the lost hunter would be liable for any damage he caused to the cabin but would not be liable for trespass. American law generally gives precedence to life over property, so someone in an emergency situation has the legal right to use the property of another to protect his own life but has a legal obligation to compensate the owner for any damage done to the property.

This principle is known as the necessity doctrine,[4] and it preserves social value in two ways: first, it allows people to protect themselves and their property in emergency situations by allowing them to temporarily use the property of others; and second, it incentivizes those in an emergency situation to consider the expected damage they would cause to the property of others, not just the benefit to themselves. This rule maximizes social value by incentivizing people to only take advantage of this rule when they expect the benefits of protecting themselves outweigh the harm to another's property.

A zombie-infested world represents a situation similar to that of a starving hunter lost in the woods. If a reasonable person is on the run from a horde of zombies, she will almost certainly break into a store for provisions rather than allow herself to slowly starve to death while avoiding the undead. Like a hunter lost in the woods, an individual in a zombie apocalypse has no idea if or when another opportunity for food might come along. She has no guarantee of food being available the next day and so would break in and take what is needed to sustain her life. In addition, it would be entirely reasonable to assume that the store and everything inside had been abandoned during the zombie outbreak and are no longer owned by anyone. (Making it legally available to the first person to find it under today's property law—more on this in the property law section later.)

This expectation that most property is abandoned comes into play with the group invading the hermit's cabin. Taking refuge within the cabin preserves their lives, and they anticipate little harm to the property of others since they believe the cabin to be unoccupied. And even if they expect the cabin to be occupied, the benefit of preserving their lives far outweighs the cost of their trespass, which makes taking refuge inside justified under the necessity doctrine. (This same analysis also concludes the hermit couldn't legally force the group off his property while the zombies remain outside his door.)

The calculus of laws relating to self-defense would also change after the apocalypse. If 99 percent of the population has turned into zombies, it is reasonable to assume anyone silently walking toward you is out to eat your brains. The onus of care would thus shift to the person approaching you to demonstrate he is not a zombie. In this case, he has the lowest cost of avoiding harm, since he knows you will likely assume he is a threat. A similar onus would be on the group as they barged into the hermit's cabin. Since strangers are often dangerous, it is rational for the hermit to assume anyone he encounters is a potential threat to his life. This cost-benefit analysis justifies the hermit's legal right to defend himself with his gun while he ascertains the motives of the group after they have barged in, armed and in a state of panic. It also justifies the group disarming the hermit, but not killing him when they could have tried to restrain him instead.

PROPERTY: POSSESSION IS NINE-TENTHS OF THE LAW

So now that we've taken a look at torts, let's turn our attention to how property law might work in this post-apocalyptic world. An example of a property rights issue in *The Walking Dead* occurs when the group discovers a farm and moves there after a member of the group receives medical treatment from the farm's owner after getting shot. While willing to help the victim, the farmer mistrusts the group and does not want them to stay any longer than necessary. Despite objections from some members, the group's leader respects the farmer's right to decide whether to allow the group to stay on his property or not, being willing to leave if the farmer asks.

The most efficient outcome would be if the group were able to compensate the farmer in some way, by giving him something he values more than the cost he bears from the group staying on his farm. (The cost to the group would also have to be lower than their benefit from staying on the farm.) In order for this type of trade to occur, people must have the ability to acquire property and transfer ownership. Property rights exist to allow people clarity of ownership and control over the use and transfer of valuable assets. Two limitations to efficient outcomes in a zombie world are the lack of clarity of ownership (no system for recording deeds)[5] and the lack of a monetary system to facilitate the buying and selling of property. With no official record of ownership, a less scrupulous group may have little respect for the farmer's claim to his property. Maybe he forcibly ousted the previous inhabitant of the property! And without money, compensating the farmer to stay on his land becomes difficult, but not impossible. It could take the form of helping maintain the farm, taking care of livestock, clearing out zombies, strengthening the farm's defenses—each of which the group does while on the farm. However, doing these chores might not be enough to compensate the farmer for the inconvenience and danger of the group staying on the farm. The farmer has to weigh the value of their work against the costs of the group consuming his resources, occupying his land, and increasing the risk of violence on his land. But even without money, it's better to respect ownership and require that only voluntary transactions occur, because that's at least more efficient than the loss of life and property that would result from endless conflict.

Another example of an implicit property right seen in *The Walking Dead* occurs when a second band of survivors comes to a prison already secured by the main characters in the show. They acknowledge that the main characters were the first to find and clear out the prison. They ask for permission to stay, but recognize ownership of the property by those who found it first. The second band of survivors does not risk conflict over the right to stay in the prison after one of the main characters (while hallucinating that he sees his dead wife) yells at them to leave. The second band reluctantly complies and leaves the prison.

This prison example represents another principle of property law that would likely continue to function after the zombie apocalypse—the right of first possession. Under common law, the first person to acquire sovereignty over abandoned or unowned property becomes the new owner. This is an efficient outcome because it incentivizes individuals to seek, acquire, make use of, and improve the value of assets that would otherwise remain unproductive. As noted above, after the zombie outbreak most property is now abandoned. Under existing laws, survivors who take possession of unowned property would legally have full rights to it, a rule that survivors in the show seem to implicitly follow. This right of first possession is yet another example of how the common law produces efficient legal rules that would still apply after the zombie apocalypse.

CONTRACTS: A WORLD OF BROKEN PROMISES

Next, let's take a look at contract law. Imagine you have survived the apocalypse, and another survivor promises in writing to give you fifty gallons of gasoline and an axe in exchange for you killing five zombies on his property. What happens if you spend a lot of time and effort killing the five zombies, only to meet afterward and discover the man you made the agreement with was only able to obtain twenty gallons of gas and a hammer—significantly less than you bargained for? You consumed fifteen gallons of gasoline killing the zombies in anticipation of getting the promised fifty gallons of gas. You are angry and demand what was promised you. But the other survivor is incapable of delivering what was promised. How should this dispute be resolved?

Welcome to the complexities of contract law. Like other areas of law, the main principles of contracts would probably remain in effect in the zombie apocalypse. Two of the foundational issues that contract law tries to answer are (1) what types of promises should be enforced and (2) what should the remedy be for a broken contract?[6] Economic theories of contract law show that any promise that is expected to make one or both parties better off without making the other worse off (what economists refer to as a Pareto improvement) at the time the promise is made should be enforced, assuming the contract does not significantly harm any third parties (such as an assassination contract might).[7]

Economic analysis also suggests that the remedy for a broken contract should be to restore a person who was relying on that promise to the position she expected to have been in had that promise been completed. If the promise can no longer be fulfilled for some reason, then the person breaking the promise should be liable for financial damages that will restore the person to the equivalent financial position she would have been in had that promise been fulfilled. These financial payments are known as *expectation damages*. The basic idea behind expectation damages is that monetary compensation can substitute for other things of value.

Consider the example above. The man whose land you cleared of five zombies owes you thirty gallons of gas or the monetary equivalent thereof. (Plus the difference in value between a hammer and an axe.) However, the amount of these expectation damages will be incredibly difficult to administer in the post-apocalyptic world due to the absence of money (and functioning markets to indicate the value of things).

With no form of currency that is generally acceptable as money, imagine how difficult it would be to adequately compensate the wronged party in a broken-contract dispute. How many chickens would it take to make up for the failure to deliver five guns? Or how much food would make up for failure to deliver gasoline? Without functioning markets to determine the value of these goods and the universal measuring rod that money provides, determining appropriate compensatory damages would be incredibly difficult, if not impossible.

The absence of money may bias post-apocalyptic law in the direction of forcing promisors (people who make promises) to fulfill their exact promises given whenever possible—a legal concept known as *specific performance*. While this may sound like a good solution, there are often times when fulfilling a promise can actually cost the promisor more than the benefit it provides to the recipient. For example, the amount of effort that the man would have to exert to acquire thirty more gallons of gas might be far greater than he expected—and the value of that effort might be much greater than the value of the gas itself. It might make more sense to spend that effort on something else, like raising chickens. But without money, it's hard to say for sure. For that reason, specific performance may become the default legal remedy for broken contracts, leading contract law to more closely resemble property law.[8]

Given these difficulties, it is likely that survivors will eventually come up with "shadow prices" for various goods, keeping track of how much of one good typically trades for another. These records of shadow prices would help facilitate an imperfect proxy for assigning expectation damages in contract disputes and might help accelerate the emergence of some form of commodity that gets used as a form of money. The shadow prices might also specify amounts of labor, so that the man might owe you a certain amount of his time—kind of like an indentured servant.

A system of shadow prices like this would probably be the best solution to the problem of the failed delivery at the beginning of this section. The man who did not follow through on his promise would have to provide you with something of approximately equal value to you (in either usage value or trade value) to adequately compensate you for his failure to fulfill his promise (expectation damages). Without a set of shadow prices, the promisor would likely have to do what it takes to fulfill his original promise (specific performance), even if that takes extraordinary efforts on his part. However, the two of you would be free to negotiate alternative terms of settlement to avoid this situation.

CRIMINAL LAW: PUNISHMENT, POST-APOCALYPTIC STYLE

In an episode of *The Walking Dead*, Shane (one of the main characters) shoots another man in the leg while they are being chased by zombies to buy himself time to get away while the zombies make a feast of the other man.[9] When Shane rejoins the main group, he lies and tells them the other man died valiantly. Eventually, Rick (one of the other characters) begins to realize the truth. If Rick could prove his suspicions to the rest of the group, how should they respond? What sort of punishment should be meted out on a man who murders another man in this type of environment?

Economic analysis of criminal law assumes that criminals weigh the benefits and costs of committing a crime when making choices about their actions. According to this theory, policy makers can reduce the incidence of crime by increasing their expected costs to criminals. (Policy makers in the post-apocalyptic world would include leaders of the various communities, such as Rick and the Governor on the show.) The cost a criminal faces for committing a crime includes actual costs involved (equipment needed, time, etc.) as well as how much he values the expected punishment of the crime. For example, a criminal in the real world who makes $20,000 per year at his day job might consider a three-year prison term equivalent to a $60,000 fine ($60,000 = 3 years × $20,000/year). However, if the criminal expects only a

50 percent chance of getting caught, he would evaluate his *expected punishment* as 50 percent of $60,000, or $30,000. If he expected to make more than $30,000 committing this crime, a rational individual with no moral compunction against committing a crime would be expected to do so. If there is uncertainty of getting convicted if caught, this would reduce his expected punishment even further.

This leaves a policy maker with three policy strings to play on to deter crime: probability of detection, probability of conviction, and severity of punishment. If any of these three becomes more costly to implement, economic theory predicts policy makers will shift toward adjusting the other two. For example, if a crime is very difficult to detect, it gives policy makers an incentive to severely punish offenders in order to deter others from committing this crime. Difficulty of detection could also incentivize policy makers to make it easier to convict potential offenders—that is, to lower the burden of proof.

The first string policy makers have to play on is the probability of detection. As previously mentioned, if civil society breaks down as portrayed in *The Walking Dead*, there will be few resources left to devote to law enforcement. This may make the probability of catching someone committing a crime significantly lower than if more resources could be devoted to this task. To the extent that crimes become harder to detect, we should expect people to respond by increasing both the probability of conviction and the severity of punishment. However, it is possible that if there are only a few individuals in a given community, it may be easier to determine who committed a crime than in a larger population with greater anonymity.

The second string policy makers have to play on is the probability of conviction. Since no system of justice is perfect, they would have to evaluate the social benefits of making it easy to convict guilty parties against the social costs of possibly wrongfully convicting an innocent person. Every system of justice implicitly balances the cost of wrongful convictions against the cost of letting the guilty go free. Because social order is so tenuous and the risk of having a criminal in the midst of a small group may leave no one safe, the survivors may come up with rules that make conviction relatively easy compared to the civil rights protections criminals enjoy today. But this is a delicate balance. If community members feel the system of justice is unfair, it may exacerbate social instability.

The third string policy makers have to play on is severity of punishment. If criminal justice becomes costly to administer, policy makers may respond by making punishments for crime incredibly severe. For example, society in the zombie world would be so constrained for resources (both human and physical) that using them to maintain a prison would probably be cost-prohibitive. (Long-term incarceration is a fairly modern idea.) As a result, punishments may change for various crimes. The death penalty may become more common, as well as societal exile.[10] Branding or maiming criminals who have committed grievous offenses may also become commonplace—a cheap way to warn others of a criminal's past in an environment where information transfer is prohibitively costly. Torture, one of the cheapest forms of punishment, may also gain widespread use as a deterrent for criminal behavior. In many ways, punishment in a post-apocalyptic environment would be like a return to the past.

Criminal law in the zombie world would likely remain intact as it is today in terms of how crimes are defined. Murder would still be murder. The legal definitions of theft and kidnapping would not change. However, criminal procedure (the rules for how crimes are prosecuted and punished) would change significantly due to changes in the post-apocalyptic costs of administration and punishment.

COMMON LAW, UNCOMMON CIRCUMSTANCES

Put into mathematical terms, the equations of the law would not need to change in a zombie-infested world—only the variables that go into the legal equations. The definition of reasonability remains the same, but its implications evolve as risks (costs) and rewards (benefits) change relative to the pre-apocalyptic world. Actions that would be unacceptable in contemporary America become quite reasonable for individuals faced with a constant threat of hostiles living and dead. Criminal law would remain the same, but criminal punishment would likely become more severe. The genius of a common-law system, like that of the United States, is its ability to apply general legal principles broadly and to adapt and evolve as circumstances change. Many of the current legal principles that have emerged through a common-law process would continue to function quite well in a zombie-filled world. The biggest challenge for survivors would not be forming new laws, but forming bonds tight enough among various bands of survivors to establish a judiciary, a system of law enforcement, and a monetary system. In a world gone mad, the reasonable man would continue to rely on the wisdom contained in the law of the past, adjusting the application but not the principles of modern common law.

Chapter Eighteen

Brain-Dead vs. Undead

Public Ignorance and the Political Economy of Responses to Vampires and Zombies

Ilya Somin

> Governments of any type are nothing more than a collection of human be-
> ings. . . . Why would they be willing to recognize and deal with an attack of
> walking, bloodthirsty corpses, when most of humanity isn't?
>
> —Max Brooks, *The Zombie Survival Guide*

In season 1 of *Buffy the Vampire Slayer*, a massive vampire uprising nearly takes over the town of Sunnydale. Buffy's friend Xander Harris is shocked that the public completely ignores the threat and does not even bother to have "an assembly."[1] Such ignorance in the face of the undead menace is all too typical. For over a century, books and films featuring the undead have shown that the public will remain ignorant about the dangers posed by vampires and zombies until it is too late. Even when voters finally do see the danger, ignorance and irrationality often lead them to support misguided policies that make the situation worse. Sometimes, the state even takes advantage of public ignorance to use the undead for its own nefarious purposes. The political ignorance portrayed in so many tales of the undead is an exaggerated but plausible extrapolation from widespread voter ignorance and irrationality in the real world.

The undead have recently been the focus of extensive scholarship.[2] Vampires and zombies have been used to analyze theories of international relations,[3] constitutional interpretation,[4] macroeconomic policy,[5] and even the rights of vampires under the Americans with Disabilities Act.[6] But the growing academic literature on the undead has neglected public ignorance and its impact on our ability to combat these terrifying threats to civilization.

181

Often, the seemingly brain-dead public is so ignorant that it is difficult to see why humanity was not completely exterminated by the undead long ago. Yet there are some possible reasons for hope. Private-sector initiatives and "information shortcuts" can sometimes mitigate the dangers caused by political ignorance. These rays of light have saved us from joining the living dead in eternal darkness. But, at least judging by movies and novels, the resulting carnage from vampire and zombie attacks has been much worse than it should have been.

WHY THE PUBLIC OFTEN SEEMS BRAIN-DEAD: THE LOGIC OF POLITICAL IGNORANCE AND IRRATIONALITY

Democracy works best with an attentive public that is knowledgeable about the issues and objectively evaluates political information. Unfortunately, most voters have little more incentive to become informed than zombies do. That's because their chances of actually affecting electoral results aren't much better than those of the average zombie.

In a presidential election, the average American voter has about a one in sixty million chance of affecting the outcome.[7] The probability is still extremely low in congressional, state, and local elections. If your only reason to acquire political knowledge is to be a better-informed voter and make sure that the government is prepared for the next zombie outbreak, that turns out not to be much of a reason at all. Even if a voter becomes extremely well informed, the likelihood that his knowledge will affect the outcome of an election remains negligible; he still has the same vanishingly low odds of casting a decisive vote as before. Thus, there is almost no payoff to acquiring political knowledge in order to be a better voter. The rational thing to do is to remain ignorant about politics and focus on decisions where your efforts can actually make a difference. When it comes to politics, most people have strong incentives to be "rationally ignorant."[8]

And that's exactly what most voters are. For decades, survey data has consistently shown that most of the public have very low levels of political knowledge.[9] A 2006 Zogby poll showed that only 42 percent of the American public can name the three branches of the federal government: legislative, executive, and judicial.[10] Even after years of controversy over the fiscal crisis, most voters do not realize that entitlement programs such as Medicare and Social Security are among the biggest expenditure items in the federal budget, even as they massively overestimate the tiny fraction of federal spending devoted to foreign aid and public broadcasting.[11] The average living citizen is better informed about politics than the average zombie but not by as much as you might think.

In addition to being ignorant, voters also often do a poor job of evaluating the information they do know. Careful, unbiased reasoning is hard work, and the electoral process gives us little reason to make the effort. Indeed, most who do take the trouble to acquire more than minimal political knowledge usually do so for reasons other than seeking out the truth about political issues. Just as sports fans follow sports because they enjoy cheering on their favorite teams even if they can't influence the outcome of games, so "political fans" enjoy following politics in order to cheer on their favorite party, candidate, or ideology.[12]

Unfortunately, people who acquire knowledge in order to enhance their fan experience are rarely scrupulous about seeking out the truth. Like sports fans, they tend to evaluate information in a highly biased way, overvaluing anything that supports their preexisting views and devaluing or ignoring anything that goes against them.[13] Committed fans of the Democratic Party greatly overestimate the inflation and unemployment rates when a Republican is in the White House, while Republican fans have the opposite bias.[14] The most avid and knowledgeable political fans usually limit their discussion of politics to fellow fans of the same team.[15]

This kind of bias is perfectly rational if the goal is to enjoy the fan experience rather than seek the truth; subjecting your views to an unbiased confrontation with the facts can easily ruin a political fan's day, almost as much as an unexpected vampire attack. Economist Bryan Caplan calls this behavior "rational irrationality."[16] For the true political fan, being logical about politics would defeat the purpose of following it in the first place. Just as vampires have an aversion to garlic, political fans have an aversion to logic and inconvenient facts.

WHAT VOTERS DON'T KNOW ABOUT THE UNDEAD COMES BACK TO BITE THEM

Ignorance and illogical evaluation of evidence are often perfectly rational behavior for individual voters. But they leave the brain-dead electorate collectively ill-prepared for coping with the living dead. This is a constant theme of vampire and zombie stories going back to the nineteenth century. Here are a few particularly notable examples:

In Bram Stoker's classic 1897 novel *Dracula*, the general public is completely unaware of the threat posed by Count Dracula and other vampires— despite the fact that the vampires eventually kill or vampirize a substantial number of people. As a result, the heroes of the story don't even seriously consider trying to persuade the British government to protect them against the undead menace. Instead, they rely on the assistance of Professor Abraham Van Helsing, a private vampire hunter.

Perhaps the most influential modern zombie movie is George Romero's 1968 *Night of the Living Dead*, which focuses on a small group of people trapped in a house during a zombie uprising. The public and the government are taken completely by surprise by the zombies. Throughout the movie, government statements about the zombies, broadcast over the radio and TV, are at best unhelpful—and at worst lead some of the characters to their deaths when they are killed by zombies while trying to reach a local rescue center, as recommended by a broadcast. At the end of the movie, the last surviving character—Ben—is shot by members of a law-enforcement patrol who mistake him for a zombie. His death and the patrol's too-late arrival are obvious consequences of government's ineffectiveness caused by political ignorance. The public is similarly ignorant, and the government equally ineffective (or worse) in Romero's later zombie apocalypse films, such as *Dawn of the Dead* (1978) and *Day of the Dead* (1985).

Public ignorance is also a major theme of *Buffy the Vampire Slayer* (1997–2003) and its spin-off series *Angel* (1999–2004). High school student Buffy Summers—the eponymous slayer—and her friends live in Sunnydale, California, a town massively infested by vampires and demons by virtue of its location on the "Hellmouth." Despite the rapidly growing body count generated by the undead, public opinion seems completely oblivious to their presence. During the first three seasons of *Buffy*, it becomes clear that both the public and most government officials in Sunnydale almost completely ignore the vampire menace, despite an extremely large number of deaths and disappearances in an otherwise normal middle-class town.

Some of this is straightforward rational ignorance. The people of Sunnydale pay little attention to political issues, including the crime rate. But some is better understood as rational irrationality. Even when evidence of vampire activity does surface in a highly visible way, the public tends to rationalize it in terms of their preexisting worldviews. Rupert Giles, the Slayer's adult mentor and Watcher, explains the town's failure to react by pointing out that "people have a tendency to rationalize what they can and forget what they can't."[17] Ignoring or rationalizing information that cuts against their preconceptions is exactly how "political fans" often address real-world political issues. In a rare episode where the public does notice the undead threat, it reacts in a highly irrational way by capturing Buffy—their best defense against the undead—and trying to burn her at the stake.[18]

The main initial consequence of political ignorance in *Buffy* is that government does little or nothing to combat the vampires and demons. But in seasons 3 and 4, the government also begins to actively exploit public ignorance for its own nefarious purposes. In season 3, we learn that the mayor of Sunnydale, Richard Wilkins III, is in fact a powerful demon himself.[19] While pretending to serve the interests of the public, he actually uses lesser undead to prepare the way for his "ascension" to godlike status and assumption of absolute power over the world. The people are so oblivious to his true nature that Wilkins has been able to dominate the town for almost a century, without anyone ever noticing that Richard Wilkins I, Richard Wilkins II, and Richard Wilkins III were all the same person. Wilkins's behavior is an exaggerated portrayal of how real-world politicians exploit ignorance to their advantage.

In season 4, the federal government begins to take an interest in Sunnydale's vampires and demons. The Pentagon establishes an organization known as the "Initiative" to deal with them. But it gradually becomes clear that the Initiative's main goal is to use the undead for the government's own purposes. Dr. Maggie Walsh, the leader of the Initiative, seeks to create supersoldiers who combine the traits of both humans and demons. Her experiments lead to disastrous results when she unwittingly creates a powerful monster—Adam—whom the Initiative cannot control. Walsh's and the Initiative's machinations would not have been possible if the public had been more aware of the undead menace in the first place, which in turn would have made it far more difficult to keep the Initiative's activities secret.

In the *Angel* spin-off series, Buffy's ex-boyfriend Angel, a rare vampire with a soul, leaves Sunnydale to fight supernatural evil in Los Angeles. The people of LA are just as ignorant about the undead as those of Sunnydale, and the government equally ineffective in stopping them. Some of the Los Angeles–based demons even use the power of government to promote their own interests. If Wilkins and Walsh represent the ability of nefarious government officials to exploit ignorance for their own purposes, the demonic law firm Wolfram & Hart represents the ability of private interest groups to "capture" the machinery of the state, while relying on public ignorance to shield themselves from any potential backlash.[20] For example, the firm develops a relationship with a corrupt senator who provides it with political support in exchange for being able to use the firm's supernatural resources in her campaigns.[21]

Political ignorance also plays a central role in the most popular zombie story of the last decade, Max Brooks's *World War Z*. In Brooks's novel, a zombie infestation threatens to engulf the whole world. The undead menace in *World War Z* develops only gradually, giving governments plenty of time to stave off the danger at a fraction of the cost it would take to combat a full-fledged zombie epidemic. Yet, with rare exceptions such as Israel,[22] most governments largely ignore the danger until it is too late—primarily because the general public also remains oblivious to it despite the accumulation of evidence indicating a serious threat.[23]

War weariness from a partially unsuccessful recent "brushfire war" leaves the public unwilling to consider expending resources on countering the zombie threat or even to recognize it as a serious danger to begin with.[24] This kind of cognitive closure is illogical but is a typical example of "rationally irrational" voters' unwillingness to consider new information. Recall the unwillingness of British, French, and American public opinion to recognize the threat posed by Nazi Germany in the 1930s—partially caused by pacifist and isolationist sentiments that flourished in the wake of the trauma of World War I. Public opinion also largely ignored the rise of radical Islamist terrorism prior to the 9/11 attacks. A more complex combination of public and elite ignorance probably also helped cause the massive financial crisis of 2008.[25]

When the zombie threat in *World War Z* becomes so clear that most of the public finally wakes up to its reality, the initial public reaction is one of irrational panic. In order to "show the people that they were still in charge, [and] get them to calm the hell down," the government decides to launch a hastily planned and ill-conceived military operation that ends in disaster.[26] Troops are sent into combat without sufficient ammunition to cope with the rapidly growing number of zombies.[27] If public opinion were less ignorant and illogical, the government would have felt less pressure to quickly "restore . . . confidence to the American people,"[28] and the military might have been able to take the time needed to mount a better-planned response.

BATTLING THE UNDEAD THROUGH PRIVATE INITIATIVE AND INFORMATION SHORTCUTS

Given the overwhelming force of rational ignorance and rational irrationality, it is difficult to understand why the undead haven't wiped out humanity yet or at least reduced us to the status of a renewable food supply, as planned by vampire leaders such as *Buffy the Vampire Slayer*'s The Master. Fortunately, the literary and cinematic canon on the undead offers two rays of hope for humanity: private-sector initiatives and information shortcuts.

In most vampire and zombie stories with happy endings, humanity is saved by private-sector initiatives, not by the government. From Van Helsing's defeat of Dracula to Buffy Summers's repeated liberation of the world from a variety of demonic menaces, a few brave private individuals have vanquished the undead where governments have failed or not even tried. *Buffy the Vampire Slayer* especially drives home this contrast between the private sector and the public when one of the military leaders heading the Initiative denounces Buffy and her friends as "anarchists," a moniker that one of them later adopts for himself.[29]

These private entrepreneurs usually succeed in part because, unlike voters, they have taken the time to carefully study the undead and figure out effective countermeasures. Van Helsing, of course, was an academic expert on vampires. Buffy relies on the expert knowledge of her Watcher Rupert Giles and on research conducted by her band of "Scoobies." Even the far less expert Ben, in *Night of the Living Dead*, quickly accumulates some knowledge on zombies, which helps him survive their attack.

In addition to seeking out relevant knowledge, Van Helsing, Buffy, and Ben usually try to evaluate the information they obtain in a logical, unbiased way. There are many scenes in *Buffy* where the Scoobies carefully analyze the strengths and weaknesses of potential opponents, often even meeting in the school library—the show's symbol of the value of knowledge and rational deliberation.

Van Helsing, Buffy, and their analogues in other stories seek out knowledge more assiduously than voters in part because they know that their decisions will make a difference. If they study the undead and figure out how to defeat them, they can actually use their knowledge to good effect. This contrasts with the average voter, whose acquisition of political knowledge has only an infinitesimal chance of affecting electoral outcomes or even of helping himself as an individual. More generally, private-sector actors "voting with their feet" have stronger incentives to acquire and effectively use information than ballot-box voters.[30] This is why most of us devote a lot more time to seeking out information when we decide what car or TV to buy than when we choose our next president. And unlike politicians, private vampire and zombie fighters don't have to cater to an ignorant electorate to stay in power. They are therefore free to adopt the most effective strategies for combating the undead, even if these approaches do not appeal to the public.

"Anarcho-capitalists" such as David Friedman have long argued that private organizations can provide security more effectively than government can.[31] Much of the vampire and zombie canon bolsters their case. Over fifty million Americans already live in private planned communities that provide various services traditionally operated by local government, including security against criminals.[32] Insecure private communities quickly lose business, as residents vote with their feet for competitors.[33] Perhaps we should also rely on such institutions to combat the undead. In *The Zombie Survival Guide*, Max Brooks recommends carefully planned private communities as a survival strategy for coping with a world where zombies have already taken over.[34] But greater reliance on private communities could also help prevent the undead from destroying civilization in the first place.

Although often more effective than government-led efforts, private responses to the undead have limitations of their own. In books and movies about the undead, private responses to vampires and zombies also often fail.[35] But the private sector still has a much better success rate than government, which almost uniformly fails. Moreover, some of the private firms that fail do so in part because their ties to the government create perverse incentives. In *World War Z*, a private firm markets a bogus anti-zombie drug that it is able to sell to the public in large part because the government promotes it and deliberately covers up its ineffectiveness.[36] Absent such government-sponsored "crony capitalism," the firm might have had stronger incentives to manufacture a cure that actually works. And crony capitalism persisted in part because of political ignorance. The public was unaware of the nature of the relationship between the government and politically favored firms.

But even relatively capable private responses to the undead have significant limitations. While the Buffys and Van Helsings of the world might effectively eliminate localized vampire and zombie threats, they may not be enough to counter a global or nationwide undead pandemic.[37] In addition, private organizations might undersupply efforts to combat the undead because they cannot "internalize" all the benefits those efforts create. When private actors nip a potential undead pandemic in the bud, they usually cannot get all of the people whose lives and property were saved to pay for their services. Although Buffy and others still fight the undead out of altruistic motives, most people are not as heroically altruistic as she is and require stronger incentives to risk their lives in the fight against the undead.[38]

At one point, Buffy's sister Dawn reacts angrily to the suggestion that Buffy charge the community for her services, protesting that "you can't charge innocent people for saving their lives."[39] But the difficulty of charging them for protection was one of the reasons why innocent lives were so often at risk in the first place. Thus, we may not be able to completely dispense with government-organized responses to the undead, especially when that menace reaches a large enough scale.

Generally ignorant voters can sometimes incentivize an effective response by using information shortcuts. In *World War Z*, one of the very few stories where it is government that ultimately defeats the undead, Max Brooks describes how most states eventually adopt a rational strategy for stopping the zombies and ultimately exterminating them. When the zombie threat reaches a truly massive scale, even ignorant and irrational voters are likely to notice and hold public officials accountable for countering the danger. As Brooks shows, the initial public response may be one of panic or irrationality. But over time, as he also describes in detail, governments have incentives to adopt at least somewhat effective solutions to large and obvious dangers, because even ignorant voters will punish them at the polls if they let the threat continue or grow. While voters may not know *why* the government has failed, the fact of the failure itself is obvious, and that may be enough to trigger punishment at the ballot box. This kind of "retrospective voting" is one of the main reasons why democratic governments are better at preventing and mitigating large and obvious disasters than are authoritarian regimes. For example, there are almost no cases where a democratic government has allowed a mass famine to occur within its borders, even though such occurrences are all too common under dictatorship.[40] Retrospective voting is one of a number of information shortcuts that sometimes enable voters to make good decisions despite having very little political knowledge. [41]

Unfortunately, retrospective voting is likely to facilitate effective policies against the undead only after the problem becomes large enough for ignorant voters to notice it. Even then, a rational public response might not arise until after an initial period of irrational panic. Although humanity ultimately prevails in *World War Z*, it is only at the cost of billions of lives that might have been saved had the electorate been less ignorant and irrational to begin with. Similarly, voters reward politicians for disaster relief spending more than disaster prevention spending, even though the latter is a far more effective way to save lives. [42]

Retrospective voting could incentivize governments to take effective precautions against the undead even if voters are oblivious to the danger. It might do so in order to forestall the massive political backlash that would occur if a major uprising of the undead occurs through its negligence. But that is only likely if the politicians perceive the coming uprising as both large enough to be noticed by the public and likely to happen during their terms in office. Governments tend to underinsure against disasters rare enough that the political benefits of preparedness are likely to be reaped by future office-holders. [43]

It is also worth noting that ignorant voters are more likely to notice zombie infestations than vampires. Most zombies are stupid and make little effort at concealment. They also usually appear in large groups. They therefore soon become noticeable to the general public, rational ignorance notwithstanding. By contrast, vampires are often highly intelligent and usually appear singly or in small groups. Many are skilled enough at concealment to pass as normal humans, so long as they avoid sunlight and holy symbols. As a result, government is likely to be particularly ineffective in combating vampires. In a world imperiled by both vampires and zombies, ignorant voters might even incentivize the government to overemphasize efforts to counter the latter danger at the expense of the former.

CONCLUSION

Public ignorance and irrationality greatly magnify the danger posed by vampires and zombies. If the voting public were less brain-dead, government might be more effective in countering the undead. The problem could be mitigated by reducing the size and complexity of government and relying more on the private sector for our needs—including combating the undead. Private-sector actors have better incentives to acquire needed information and use it rationally. In addition, reducing the amount of government activity voters must keep track of might enable them to focus their limited attention on the truly essential functions of government, including combating vampire and zombie attacks that are too large-scale for private initiatives to handle. Rationally ignorant voters can do a better job of monitoring government when there is less government to monitor. [44]

So far, civilization has survived by relying on a timely combination of private initiative and information shortcuts. But, as numerous works about the undead suggest, it has done so only at unnecessarily great cost. With any luck, we can go on avoiding an undead apocalypse. But in the meantime, political ignorance will continue to exacerbate a host of other public policy problems, ranging from America's fiscal crisis to the ongoing harm caused by protectionism and immigration restrictions. [45] Not to mention the looming menace of werewolves and orcs, which the public is even more ignorant about than it is about the undead. . . . [46]

Chapter Nineteen

Sinking Our Teeth into Public Policy Economics

A Taste of Immortality

Fabien Medvecky

Vampires aren't just bloodsucking, powerful, sexy, immortal creatures; they are also deeply social and political creatures. In the movie *Underworld*, vampires refer to themselves as "the Vampire nation" and are led by elders and a council. Similarly, the vampires in the HBO series *True Blood*, who also live in and openly interact with human society, have their own parallel government. So what would happen if a vampire were to become, say, secretary of the treasury? What public policy would she push for? Would vampire policies be any different from human policies?

Let's consider one of the most topical and difficult public policy questions around: what to do about climate change. As it stands, the two sides of the (north) Atlantic couldn't be further apart on climate change policy. European nations have, largely, ratified the Kyoto Protocol with binding targets (period 2: 2013–2020), while no North American country has done so. But how would things have turned out if vampires had been running the show instead of humans? If Dracula and company had been in charge, would there have been a stronger consensus over action on climate change? If there is a difference in the way vampires approach climate change policy decisions, it is not likely to be because of any natural affinity vampires have for the environment or because of any altruistic or cooperative traits vampires might exhibit in international negotiations. The reason, I'll suggest, comes down to economics: economics and immortality.

Climate change should whet our appetite for the effects of immortality on other public policy decisions. In order not to leave us hungry for more, we will sink our teeth into another policy area where life expectancy matters, namely Social Security. Here again, fanged policy makers would need to grapple with questions less obviously relevant to us. Yet, as with climate change, humans could learn much from vampires. As our life expectancy and our capacity to foresee the long-term consequences of our actions increases, the questions vampires face—and their answers to these questions—become increasingly relevant to us.

CLIMATE CHANGE

Let's start with an assumption that there is no disagreement over the facts concerning climate change; Democrats, Republicans, and vampires all agree that climate change is happening, all agree that it is human caused, and all agree on how much damage it will do to the planet. Even under these seemingly heavenly conditions, consensus on public policies is unlikely. Two big stumbling blocks stand in the way to some form of consensus: first, what form should our mitigation policy take, and second, how much should we be willing to spend on said policy. With regard to mitigation policy, we'll focus on the policy package recommended by the Stern Review (more on this later). The Stern Review recommends (1) carbon pricing, most likely in the form of taxes that encourage people to reduce their use of carbon-based fuels; and (2) subsidies for research and development of carbon-capture technologies and green technologies such as solar, wind, and tidal energy. These policies will be costly because they divert people from using the energy sources that are *currently* the most economical, and as a result they may reduce economic well-being and economic growth. Now let's sink our teeth into the second question—how much should the government be willing to spend on these policies—and consider what our fanged treasurer might have to offer in response.

VALUING CLIMATE CHANGE AND DISCOUNTING

Determining how much we should spend on climate-change mitigation policies is incredibly complex, largely because the costs and benefits of the various policy options are spread over very long periods of time. Take two extreme options: business as usual versus a serious mitigation policy. Business as usual comes at no current cost, while a serious mitigation policy would come at a high current cost. According to the Stern Review, the British government's main report on the economic impact of climate change, serious mitigation efforts would reduce world output by about 1 percent per year (2006 figures), meaning a total annual cost of over $486 billion compared to business as usual.[1] However, a serious mitigation policy would avert large harms in the future from rising temperatures. Business as usual, on the other hand, will mean a rather bleak future and will affect our future economic capacities as land is lost to sea, health impacts are exacerbated, and so forth, leading to a 20 percent loss in world output by 2200 compared to a serious mitigation policy (estimated at a total annual cost of about $135 trillion).[2] Table 19.1 shows the two positions:

Table 19.1.   Comparison of Costs of Climate Policies

	Current costs	Future costs in 2200
Business as usual	none (baseline)	-$136 trillion
Serious mitigation	-$486 billion	None (baseline)

Of course, these are two extremes, and our likely policy choice will lie somewhere in the middle. Still, in order to work out how much we should spend on climate-change mitigation policies, it will be useful to work out how much the cost of business as usual—that $136 trillion in 2200—is worth to us today.

A core disagreement in climate change negotiations is over how future costs and benefits should be valued relative to current costs and benefits. Put simply, how much should we care now about the $136 trillion loss of wealth that will occur in 2200? In economics, the answer to this lies with a process called *discounting*. Discounting is an economic tool that decreases future costs and benefits by a yearly rate, known as the discount rate. This process permits comparison of costs and benefits occurring at various points in time. But why shouldn't all costs and benefits be valued the same, regardless of when they will occur? One commonly stated motivation for discounting is that all things being equal, individuals prefer earlier rewards over later rewards; after all, wouldn't you rather drain that human now rather than wait a year to do it? If individuals prefer earlier rewards to later rewards, then conversely later rewards are valued less highly than earlier rewards.

Intuitively, the discount rate can be thought of as a reverse interest rate. At an interest rate of 10 percent per year, putting $1,000 in the bank today will return us $1,100 next year. Now imagine you expect to receive $1,100 in the future; we can think of $1,100 next year as being equivalent to $1000 today if we reverse the process—that is, if we discount the $1,100 at an annual discount rate of 10 percent for one year.[3] And like the interest rate, which determines how much current amounts will be worth to us in the future, the discount rate determines how much future costs and benefits are worth to us today, and consequently, how much we should care about them. If we were to discount $1,000 for ten years at 5 percent per year, the *net present value* of the $1,000 (what it is worth to us today) would be $613.91. In other words, if you wanted to have $1,000 ten years from now, and your bank offered you a fixed rate of 5 percent per year, you would need to invest

$613.91. If, on the other hand, we were to discount $1,000 for ten years at 10 percent per year, the *net present value* of the $1,000 would only be $385.54—in other words, if your bank offered you a rate of 10 percent instead of 5 percent, you would only have to invest $385.54 to end up with $1,000 in ten years. So, the higher the discount rate, the less future costs and benefits are worth to us today.

In the debate over climate-change policy, choosing the right discount rate is without doubt the most contentious economic issue. This is because for us to know how much we should be willing to spend on mitigation policies, we need to know the cost of the alternative. This means we need to work out the cost of not mitigating, and to do this, we need to discount the $136 trillion loss of output in 2200 to get its net present value. Since the value of the discount rate determines (in large part) the current value of these future costs, much of the disagreement turns on what rate should be used for discounting and the related question of what counts as a good justification for discounting. Without agreement on this, there can be no agreement on what the cost of climate change is and thus no agreement on how much we should be willing to spend on policies to combat climate change.

LIFE, IMMORTALITY, AND DISCOUNTING

As stated above, discounting is often motivated by appealing to individuals' desire and preference for immediate consumption—that is, our impatience, which economists refer to as *pure time preference*. Not everyone agrees with this. A number of economists claim that impatience is never a good motivation for discounting in social decisions because it is ethically indefensible. From a social perspective, when an event occurs seems to be irrelevant to its value; one million deaths due to famine now are no worse than one million deaths due to famine in a hundred years. Others say that since most people are in fact impatient, it is perfectly fine to discount for impatience; after all, we live in democratic societies and the wishes and whims of the body politic are what should be enacted. So what would our bloodsucking treasurer do? Surprisingly, this would not be a sticking point for vampires; here is why. Studies have shown that our rate of *pure time preference*, our impatience, changes as we progress through our lives. In fact, there seem to be two drivers that affect our degree of impatience: life experience and life expectancy. In humans, the elderly discount the future most heavily because of their limited life expectancy, and young people are the second-heaviest discounters because they have a substantially more limited range of comparison. The lowest discount rate is found among middle-aged individuals who have both substantial life experience and some reasonable life expectancy.[4] So, on both counts, we humans are likely to do worse than vampires. Given that we blunt-toothed humans tend to be younger than most of our fanged friends, it seems reasonable to assume we may lack their patience (except when it comes to feeding, where the bloodsucking fiends more than match our impatience). Second, we have limited life expectancy, and we need to cram all our desires into a relatively short time. In a fleeting eighty-odd years, we must try to do everything we want to do, see everything we want to see, and experience all the richness life has to offer. We better hurry! By comparison, when we meet Louis, at the beginning of *Interview with the Vampire*, he is over two hundred years old and still going strong. With no foreseeable end to one's existence aside from foul play or lack of food, the sense of urgency that drives humans loses pertinence. That holiday to Kilimanjaro to taste the locals can be had next year or next century, for that matter. More to the point with regard to climate change, the Nosferatu decision maker is likely to still be around when the consequences of our decisions take effect. With such longevity, vampires' rate of impatience is likely to be very low, and that has an enormous impact for public policy.

IMPATIENCE AND CLIMATE-CHANGE POLICIES

Impatience plays a big role in the discount rate debate in climate-change policy decisions, and while humans are not immortal, we often have a sense of caring beyond our own lifespan. This is often stated in terms of our interest in the well-being of our progeny or through some other sense of a bond with the rest of humanity. But interest by proxy is substantially more limited than having an interest for yourself, and this form of care has a poor historical record; there was a time when men claimed they "incorporated" their wives' views and interests into their decisions, making universal suffrage redundant. Back to climate change, those who think impatience is a good reason to discount support a relatively high discount rate, whereas those who don't claim the discount rate should be relatively low. In fact, impatience is the main point of difference between two of the most prominent economists working on climate change, Nicholas Stern and William Nordhaus. Stern rejects impatience as a reason to discount while Nordhaus accepts it, claiming that "the [Stern] Review's radical view of policy stems from an extreme assumption about discounting."[5] Rarely do economists bare their teeth so publicly, but impatience is all-important here. The discount rate is (classically) made up of a number of parameters, most notably the previously discussed *pure time preference* and *expected economic growth*. We discount for economic growth because growth will lead to future people being better off, so they will be able to more easily pay for goods than we can. Indeed, the current world mean yearly income is about $7,000 US per person; by 2100 it is estimated it will be $100,000 US per person.[6] Stern and Nordhaus largely agree on the other parameters; their major disagreement is over the rate of pure time preference. In keeping with that, let's adopt their shared projected values for economic growth of between 1.5 percent and 2 percent. Nordhaus combines this 1.5–2.0 percent growth rate with a rate of pure time preference of 3 percent to get a combined discount rate of between 4.5 percent and 5 percent. Stern uses the same growth rate, 1.5–2.0 percent, but argues that pure time preference is not a good reason to discount and so uses the minimal rate of 0.1 percent to give a combined discount rate of between 1.6 and 2.1. This means that pure time preference accounts for more than half of Nordhaus's discount rate, making his rate more than double Stern's. As a result, Nordhaus values future costs much less than Stern. Every $1,000,000 of loss that occurs in one hundred years is equivalent to a current loss of $7,604 for Nordhaus, while for Stern, it is equivalent to a current loss of $138,033. In terms of policy difference, this means that Stern would support incurring costs (from high carbon prices and alternative-energy subsidies) that are eighteen times greater than what Nordhaus would support.

But this is a human squabble. It stems from our limited life expectancy and its accompanying impatience. If we shared our immortal companions' life expectancy, we would not have such strongly divergent views over pure time preference. With regard to the cost of climate change and the related issue of how much we should be willing to spend on it, we would expect vampires to place a higher value on the future than we do and, as a result, to be more agreeable to climate-change mitigation policies, even if these policies came with a higher current price tag. Of course, even once we agree on how much we should spend on climate-change mitigation policies, there is still a debate to be had about exactly how this money should be spent; agreeing on a discount rate is only part of the battle. But at least as far as discounting is concerned, immortality breeds consensus.

IMMORTALITY AND SOCIAL SECURITY

As with climate change, there are many decisions that involve an element of time: saving for the future, investing in research, and countless others. One of particular interest at the moment is Social Security.

First, let's get the mechanics of Social Security clear. Social Security is a federally administered program that collects money through taxes and redistributes it to the elderly, disabled, or widowed members of society. By far the largest group of beneficiaries of Social Security are the elderly, who benefit mostly in the form of retirement benefits. Practically, what this means is that Social Security is a continuous intergenerational transfer mechanism; the younger generation in the workforce funds the program that supports the older generation, who are no longer in the workforce (just as that older generation had to support the previous generation in their youth). As long as there are a steady number of taxpayers to fund a similarly steady number of retirees, then all is well and good. But the challenge for policy makers, and the debate among economists, is that changing demographics mean we are unlikely to see consistent numbers of taxpayers and retirees. Instead, we are likely to see a thinning percentage of taxpayers carrying the burden of funding an increasingly large population of retirees. There are two reasons for this change in demographics: first, the aging of the Baby Boomers, and second (and more importantly), our increasing life expectancy.[7]

But Social Security is hard to think through clearly for us because our life expectancy creeps up gradually from generation to generation. When Social Security was first introduced in 1935, the life expectancy was just under sixty-two years of age, three years less than retirement age. This meant very few got to live long enough to get access to the benefits. By comparison, current life expectancy is just under seventy-nine years of age. And unlike bloodsucking immortals, whose life expectancy is, well, equally immortal across all generations, our generation is likely to live four to six years longer than our parents. However, the increase in life expectancy from one generation to the next is too small and gradual for most of us to notice. And to double the trouble, while we can't fully appreciate our increasing life expectancy, we can and do remember that when we entered the workforce, people were retiring at sixty-five—and we feel a slight injustice at having to put in more years of work than they did. So what policy options are available, and what might the Nosferatu treasury secretary do? This will largely depend on *who* the policy is aimed at: vampires only, humans only, or a mixed population. I'm especially interested in the last case, but first, let's lay down the policy options available to our treasurer.

PENSION AS REWARD OR PENSION AS SUPPORT

There are three policy options usually bandied about for adjusting Social Security policy in light of demographic change: do nothing and hope for economic growth, increase the tax contribution of the working population, and/or increase the retirement age. While everyone desires economic growth, few advocate the first response, as it requires not just continuous economic growth, but also that the growth be reasonably high (somewhere above 2 percent per year). For immortals like Eric Northman, a Nordic vampire in *True Blood* born around 900 AD, such optimism in economic growth would seem a poor bet, given that he remembers firsthand that between 1000 and 1820, the annual growth rate of the Western countries (plus Japan) was only 0.13 percent per year, slightly better than the world average of 0.05 percent.[8] Indeed, substantial growth—growth of over 2 percent per year—is only a fairly new phenomenon and statistically seems to have peaked in the mid-to-late last century (1950s to 1970s). So what of the other two options?

The other options—increasing tax contributions and increasing retirement age—turn on a philosophical question about fairness in retirement. The fundamental question is: should retirement be based on years spent working or on the proportion of one's life spent working? If we set the retirement age at sixty-five, is it because we think once you've worked a set number of years (say forty-five years), you deserve a break no matter how much longer you are likely to live? Or is it because we think once you've worked a set proportion of your adult life, such as 75 percent (no matter how many years that may take), you deserve to have a break? If we take the first view—that retirement is deserved once a set quota of work years is fulfilled—then, as life expectancy increases and the population ages, we need to increase our tax contributions to fund Social Security. This is because the numbers of work years per person will diminish compared to the number of years the average person spends in retirement. If, on the other hand, we take the second view—that retirement is deserved once a set proportion of adult life has been committed to working—then we need to increase retirement age as life expectancy increases to keep the ratio of work life to retirement constant. To try to help our treasurer decide on the best policy course, let's consider two extreme scenarios—one being an all-human world with a fixed lifespan, and the other being an all-vampire world with infinite life expectancy—and then we'll consider the middle ground, a mixed-population world.

In the all-human world with a fixed lifespan, there would be no problems with Social Security as it is, because the fixed lifespan would ensure that the retirement payments are matched by a consistent revenue stream. The catch would be to ensure the tax rate is sufficiently high to cover the expected payments. On the other hand, for the vampire-only world, things aren't that simple; for Nosferatu, the philosophical issue is subservient to practical considerations. Imagine Viktor, an elder in *Underworld*, designing a Social Security policy for his vampires. If he were to take the view that after, say, sixty-five years of work, vampires earn the right to retire, then the government would eventually need a near-infinite sum of money to fund potentially near-infinite retirements. This, in turn, would require unreasonably (if not impossibly) high tax contributions from the working population. Indeed, it seems that in the vampire-only world, Social Security makes no sense.

Now consider the mixed-population world. In such a case, the best policy will largely depend on how the population is made up. If retirement is set at sixty-five, then vampires' very lengthy period of rest will be a burden on the rest of society, and the more vampires there are, the more unsustainable the situation becomes. Interestingly, having a greater proportion of vampires in the world is much like having a longer life expectancy. In order to avoid Social Security being an unacceptable strain on the public coffers, the only option available to the bloodsucker treasurer is to take life expectancy seriously into consideration and to use that as a basis on which to set the retirement age. If life expectancy increases, then retirement should likewise increase, and if life expectancy decreases, then retirement age should likewise decrease. While there is a debate to be had around the correct proportion of work life to retirement, the need to set retirement age as a proportion of life expectancy seems unavoidable to the budget-conscious immortal. Here, as with climate change, immortality brings clarity to the issue—a clarity that is harder for us short-lived humans to see.

CONCLUSION

We blunt-toothed mortals could do well to learn from our fanged treasurer's considerations on public policy. In particular, the bloodsuckers' immortality brings clarity to a number of issues we find perplexing. Our limited life expectancy hinders our capacity to make long-sighted decisions, while their immortality leads them to better decision making. Our fanged friends can also teach us to place more value on the future, to be careful not to forget the past, to keep in mind that the current situation may not be the norm and may not continue unabated, and to be mindful of slowly creeping changes to our world. So, while we're unlikely to turn immortal anytime soon (unless the undead descend upon us), maybe we should try and think a little more like our immortal brethren when we sink our teeth into public policy questions.

Chapter Twenty

Where, Oh Where Have the Vampires Gone?

An Extension of the Tiebout Hypothesis to the Undead

A. L. Phillips, M. C. Phillips, and G. M. Phillips

> Where, oh where have the vampires gone?
> Oh where can the undead be?
> Where their thirst is slaked
> They will make their home—
> Are they amongst you and me?
>
> —with apologies to Septimus Winner

The question of where vampires and zombies can be found—where they unlive, that is—is of immense importance for slayers and average Americans alike. There are two possible answers to this question: first, that the undead are distributed proportionally around the United States, meaning that anywhere you live, you are in equal danger of being turned in the night. Alternatively, the undead might be more concentrated in certain areas than others, leaving residents of some states in relative safety even as they threaten others.

According to economic theory, the second is far more likely. Economist Charles M. Tiebout[1] theorized about why people choose to live in particular places and how local communities distinguish themselves from each other. Communities, he said, choose to offer specific benefits that will appeal to the types of residents they want to live there, and individuals, recognizing these differences between communities, purposefully select the communities in which they will be most satisfied. Together, these observations are known as the Tiebout hypothesis.

However, Tiebout only studied, theorized, and referred to those who "live" in a community. In this chapter, we generalize Tiebout's hypothesis to the undead. Though these individuals do not "live," they may still attempt to maximize their well-being by choosing a place to spend their existence based on its inherent attractiveness. The attractiveness of a community can be described in terms of its characteristics, called "local public goods," which are inherent to a particular community and are generally available to everyone who resides in that community. There are two types of local public goods—those naturally occurring and those created by its residents. For instance, the cloud cover in Forks, Washington, is a naturally occurring local public good and supposedly a strong draw for the vampires whose unliving patterns were observed by Stephenie Meyer in her *Twilight* series. Alternatively, if a city offered Meals on Wheels and other services attractive to senior citizens, those policies might attract vampires with the promise of a well-fed supply of victims. (Of course, these are "public goods" from the perspective of vampires. From the perspective of humans, policies that attract vampires might constitute "public bads.")

If the Tiebout hypothesis holds for the undead, we would expect to find:

1. Migration over time by the undead to areas with local public goods attractive to them, and corresponding migration by the undead out of less attractive areas.
2. A geographical distribution of the undead across the fifty United States that is not proportional to the distribution of the living—that is, the number of undead per capita is not the same across the fifty states.

We explore in this chapter, then, the question of whether the undead choose to unlive in different types of locations, represented by different percentages of undead per capita in the population, and then use two statistical methods to explore possible local public goods that might attract or repel the undead population.

Of course, identifying the number of undead residents in a particular state can present a challenge: vampires and zombies don't tend to respond to the U.S. Census, the American Community Survey, or other national statistical studies. It is thus very difficult to survey the population about their behavior patterns, interests, or reasons for unliving anywhere. Further, none of the authors of this chapter is undead, and we were unable to contact any vampires or zombies to interview for this chapter.

Fortunately, the undead have chosen to reveal their presence in a highly visible and quantifiable location: the voting booth. Using the official report by the prestigious Pew Center on the States on the status of the "graveyard vote" in the United States—that is, the number of dead registered voters in each U.S. state in 2012—as well as state and national population and voter registration rates, we are able to discover where the undead are unliving, test the Tiebout hypothesis, and identify what local characteristics may be drawing the undead to particular communities.

THE VOTING DEAD

Since the earliest days of the United States, the undead have been an active part of the political process. For example, an investigation by the *Chicago Daily Tribune* in 1891[2] identified that in some precincts as many as a quarter of the voters were dead, while others were not known to be dead but had as their addresses empty lots, abandoned buildings, and "vacant quagmires." Around the country, newspapers and political analysis have long referred to this phenomenon as the "graveyard vote," "tombstone vote," "cemetery vote," or "voting dead," with some commentators directly referring to zombies exercising their vote.[3]

It is not surprising that the undead garner so much media attention: in many cases, political victories would not have been won if the undead had not participated in elections. For instance, Republicans blamed graveyard voters for the poor performance of Richard M. Nixon in the 1960 presidential election. As historian Robert Weisbrot recorded, "On election day Kennedy won the smallest of pluralities over Nixon, scarcely 100,000 votes out of some 69 million cast. Any of numerous groups could claim to have decided his victory—Irish, Italians, Poles, Catholics, Jews, and, as some pundits whispered, the heavy graveyard turnout in parts of Texas and Cook County, Illinois."[4]

Prior to the next presidential elections in 1964, the Republican Party acted on its fears of undead participation in politics and attempted to ensure that no ballots were cast by "tombstone voters" in Atlanta, Baltimore, Boston, Chicago, Detroit, Kansas City, Milwaukee, Los Angeles, New York, Newark, Philadelphia, Pittsburgh, St. Louis, and San Francisco, all of which had been carried by Kennedy over Nixon in 1960.[5]

More recently, according to director Joe Dante in "Homecoming,"[6] many deceased members of the American military reanimated as zombies to participate in the 2004 presidential election. Even today, the impact of the undead's vote can be felt: San Antonio, Texas, is the subject of a current examination by the Texas secretary of state, which discovered that thousands of mail-in absentee ballot applications in Bexar County all had the same cemetery as an address.[7] The cemetery management is reported to be involved in the Bexar County Democratic Party's vote-by-mail initiative.

The undead, it is worth noting, vote for both Republicans and Democrats. In Philadelphia, it was reported in 1963[8] that the once heavily Republican Fifth Ward had become overwhelmingly Democratic, with extensive dead voters and registered Democratic voters "listed at addresses that turned out to be parking lots, street intersections, condemned buildings, empty lots, and a wholesale chicken house." However, in upstate New York, it was observed by Democratic representatives in Albany that dead voters formed a "considerable portion" of the voters in smaller upstate communities, and that these dead voters routinely voted Republican.[9]

Upon occasion, the undead have even managed to run for office, though it remains unclear whether any have been elected. For instance, the deceased sheriff's candidate J. K. Towne in Carroll, Iowa, received 1,710 votes in an election some weeks after his death in 1938,[10] and Horace Greeley, a Democratic candidate for president in 1872, received numerous electoral votes in his bid for presidency despite his demise before the electoral college met.[11] In contrast, in 1961, Johnstown, Pennsylvania, voters "rejected a plea of party leaders and refused Tuesday to renominate a councilman who died of a heart attack May 4."[12]

To respond to the threat of the graveyard vote, many initiatives have been put forward that would keep undead individuals from voting. Most drastically, the Canadian government during World War II sent sixteen thousand of its zombies overseas in support of the war effort.[13] In this country, Abraham Lincoln, sixteenth president and reputed vampire hunter, purposefully opposed the agenda of the undead by supplying Union forces with silver weapons to face and defeat the Confederate vampires who wanted to take over the country.[14]

Since Lincoln's death, however, efforts in the United States have been limited primarily to forcing the removal of dead voters from registration lists, which has substantially reduced the graveyard vote.[15] It is also worth noting that some anti-undead legislation did not pass. For instance, an amendment to the 1964 Civil Rights Bill offered by Texas representative John Dowdy would have prohibited counting "any vote except that of a living" voter. He further explained, "I should like to have it understood that my amendment is nondiscriminatory in nature. It would apply to dead white folks as well as to dead colored folks."[16] Since this amendment was not approved, it seems likely that Dowdy's view of "discrimination" was not shared by the undead or their supporters.

Even today, some states take differing sides on the issue of undead voting: Kentucky, Nebraska, and New York mandate that individuals must "live" in their state to be eligible to vote, while the rest of the states merely demand that individuals must be "residents" of the state. In some instances, the undead have fought against discriminatory practices. In 1968, for instance, in Gallup, New Mexico, three individuals listed as being dead showed up at a county clerk hearing to protest their removal from the voter roster.[17]

Today, in spite of attempts to limit voting by the undead, the deceased are still present and accounted for in elections. According to a 2012 report by

Pew Center on the States, there were more than 1.8 million deceased individuals registered to vote for the 2012 U.S. presidential election, or about 1 percent of the total U.S. voting population.

With these data and the historical support they give us, we can begin to discover where America's undead are unliving and what local public goods they may value.

THE BODY COUNT: WHERE THE UNDEAD UNLIVE

Recent studies by Pew and Harvard University have published information regarding the extent of registered voters who are not living.[18] We obtained those data, adjusted for the voter registration percentage in each state, and thus computed the number of undead in each state, as well as the number of undead per capita in each state. These data are shown in figure 20.1 below.

Viewing this chart, it appears that there are substantial differences from state to state in the undead per capita. Later in this chapter, we perform statistical tests to show these differences are not due to mere chance.

As shown in figure 20.1, there are quite a few states that appear to be relatively attractive to the undead, while others do not seem to encourage residence. It is worth noting that Washington and Louisiana—both sites rec-

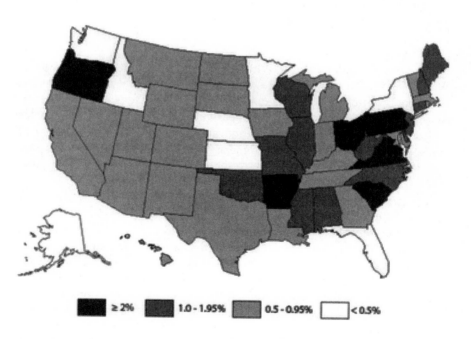

Figure 20.1.   Per Capita Concentration of Undead in the United States

ognized in popular culture as having high numbers of vampires—are less densely populated by the undead than are their neighboring states of Oregon and Arkansas. This leads to the possibility that the locations of the events described in the *Twilight* and *True Blood* series may have been purposefully changed to protect the anonymity of the individuals involved.

More important than the potential misrepresentation of the undead in popular literature, however, are the actual findings of which states in the United States are most attractive to the undead. Citizens, after all, should be concerned with the immediate threat of having their blood sucked out or brains eaten. Following, then, in table 20.1 is a list of the ten states with the highest proportion of undead per capita—that is, the states in which you're most likely to need to carry garlic and your zombie-killing weapon of choice. We follow this with a list of the ten states with the lowest proportion of undead per capita, perhaps those states where vampire hunts have been most successful over time.

Using a chi-squared test, we find that these concentrations of the undead are statistically significantly different from what would be expected if the undead chose their states of residence by chance.[19] Specifically, the undead density in the top ten states is significantly larger than it is in the bottom ten states, showing that the undead are not a constant proportion of the population. Similarly, using a t-test for the difference in mean percentages between the top ten and bottom ten states, we conclude that the percentages are statistically different.[20] From these tests, we conclude that the Tiebout hypothesis can, indeed, be extended with confidence to the undead as well as to the living.

One final question remains. What attracts the undead to certain locations? We answer this question at a state level by identifying local public goods that are strongly correlated to higher concentrations of undead per capita. Specifically, we identify the mean value of measures of local public goods for states with a high undead concentration and also for those with a low undead concentration, then divide the high mean by the low mean. Ratios over one indicate that the good is attractive to the undead, as the level of that good tends to be higher in areas where the undead congregate.

Local public goods can be divided into three basic types: those related to natural phenomena (e.g., weather), those related to sociodemographics (e.g., diet), and those related to policy decisions (e.g., tax rates). In terms of natural phenomena, we can see from table 20.1 that the undead can survive in a number of geographic locales, from cool, rainy states such as Oregon to the hot, humid south of South Carolina. Popular culture, if its settings are accurate, informs us that the undead can survive in such varied locations as dreary Forks, Washington,[21] sunny Sunnydale, California,[22] humid Bon Temps, Louisiana,[23] and the stormy seas of the Caribbean.[24] Characteristics not related to natural phenomena, however, can give us valuable insight into the less

Table 20.1. Top Ten and Bottom Ten States by Percentage of Undead in 2012

The Top Ten			The Bottom Ten		
1.	Ohio	2.4%	1.	Washington	.001%
2.	South Carolina	2.1%	2.	New York	.001%
3.	Virginia	2.1%	3.	Florida	.001%
4.	Arkansas	2%	4.	Alaska	.003%
5.	Oregon	2%	5.	Minnesota	.0035%
6.	Pennsylvania	2%	6.	Nebraska	.0045%
7.	Connecticut	1.7%	7.	Kansas	.0045%
8.	Mississippi	1.7%	8.	Idaho	.0045%
9.	Alabama	1.6%	9.	Nevada	.005%
10.	Illinois	1.5%	10.	North Dakota	.005%

well-explored preferences of the undead. A list of sociodemographic and policy-related characteristics with ratios of over one, indicating a relative preference by the undead, is shown below in table 20.2.

Table 20.2.   Local Public Goods Attractive to the Undead

Sociodemographics	Ratio: Mean High/Mean Low
Religiosity index	1.39
Funeral expenses (dollars spent)	1.11
Cigarettes (dollars spent)	1.11
Prescription/over-the-counter drugs (dollars spent)	1.11
Steak (dollars spent)	1.11
Total population in local area	1.11
Sweet rolls, coffee cakes, doughnuts (dollars spent)	1.1
Potato chips, nuts, other snacks (dollars spent)	1.1
Nursing homes (dollars spent)	1.08
Individuals 75+ years	1.06
Policy-related	
Fireworks (dollars spent)	1.19
Property taxes (dollars spent)	1.1
Public transportation (dollars spent)	1.04

As shown in table 20.2, there are several types of local public goods that make certain communities attractive to the undead. First, it should be noted that the strong association of religiosity with the presence of the undead may be a reaction to the presence of vampires in an area rather than a local public good that attracts vampires. On the other hand, in a highly religious area, those who are not religious may have less support from the establishment than they would in other locales, thus making them easier targets for the undead. If so, it is possible that vampires do choose these locations for the purpose of preying on the nonreligious minority.

It does appear clear, however, that undead tend to prefer states with higher funeral expenses and older, sickly populations. Communities that are already spending a great deal of money on funerals—indicating a high number of deaths already taking place—may be less likely to notice a few more due to vampirism or zombie attacks. Additionally, nursing homes may present especially tempting targets, as nursing homes have an abundance of elderly patients who cannot run and may not have family close by. It is also not unexpected for this population to die suddenly, thus helping undead predators keep from being discovered.

Next, the undead appear to choose locations based on the food and lifestyle that they provide. More densely populated areas are likely preferred for the simple reason that there are more opportunities to find an ideal victim—not just a human who won't be missed, but one who tastes good. As Joss Whedon revealed in *Buffy the Vampire Slayer*, vampires can taste steroids when they are present in human blood.[25] It appears that the same holds true for other substances that humans consume: steak, junk food, drugs, and cigarettes. (This provides just one more reason to skip dessert—your blood will be less attractive to vampires.) In addition, vampires cannot be affected by narcotics unless they are present in a victim's bloodstream.[26] Any vampires who wanted to experience the effects of drugs (and then avoid withdrawal symptoms) would need to unlive in an area where humans were routinely using the desired substances.

It also appears that the undead appreciate communities' efforts to make their existence enjoyable and easy. A high amount of money spent on property taxes indicates the presence of wealthy neighborhoods, which in turn are likely composed of nice homes—and graveyards. Records show that vampires in particular enjoy finer locales in which to unlive. Count Dracula, the first of all great vampires, enjoyed residing in a castle of his own in Transylvania, and when he chose to move to England, he picked a fine gated estate, Carfax near London.[27] What vampire wouldn't choose to follow in his shadowy footsteps and dwell in a mansion or marble crypt if given the opportunity? Public transportation also provides a convenient way for the undead to travel (especially if drivers' licenses have expired) and a handy place to grab a midnight snack. Finally, fireworks displays—late-night events where large crowds stand around in the dark for long periods of time—provide ideal opportunities for the undead to grab a straggler or five.

PULLING UP STAKES: CHOOSING WHERE TO LIVE

As shown, the Tiebout hypothesis does accurately describe the unliving patterns of America's vampires and zombies: not only do the undead prefer certain types of locations to others, they act on those preferences and move to those areas that are more undead friendly. Future research could extend these findings by using qualitative methods, such as in-depth interviews of the undead or direct observation of their unliving habits, to gain a deeper understanding of why the undead make the choices that they do. (Please note that such research should be undertaken with extreme caution.)

We believe that our findings will prove useful to the American population as a whole, as well as to more specialized groups. Individuals who want to minimize their danger from the undead can now make better-informed decisions as to where to live. On the flip side, slayers and other fighters of the undead can now be more effective in their choice of new hunting grounds. Anthropologists, ethnologists, and other academics who study vampires or zombies are given new research questions to explore. And if you're a Twihard who wants nothing more than to be turned, just head over to a high-density area with lots of religious people and a thriving funeral parlor, eat more steak and tasty snacks, and remember to always take time to go see the fireworks.

Part V

Brain Food

People don't just trade goods and services; they also trade in ideas. Economics has exchanged ideas with a number of other disciplines, including math, psychology, history, and biology, to the benefit of both sides. Sometimes this has involved economics importing methods or ideas pioneered elsewhere. Other times, economic theory has been exported for use in areas that initially seem to have little to do with economics (we've given you a taste of that in the first section of the book). In this section, we offer more examples of the benefits of trade in ideas and the resulting diversity of analytical approaches.

One of the defining features of vampires is their addiction to blood. Ian Chadd—venturing into the intersection of economics, psychology, and biology—shows how you can use economic theory to understand the decision making behind addictive behavior, whether it's blood you crave or just coffee and cigarettes.

While most economic theorists use logical and mathematical models that can be solved by hand, sometimes higher-tech tools are called for. Using computer simulation techniques to combine insights from both economics and ecology, Daniel Farhat shows how vampires and humans might coexist in a city and how the city's economic landscape would evolve over time.

We finish the volume with one of the classic horror stories of all time: *Dracula*. Hollis Robbins shows how Dracula arrived at a key point in economic history, when the economy was changing from mostly rural communities to a modern industrialized society. Part of this process was a change in timekeeping standards. The epic struggle between the Count and Dr. Van Helsing captures that changing notion of time.

—GW & JD

Chapter Twenty-One

The Economics of Bloodlust

Ian Chadd

And all the while, as the death wish caused me to neglect my thirst, my thirst grew hotter; my veins were veritable threads of pain in my flesh; my temples throbbed; and finally I could stand it no longer.

—Louis, in Anne Rice's *Interview with the Vampire* (1976)

In the early days of Louis's transformation, he laments his newfound urge for blood. Driven to vampirism by severe depression following the death of his brother, he comes to regret welcoming this change after he realizes its cost. Newly undead, he hunts at night with his partner Lestat and the two wreak havoc on the citizens of New Orleans. Though he attempts to remain abstinent, choosing to drink animal blood rather than humans, his insatiable thirst for the warm blood of the living eventually causes him to take the life of even the most innocent: the life of a child.

The vampire has an inherent dichotomy that has simultaneously made him a tragic and terrifying character. On one hand, he has a human essence; he yearns for companionship, for aspirations, and, at times, for mortality. On the other hand, he possesses the capacity for truly horrifying acts; his vampiric desire for blood could overcome whatever rationality or lingering human elements that may seem to guide his everyday actions. It is precisely this capacity that makes the vampire such a creature to be feared. While some vampires exist for years only drinking what they must to survive (or to avoid desiccating, depending on the individual vampire mythos), few avoid going on a blood "binge" at some point, or worse. Most will exhibit an animalistic urge for human blood at some point, disregarding all sensibilities left from their previous human existence to unceasingly pursue their victims. At first glance, bloodlust appears to be inexplicable when analyzed in the context of human behavior. It is almost as if the vampire succumbing to bloodlust is a separate being entirely from the being who appears as he did in his previous life as a human. However, have humans never exhibited such a duality? In fact, such behavior can easily be explained using economic models of human addiction. Specifically, the work of the economists Gary Becker and Kevin Murphy on rational addiction does a fine job explaining vampiric bloodlust. While the implications of their work have caused some controversy in the field of human addictive behavior, they can explain a great deal of the peculiar aspects of bloodlust in vampire lore. By viewing the vampire as a rational addict of human blood, we see some perplexing behavior as the result of a rational economic choice.

RATIONAL ADDICTION AND RATIONAL REVENANTS

The traditional economic view of choice maintains that consumers possess an inherent rationality. In this context, rationality simply means that consumers are forward looking and should respond to changes in price, taking into consideration all costs and benefits of their actions and maximizing their happiness thereafter. If a rational consumer purchases some number of DVDs at a price of $10 each, she should purchase fewer if the price increases to $15 and more if the price decreases to $5. Further, if a consumer is forward looking, she should not only respond to price changes that occur in the present, but also to expected price changes in the future. For the most part, this theory is remarkably useful in explaining everyday consumption patterns, whether human or vampiric, and is actually quite simple. However, what happens when we observe behavior that, to the naked eye, seems wildly irrational? When it comes to addictive behaviors, this theory of rational choice at first seems to be less useful.

It is easy to dismiss addictive behavior as "irrational" by most conventional definitions. If a heroin addict is in and out of rehab, loses friends and family members, or suffers negative health consequences due to her use of such a drug, why would she continue to indulge in such activities? For many years, it was thought that rational choice theory as briefly described above was inadequate for explaining addictive behavior—how could a consumer be considered rational by any definition of the word if she seems to ignore such obvious negative future consequences?

A common way of explaining addictive behavior is to pass it off as myopic; addicts simply disregard the future consequences of their actions, being tempted by the short-run euphoria experienced under the influence of an addictive substance. This explanation could certainly be sufficient to explain many behaviors associated with addiction. For example, it is certainly plausible, and even anecdotally confirmed in many cases, that tobacco smokers simply ignore the negative consequences of current consumption—the increased likelihood of various forms of cancer, general decrease in life expectancy, and the deterioration of general health—in favor of experiencing the effects of smoking cigarettes, which become increasingly difficult to resist the greater the addiction.

The early literature in economics on the consumption of addictive goods attributes such actions to the formation of habits.[1] Building upon these approaches to describing unique consumption patterns and breaking from the traditional view of addictive behavior as purely irrational, Gary Becker and Kevin Murphy provide a model of "rational addiction."[2] Essentially, they claim that addicts are indeed rational in the sense that they are forward looking and seek to optimize their own enjoyment of such goods over time. Becker and Murphy's work has gained traction since their original publication in the 1980s. As recently as September 2013, a researcher has found convincing evidence that crack and methamphetamine addicts act rationally in response to price changes. While conventional wisdom and policy are generally guided by the assumption that such addictions are irrational in nature, the idea that rationality guides such choices is gaining popularity.[3]

One key aspect of addictive consumption that must be understood is that of a *stock of addictive capital*. In essence, this stock of addictive capital is a measure of the intensity of the addiction to some good. The term "addictive capital" refers to the fact that past consumption of the addictive good affects the enjoyment of future consumption. It is important to note that, to economists, "capital" simply refers to the accumulation of something that will affect the future in some way. This addictive capital is accumulated as a total "stock" that is used in the calculation of the enjoyment of present consumption of the good. For example, we can talk about a stock of (nonaddictive) capital as an acquired taste for fine cheese or art; the more brie someone consumes, the more she will enjoy consuming it in the future, or the more opera you have experienced in the past, the more you will enjoy it now. For the consumption of addictive goods, it is easy to see how this concept is useful.

Consider a consumer who is addicted to gambling. Every time she hits the craps tables and makes bets, her stock of addictive capital with respect to gambling increases, feeding back into her addiction. The next time she decides to gamble, her stock will already include this previous experience and will increase. Thus, this stock will accumulate all instances of consumption of the addictive good. However, this stock has a leak, which causes it to decrease at a given rate. This abstract leak is called a *depreciation rate* when referring to these capital stocks; it is the rate at which the stock diminishes over time. In order for the gambler to stay at the same level of addiction, this depreciated stock of addicting capital must be periodically replaced (by consuming the addictive good). Thus, if our consumer's depreciation rate is one unit (in the abstract) of addictive stock every month, she must gamble once per month to stay addicted to gambling at the same level.

Addictive consumption involves the interplay between two forces: tolerance and reinforcement. *Tolerance* means that higher past consumption leads to lower enjoyment in the present. In this model, this is captured in the effect that the stock of addictive capital has on current satisfaction. When the stock is higher, the consumer's tolerance for this addictive good is higher, which causes the enjoyment of consumption to be lower. Imagine a smoker who begins by smoking one cigarette each afternoon. After a certain period of time, the smoker's tolerance to cigarettes will increase, and she will need to smoke more with each session to stay satiated. Thus, the higher the stock of addictive capital, the *lower* satisfaction she will get from the same level of consumption; the more our smoker has smoked in the past, the more she will need to smoke now in order to be satisfied.

Reinforcement refers to the effect of this same addictive capital on satisfaction gained from a single unit of consumption of the addictive good. In this phenomenon, past consumption raises the stock of addictive capital as above, but this stock has a positive effect on the enjoyment of each additional unit of the addictive good. Though our smoker now needs more cigarettes to be satisfied (because of her higher tolerance for nicotine as described previously), she also enjoys each individual cigarette more than she would have without having smoked before. Anecdotal evidence definitely confirms this fact, as first-time smokers often have negative initial reactions to smoking but grow to savor each cigarette as smoking is reinforced with continued use. We can think of this as an "acquired taste" for the addictive good. In order to truly enjoy an additional unit of the drug, for example, a consumer must have consumed it to some extent in the past.

At first glance, tolerance and reinforcement might seem contradictory. But in fact, these two phenomena can and do coexist. Consuming an addictive good is somewhat like filling a hole with dirt. In order to be fully satiated, you must fill the hole completely. Tolerance for this good (which is a result of past consumption) causes the hole to get deeper: you are more tolerant of the good and thus will require more of it, in total, to be satiated. However, reinforcement of this good (also a result of past consumption) causes your shovel to get larger; consuming this good gives you more satisfaction from each unit. Thus, you will have to dump more dirt in total into the hole to be satisfied, but the tool you're using to fill the hole has gotten better. Depending on the magnitude of the tolerance and reinforcement you experience, it may then be easier or harder to fill the hole.

For a brief example of these two concepts, consider the vampiric pair in Anne Rice's *Interview with the Vampire*: Louis and Lestat. Just following his conversion to vampirism, Louis would have possessed a relatively low level of this stock of addictive capital with respect to blood. Lestat, already a vampire for some years prior, had a much higher stock of such capital at that point in time. Because of his previous accumulation of stock, Lestat would have had a high degree of tolerance but also a high level of reinforcement. His great level of tolerance for blood would indicate that he needs to drink a larger amount of blood to stay at the same level of euphoria. This is somewhat counteracted by the reinforcement indicated by his stock of addictive capital, which would cause the enjoyment of each kill to be greater than that experienced in its absence. Thus we see Lestat dining on no less than four humans per night (a large number required to stay at a given level of satisfaction based on his tolerance for blood), while enjoying each kill significantly more than Louis, who possessed a much lower stock of addictive capital (higher levels of the stock lead to higher satisfaction per unit of blood consumption).[4]

While all of these aspects of addiction are highly illuminative and can describe a variety of addictive behaviors, the real insight of the Becker-Murphy model is what it tells us about the future costs and benefits of consuming addictive goods. Though the concept of rationality is heavily contested in economics, a decent simple definition of a rational consumer is one who weighs all costs and benefits of consumption and maximizes her own enjoyment thereafter. By this definition, addictions seem to be entirely contrary to rationality—how can it be said that an addict is looking forward at all of the possible costs of current consumption of an addictive good and still chooses to partake? However, the mathematics behind the Becker-Murphy model, which lie beyond the scope of this essay, suggest that addicts are indeed maximizing their enjoyment over time and respond as expected to changes in the price of this consumption—whether monetary or psychological. With regard to human addictions, such a result implies that people should consume more of the good when the price goes down and less of the good when the price goes up. While highly controversial, several empirical studies based on this model of rational addiction seem to confirm that this is indeed the case; consumption of alcohol, cigarettes, and caffeine changes significantly in reaction to changes in the price.[5] How vampires may react to such changes in price is discussed below.

THE LOGIC OF BLOODLUST

While the constraints on human behavior differ greatly from those of the vampire, these creatures exhibit addictive tendencies that can readily be modeled using the above analysis. For the vampire, both reinforcement and tolerance can be quite severe, while the relevant costs and benefits extend over eternity rather than a single lifetime. Becker and Murphy's model is quite useful for analyzing undead consumption patterns because it is highly adaptable to the individual vampire. Remarkably, it can easily describe the reasons for a variety of bloodlust behaviors.

The Vampire in Infancy

The birth of a vampire is a chaotic and tumultuous event. In most lore, this occurs when the "victim"[6] drinks the blood of her attacker after being drained nearly to death. Depending on the individual mythos, the victim then either dies as a direct result of this influx of vampiric blood or must be killed with the vampire's blood in her system. In either case, what usually follows is a deep thirst for human blood as the newborn vampire yearns with animal frenzy for her first independent taste of what sustains her. This initial onset of bloodlust can be easily explained using the Becker-Murphy model of rational addiction.

Becker and Murphy provide illuminating examples of life circumstances that can *instantly* affect the level of addiction to a particular good. People often find themselves most vulnerable to addictions following traumatic events such as divorce, wartime military service, and job loss. Directly following the trauma, this person's stock of addictive capital increases suddenly and significantly, simultaneously causing her to become more tolerant of the addictive good and also to have a large "previous" reinforcement of its use.[7] For the newborn vampire, this means that the enjoyment of a fresh pint of blood would be much higher than before (for most humans, the enjoyment would have been zero or negative). This young vampire, however, is less easily satiated by such consumption than before (assuming humans are happy not drinking blood at all).

For the vampire in infancy, this translates into an insatiable urge for blood immediately following a complete transition to vampirism, with the vampire often lacking any sort of intellectual understanding of why this is the case. In *The Vampire Diaries*, when the character Caroline first becomes a vampire, she is initially unaware that any change has actually occurred.[8] Drawn to a blood bag in her hospital room upon awakening, she drinks her first meal as a vampire in transition. Her bloodlust then increases over the next several days, with her becoming increasingly violent with each instance of feeding, until she is driven to indiscriminately kill an innocent human. This example perfectly illustrates the instantaneous change in subconscious preferences that occurs when a vampire is born. At the time of her transition, Caroline's stock of addictive capital with respect to blood increases significantly; all at once, she becomes highly addicted to blood without having previously consumed it.

A Discriminating "Shopper"

As mentioned earlier, the key insight of the Becker-Murphy model is that addicts can and do respond to changes in price. This result applies to both monetary prices and other negative effects or expectations. While the former doesn't necessarily apply to bloodlust because blood is typically not available for sale, the latter is especially helpful in explaining variations in drinking patterns. The price of obtaining and drinking blood is the psychological effect of taking a human life, the threat of being discovered and/or killed, and the general physical exertion of killing one's prey. Several contemporary vampire mythoi provide wonderful examples of how vampires indeed take morality or a psychological price into consideration in their eating patterns.

The Cullens in the *Twilight* saga are unique in their vampire vegetarianism; they completely abstain from the taking of human life for sustenance, opting to feed from animals instead. For such vampires as Edward Cullen, the psychological cost of taking a life given his moral character is simply too high. Thus, abstention is the only viable option for vampires with such remnants of their human pasts.

The *Vampire Diaries* mythos provides a number of illuminating examples and presents an interesting interpretation of the question of morality. In this work, vampires possess the ability to "turn off" their humanity so as to relieve themselves of all empathy when taking human lives to survive. The two brothers, Stefan and Damon Salvatore, act as the poster children for each respective way of vampiric life: Stefan lives with his humanity intact, choosing to live a Cullenesque vegetarian lifestyle, while Damon has turned off his humanity, embracing the darker aspects of this vampiric existence. While the polarizing nature of their individual lifestyles makes for a wonderful contrast between two different forms of bloodlust, it is Stefan who truly illustrates the rationality of addiction. At one point, as part of a desperate bargain to save his brother's life, Stefan agrees to serve as another vampire's right-hand man, a post that will require him to take many lives and relive his days as a "ripper."[9] Having previously abstained from drinking human blood because the psychological cost or guilt associated with such consumption was too high, he then faces a dilemma: continue to wreak havoc with his humanity intact, suffering the mental anguish associated with such guilt, or turn off his humanity so as to reduce the permanent psychological price of such actions? He chooses the latter and becomes a ripper once again until he has an opportunity to return to his vegetarian lifestyle.

Stefan's addiction is always portrayed as very intense—it is indeed this intensity and his past crimes that prevent him from normally taking a human life to survive lest he "fall off the wagon" again. However, in this period in which he is forced to drink from humans, would he care about the psychological cost of such actions if his addiction were irrational? The sheer fact that he took measures to decrease the psychological cost of drinking blood (turning off his humanity) indicates that he was going through some sort of satisfaction-maximizing, or cost-minimizing, calculation. This points to rationality at work.

A Variety of Addicts

Human addiction can run the gamut from casual but habitual use of an addictive good to very high levels of consumption. For example, we see smokers who only smoke one cigarette per day but will never stop and others who smoke a pack per day but may stop after several years of use. The key aspect of addiction to note here is that each is unique, with an individual addict's behavior able to differ greatly from other addicts of the same good. The Becker-Murphy model provides a number of explanations for the variety of addictive consumption patterns. For our purposes, it suffices to discuss two of these factors: the depreciation rate of the stock of addictive capital and the individual's preference for present consumption. These factors, as well as some others, determine the level of addiction to a particular good, and each factor influences the nature of the addiction in different ways.

Goods that are particularly addictive, such as heroin for humans and human blood for vampires, have relatively low depreciation rates for their stocks of addictive capital. Consequently, their stocks are easily accumulated, causing past consumption to have a large effect on current consumption—in this case, we say that past consumption of these goods reinforces future consumption to a great degree. However, different individuals may exhibit different reactions to the consumption of these goods, meaning that the depreciation rate may vary between individual consumers as well as individual goods. For example, drinking human blood highly reinforces bloodlust in some vampires but has little effect on others. In the movie adaptation of Anne Rice's *Queen of the Damned*, Akasha, the original vampire, exhibits a strong reaction to drinking blood after waking from her centuries-long slumber. Here, Akasha's depreciation rate is quite low. Even after centuries without tasting blood, her stock of addictive capital is very high. Driven by her strong addiction, she even takes to drinking the blood of other vampires for sustenance, an act that is condemned in most vampire circles. Compare this experience to that of the level-headed Maharet, who is constantly mindful of the delicate nature of a human life and easily able to control her hunger. This would indicate that her depreciation rate is very high, causing the effects of drinking blood to fade away from her quickly.

The strength of the individual's preference for present consumption relative to future consumption also affects the nature of the addiction. For an individual who highly values consumption of a good now rather than delaying this into the future, we say that she highly *discounts* future consumption.

That is, for the myopic vampire, a pint of blood today is much more satisfying than a pint of blood in the future, other things being equal. In general, people with a particularly high preference for current consumption are much more susceptible to addiction, as they steeply discount the future costs of current consumption. For example, if one potential future cost of smoking crack cocaine now is a $5,000 fine, the myopic consumer would only value this cost at, say, $3,000—because of her preference for the present, the future costs and benefits are heavily discounted. Compare this to a less myopic crack user, who may value this $5,000 fine in the future at $4,500. If these two users both value the present consumption of crack at a total value of $4,000, the first would light up while the second would abstain. For her, the cost of this consumption is higher than its benefit. Similarly, if the cost of killing a human now is the future possibility of being discovered and killed by angry villagers, the myopic vampire may exhibit a level of disregard for these consequences if she values the present highly enough, while the more patient vampire would tend to be more careful.

It is the interplay between these two forces, as well as several others that are beyond the scope of this chapter, that can determine long-term patterns of addiction. Because each individual may exhibit different rates of depreciation of the stock of addictive capital and preferences for present consumption, a great variety of consumption patterns with respect to addictive goods may emerge. Though the variety in vampire lore can be attributed to the creativity of each author or screenwriter, individual behaviors can be easily explained within the framework of the Becker-Murphy model.

We now return to one of the classic pairs in vampire lore: Lestat and Louis, archetypal vampires in Anne Rice's *Interview with the Vampire*. Lestat is highly addicted to human blood, often taking many souls each night to satiate his hunger. Louis, however, is a thoughtful, almost human vampire who nearly abstains from killing humans to sustain himself. Within our framework of rational addiction, this difference in bloodlust behavior can be attributed to differences in their respective preference for present consumption. Louis seems to exhibit a lower preference for present consumption, mentioning often his desire to delay imbibing human blood until he is fully acclimated to his vampiric form. "I should never have started with human beings," he notes as he tells the tale of his first kill.[10] This, combined with his consumption of only animal blood for much of his undead life, is indicative of his lack of preference for current consumption of human blood. In contrast, Lestat easily succumbs to the immediate desire for human blood, relishing the opportunity to overpower a victim to excess.

THE THINKING DEAD

While bloodlust may seem to be the manifestation of an animalistic desire for blood, it can be easily explained in the context of rational addiction. The Becker-Murphy model equips us to understand the variety of bloodlust behaviors in vampire lore by considering the factors of addiction, including the stock of addictive capital, preference for current consumption, and instantaneous changes in life circumstances. Where the applicability of this model truly excels, however, is in its ability to show that addicts can and do respond to changes in prices—including psychological and nonmonetary prices—in a rational manner. While this conclusion has been relatively controversial with regard to human addiction, it can be especially useful in an analysis of vampiric bloodlust. The vampire can be seen as an actor responding to life and economic changes in a rational manner.

Chapter Twenty-Two

Between Gods and Monsters

Reason, Instinct, and the Artificial Vampire

Daniel Farhat

What determines how often vampires feed and where they go to hunt? When will a vampire "turn" a human and when will he allow his victim to perish? What affects how much time and energy humans invest in defensive (garlic and holy water) and offensive (stakes) anti-vampire equipment? When do humans flee from vampires and when do they stay and fight?

Scientists interested in answering these questions would typically rely on the scientific method to guide their research. This practice involves building a *model* of the human-vampire ecosystem. Models are abstract representations of reality; they contain only a few necessary details about the way a researcher believes things may work. Once a model is constructed, scientists derive implications and predictions from their model and then test these with data. If the data suggests their model is reasonable, the scientists can argue that they have uncovered an important truth or useful insight. But what sort of model is suitable for the "science of vampires"? Economics studies how people allocate limited resources among alternative uses. Ecology studies how different species interact within their environment. If we want to find a model that can help us understand the decisions made by both humans and vampires as they intermingle, these disciplines seem the best place to start.

When we dig into ecologic and economic model making, however, we don't find quite what we're looking for. Ecological models are often used to study beings that rely entirely on instinct to guide their choices ("animals"). If organisms simply respond to their surroundings according to natural urges, then the state of their population as a whole can be described using environmental factors and biological attributes (like the amount of food available in the local area, the likelihood of death from a predator attack, and the species

223

reproduction rate). Economic models, on the other hand, are used to study creatures that rely on perfect reason and plentiful information to make decisions ("gods"). The benefits and costs of each choice are meticulously evaluated so that the absolute best actions can be taken. Both humans and vampires fall somewhere between these two extremes (see figure 22.1).

Humans appear to be evolving away from "animals" toward "gods" as their cognitive abilities develop. Because of this, economic models may be appropriate for some types of human activity, and if we continue on this path they will become even more suitable in the future. However, we're not entirely there yet. Human decisions tend to be ill-planned, guided by fear or hate, or based on incorrect or incomplete information. We see this often when we observe how humans interact with vampires in books, movies, and TV shows. Vampires are not following the same path to godliness as humans. In lore and popular culture, vampires are often portrayed as being *more* intelligent than humans (likely due to their unnaturally long lives) but also as slaves to their urges: the uncontrollable desire to feed. We call such creatures "monsters"; they are strategic and forward thinking, yet primal and compulsive.

If humans and vampires are semi-instinctual, semi-rational beings, then we might not get a good representation if we use a basic ecological model or a standard economic model to study their choices. So what should be done? Advances in computer science have given scientists a promising new modeling tool: computer simulation. Since the 1990s, some researchers have fabricated entire artificial societies composed of synthetic individuals in an at-

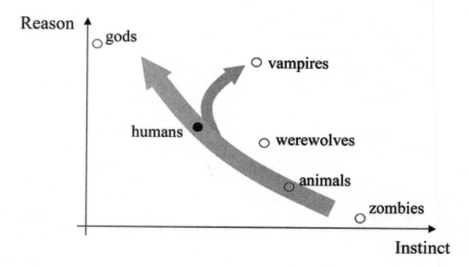

Figure 22.1.   Reason versus Instinct in Decision Making

tempt to understand real social activity. This method, known as *agent-based modeling*, involves populating a virtual environment with interacting autonomous agents, each with their own information and objectives to achieve. As the synthetic individuals interact, digital communities form and patterns start to emerge, both for the population as a whole and for the environment.[1]

Agent-based simulation models have much to offer. The researcher is free to choose the behaviors of the synthetic agents and the makeup of the artificial environment with little restriction. They can include elements from standard ecologic and economic models but can also incorporate aspects of the real world that don't easily fit into these standard frameworks. For example, the agents in these models can each be unique (or *heterogeneous*); the computer can easily record and monitor differences among thousands of entities. Also, these models generally showcase *complexity*: many small pieces come together in intricate ways to make up the whole. As a result, the patterns that emerge from agent-based models tend to be rich and surprising. Further, since the structure of the environment, the nature of the agents, and the *algorithm* (a repeating sequence of events) guiding all activity in the simulation are developed by the researcher, these models provide more detailed and complete descriptions of *how* discovered patterns come to be.[2] Agent-based modeling seems ideal for merging together untamed urges with semi-economic decision making. In fact, we actually get more than we bargain for: realism, complexity, and understanding.

This chapter focuses on *artificial vampirism*. What can we learn from building synthetic communities comprised of semi-rational artificial humans and vampires? What patterns do these clashing communities generate? Further, what do these patterns *mean*? In the discussion below, I briefly summarize and compare the ecological, economic, and simulation approaches to understanding vampire communities. To illustrate the benefits of simulating artificial human-vampire ecosystems, I actually build an agent-based model with vampirism. I draw connections between the patterns produced by these synthetic communities and how some humans in the real world interact with each other, with intriguing results.

BIOLOGICAL, ECONOMIC, AND COMPUTATIONAL MODELS OF VAMPIRES (AND HUMANS)

To model how the population sizes of two species change over time, an ecologist may choose to use a set of mathematical equations. One of the simplest examples of these types of models, known as a *predator-prey model*, seems most appropriate for the study of vampires. Predator-prey models were initially developed in the 1920s and consist of only two equations: one describes the growth rate of a prey population while the other describes the growth rate of a predator population. How quickly the prey population increases depends negatively on the number of predators around (too many wolves in the forest drives down the rabbit population, for example). The growth rate of the predator population depends positively on the amount of prey (rabbits in large supply will support a greater number of wolves).[3] A set of environmental parameters and biological characteristics, such as the carrying capacity of the landscape and the birthrate of prey, appears in the equations and dramatically influences how each population grows (see figure 22.2a, b, and c for examples).

Figure 22.2a shows a stable relationship between the two populations appearing after an initial transition period. When it comes to vampires, we might think of this as a sort of orderly coexistence with humans (as seen in *Vampire Chronicles*, the *Twilight* saga, and *The Vampire Diaries*, for example). Figure 22.2b shows large periodic fluctuations in numbers. We might think of these as extensive "awakenings" or "revelations" of the vampire community that produce fluctuations in population sizes through large-scale conflict (with different points in these cycles apparent in *Buffy the Vampire Slayer*, especially seasons 1 and 7; *True Blood*, both the *Underworld* and *Blade* series; and more recently in the film *Abraham Lincoln: Vampire Hunter*). Figure 22.2c shows the predator population overexploiting its resources then starving to extinction (a central theme in the film *Daybreakers*).[4] Is this why we don't come across vampires today: did their greed drive them to annihilation?

Although it is possible to use such models to describe the symbiotic predator-prey relationship between humans and vampires, a social scientist might hesitate to do so. The role that the environmental parameters play is too strong; there is little scope for heightened awareness and independent choice. Humans and vampires differ from animals in that they contemplate their circumstances and exert some control over their actions. Wolves, for example, rarely collect data on the size of the rabbit population and then voluntarily cut back on their consumption when stocks are low. Humans, however, do monitor their resources and plan for the future; vampires may, as well.

Economists prefer to use models where agents are fully aware of their constraints and make decisions optimally. The best choice available is always selected. Several restrictive assumptions are built into these models, either to ensure a logical outcome or for convenience in deducing the model's implications. For example, it is often assumed that agents have access to large amounts of information about their environment, much more than the average person would have in reality. This guarantees that agents can fully identify all of their available options, without which decision problems become much harder (if not impossible) to solve. It is assumed that agents can perform vastly complex computations costlessly. This allows economists to

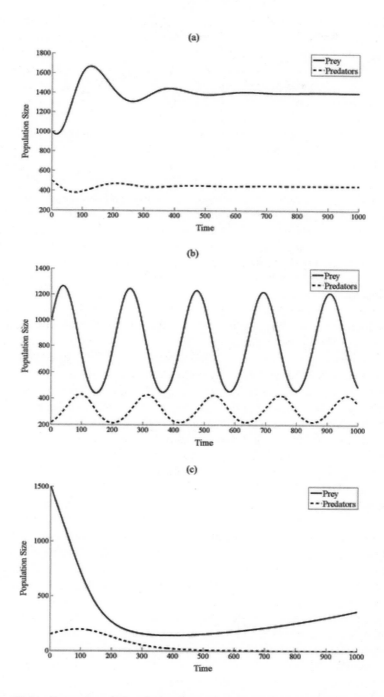

Figure 22.2.   Examples of Population Dynamics from a Predator-Prey Model

model precise choice problems mathematically. It is often assumed that all agents are identical in nature (or *homogeneous*). Economists can then reduce the amount of time they spend calculating solutions by focusing on the decisions made by a single individual (known as a *representative agent*) to understand the choices made by the community as a whole. Some economic models even assume that agents live forever, a reasonable assumption if the agents under study are vampires, but less so for the agents that most economic models are designed for: nondurable humans. Assuming agents are immortal, however, allows economists to use special mathematical tools to solve their models quickly.

In other words, economic models are designed to capture the decisions of a particular type of individual: rational, calculating, all-knowing, and immortal . . . namely, "gods" (to avoid religious connotations, economists prefer the term *homo economicus*). While the assumptions that economists make seem unrealistic, fairly accurate predictions can be derived from these sorts of models provided real people are sufficiently reasonable and informed. In our current state of evolution, economic models function fairly well in some settings. If our mental faculties continue to evolve, they will capture our behavior even better.

Economists have relied on models like these in past studies of vampires. For example, Hartl and Mehlmann (1982) and Hartl, Mehlmann, and Novak (1992) build models where vampires need to decide how to optimally use their human resources (literally, the optimal rate of blood sucking).[5] Periodic fluctuations in vampire activity (or *cycles of fear*) are produced by these models under certain conditions. Dennis Snower (1982), on the other hand, chooses to advise humans on the optimal destruction of vampires.[6] He constructs a model where humans have to split their time between hunting vampires and economic production. It can be shown that completely eliminating the vampire threat is too costly, and thus not optimal.

Using a standard economic model for the human-vampire ecosystem can draw criticism. First, it seems that "rationality" or "reasonableness" should be off the table once vampires arrive on the scene. Human choices are often influenced by fear, prejudice, vengeance, or righteousness. Substantial investments in the destruction of vampires as seen in *True Blood* (as fear drives the townsfolk to arm preemptively and the Light of Day Institute grows in influence), *Bram Stoker's Dracula* (as Lucy's suitors seek revenge for her demise), and *Van Helsing* (as the Vatican sends Van Helsing to destroy Dracula out of obligation to the Valerious family) are examples. Meanwhile, vampire decisions are shaped by a powerful need to feed. *Dracula*, the *Vampire Chronicles*, the *Twilight* saga, *Buffy the Vampire Slayer*, *True Blood*, *The Vampire Diaries*, the *Underworld* and *Blade* series, and *Cirque du Freak: The Saga of Darren Shan* all portray vampires as highly strategic and insightful people who nevertheless struggle to control their appetites and resist their urges. This "dieting narrative," as described by Sandra Tomc (1997), is often motivated by moral (staying pure), political (staying hidden), and emotional (for love's sake) factors.[7] In many cases, the dieting vampires break down and fill their plates at the human buffet regardless of whether they really want to or not.

One approach used among some economists to account for these sorts of limitations is to evaluate the biological and psychological makeup of decision makers and then refine standard economic models accordingly. This is an objective in the blossoming field of *behavioral economics*.[8] Typically, the refinements made to standard models are based on findings from field experiments or lab experiments. These can be collected from the human community relatively easily; however, it would be troublesome (not to mention incredibly dangerous) to acquire these from the vampire community.

A second criticism of using standard economic models to study vampirism has to do with homogeneity and the use of representative agents. Any model that assumes all agents are identical overlooks the personal characteristics of individuals and the one-to-one interactions that define relationships, both of which can affect decision making. For example, a thirsty vampire will not necessarily partake of the human nearest at hand because he or she is a love interest,[9] friend, or caretaker and the vampire feels this relationship will be damaged during the feeding process.[10] Alternatively, a nearby victim may be a powerful enemy and the vampire may think the chance of a successful kill is low. In the human community, a vampire hunter's willingness to vanquish often depends on whether he or she has romantic, friendly, or adversarial affiliations with particular vampires.[11] Hunters may also be selective in choosing their targets based on their enemies' traits (either going after vampire "bosses" to cut the organization off at the top or eradicating small-fry vampires first to weaken the organization's base). Models where all humans are identical, and one vampire is the same as any other, do not capture such things and may not accurately predict the behavior of the community at large as a result.

Agent-based simulation models are capable of more realism than we might get from traditional ecological and economic models. In these models, synthetic individuals are constructed. Each agent has his or her own personal characteristics, histories, and relationships with others. These are recorded and used later to influence decisions. Individual agents are allowed to interact with each other according to "rules" chosen by the researcher; these rules can be quite simple or quite sophisticated depending on the researcher's interests. The researcher also builds the virtual environment (where agents interact) and can select its features as well. In other words, this modeling approach allows us to create artificial vampires and humans who are neither perfectly rational "gods" nor completely instinctual "animals," but something in between. We can select features consistent with vampire lore to incorporate into these models as we see fit. We can then watch these artificial agents and see not only *how* they form communities but also how these communities co-evolve over time (with surprising results). To illustrate all that an agent-based model of vampirism has to offer, why not just build one?

VAMPIRISM AND COMMUNITY SAFETY: A SIMPLE MODEL

For this exercise, let's focus on a single aspect of the human-vampire rela-tionship: defense against the vampire scourge. The model will attempt to identify how vampire attacks affect investment into local safety measures and what this might mean for the community at large. Imagine that there exists a large village that is subdivided into small districts or "lots." Some lots are better rated in terms of security than others (as measured by how well-lit the area is, how many private security guards are on patrol, etc.). As you would expect, lots with more safety features are more expensive to live in. We can construct a "virtual village" that looks exactly like this: a simple geometric space that is subdivided into lots, with each lot being assigned a numerical safety rating and corresponding rental cost. We need only populate this village with artificial humans and vampires, select the characteristics and behavioral rules that each type of agent follows, and settle on the sequence of events guiding activities within the virtual village to complete the model.

For agent characteristics, let's keep it simple. Suppose that each human has a different income level that is randomly assigned to them. Suppose each vampire has a different hunting skill level (also randomly assigned). We can scatter a large initial population of humans across the village along with a small fixed population of vampires. Each agent then has only two character-istics: a budget (for humans) or killing ability (for vampires) and a location in the village. These differ from agent to agent.

For the model algorithm and agent behaviors, the following suffices:

1. Daytime. Each human measures the "desirability" of each lot in their immediate vicinity by looking at those lots' safety ratings. If a vam-pire-related homicide has ever occurred in a lot, the human adjusts the desirability of that lot by planning to spend her excess income on improving its safety level. Humans move to the most desirable lot that they can afford and any planned investments into safety improvements are performed. This step captures settlement patterns of the human population: finding desirable areas nearby, moving to them, and in-vesting in security if a suspicious murder has occurred in their new home.

2. Nighttime. Each vampire measures the "expected catch" they can get in each lot in their immediate vicinity. This depends on the lot's safety

rating and how many people live there. Vampires move to the lot with the highest expected catch and attempt to hunt. Their success depends on how well they overcome the lot's defenses (determined by the lot's safety rating) and their abilities (determined by their private hunting skill level). This step captures vampire feeding behavior: find a rich hunting ground and attempt to procure a good meal.

3. Dawn. Some humans reproduce and others die from natural causes. The safety ratings in each lot are updated: each successful vampire kill reduces the lot's safety rating, and a high population of survivors in the lot raises the safety rating while a small population lowers the safety rating (to capture "safety in numbers"). Rental costs adjust to reflect the new safety ratings. The algorithm then repeats at step 1 above.

We can easily add many more bells and whistles, but this is enough to start.[12] The computer program that simulates this virtual world first sets up the environment, then runs the sequence of events over and over again (day . . . night . . . dawn . . . day . . . night . . . dawn . . .).[13] As promised, the agents in our model are only semi-rational. They attempt to use their resources wisely and to improve themselves by evaluating their surroundings, yet they do not do so perfectly; no one can see the whole village and no one calculates how a choice today affects the entire sequence of future choices. Also, each agent is a separate entity. An agent's individual outcome depends on his own characteristics and circumstances.

A few exact details are needed to construct a functioning computer program for this model.[14] Once these are in place, we can see what happens to both populations and the safety levels for each lot in the village as the program runs. When we inspect the results, we can see two particularly interesting trends. First, this model appears to produce urban stratification: "rich" and "poor" areas develop. Second, the presence of vampires leads not only to a reduction in the total size of the human population, but also to an increase in the dispersion of the population across the village—people tend to spread out when vampires are present. Let's look at each of these in turn.

To show the division of urban space, the safety levels (and thus rental prices) in the simulated village are plotted for day zero and day five hundred in figure 22.3a and b. Light areas indicate high security and expensive rent, while dark areas indicate low security and cheap rent. The human population is represented in the figure by man-shaped markers. At day zero, the high-safety and low-safety areas are evenly distributed across the village, as is the human population. By day five hundred, a distinct clump of unsafe neighborhoods—a "ghetto"—has appeared. As agents attempt to move to high-safety areas in the hopes that local defenses will protect them from vampires, the less-safe neighborhoods are left to deteriorate. Rents are low in this emerging

(a)
Day 0 (set-up)

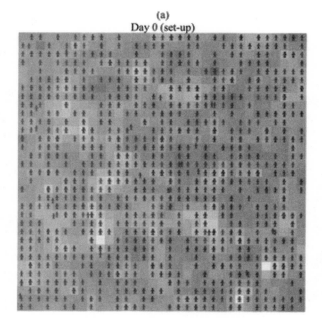

(b)
Day 500

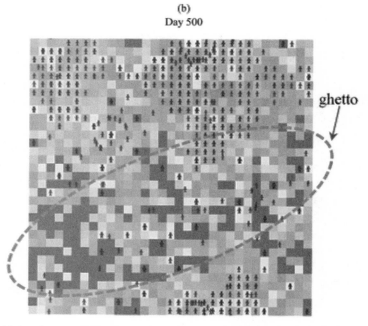

ghetto

Figure 22.3.   Simulated Safety Levels and Location Choices for the Virtual Village with Vampires, Day 0 (set-up). Dark areas indicate low safety ratings; light areas indicate high safety ratings.

ghetto, which caters to the relatively poorer agents, and the only anti-vampire strategy there is "scarcity": the ghetto population's best hope is to remain scattered enough so as not to attract much interest from vampires.

In the areas where lot safety improves (either from defense investment or from "safety in numbers" effects), rents start to rise. Richer agents are attracted to these areas, resulting in the appearance of high-class and middle-class neighborhoods. For the population living in affluence, all may not be well. Lots with high safety ratings are not necessarily "safe" since a large number of humans densely packed in a small area may entice a vampire attack despite a high level of security. Evidence of exactly this appears when we look at vampire attacks in books, films, and television. Victims are often upper- and middle-class citizens who live in what are thought to be relatively nice neighborhoods (including both Lucy and Mina in *Bram Stoker's Dracula*, Buffy and friends in *Buffy the Vampire Slayer*, and Elena in *The Vampire Diaries*). Vampires have even been known to adopt aristocratic personas to increase their chances of a good meal in upper-class society (the most well-known example being Lestat in *The Vampire Chronicles*).

To evaluate the impact that vampires have on the number of humans and the dispersion of humans across the village, we can look at the village census in simulations with and without vampires (see figure 22.4a and b). With no vampires, the human population perpetually grows, as does the average number of people in each populated lot. In a village plagued by vampires, the size of the human population is lower (which is expected since vampires are killing people) yet still manages to perpetually grow. The average number of people in each inhabited lot, however, behaves strangely. Kills made by vampires initially force the population to band together (days 50–200). These same kills encourage people to invest in security, which pushes up rental prices. Income constraints then take effect, and some people are forced to move to cheaper lots nearby, leading to dispersion. In the end, humans tend to be more tightly clustered if there are no vampires present and more evenly spread out if vampires are on the scene.[15] It is not easy, however, to see this trend occurring in vampire media (as we would have to compare the size of towns in vampire movies to those in nonvampire movies).

With insight into how vampires affect security, property values, and population density in the virtual village, we can begin to think about effective urban policies for the human community. One program that immediately comes to mind is *public defense*. If the village decided to impose a small income tax on each inhabitant and then spend the revenue on improving security in all lots evenly (by establishing a village police department, for example), would the outcomes change any? Figure 22.5a, b, c, and d show what happens to the artificial human-vampire ecosystem when this policy is in place.[16] A ghetto still emerges after five hundred days (see figure 22.5a), but the security levels there seem a bit higher than they were with no public

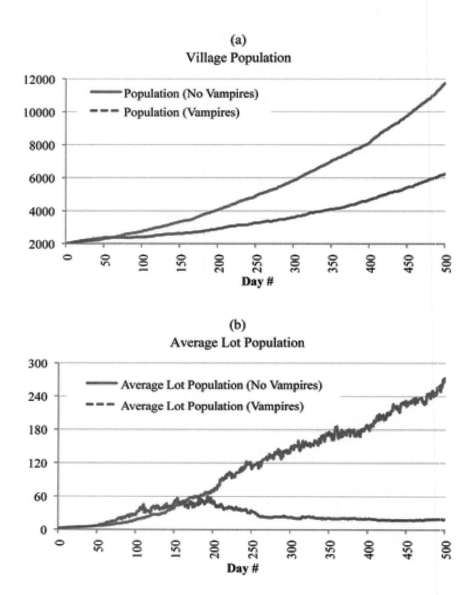

Figure 22.4.   Simulated Population Dynamics for the Virtual Village with and without Vampires.

defense (see figure 22.3b). Figure 22.5b, which shows the total population size with public defense and without (from figure 22.4a), indicates a small yet positive improvement in human numbers. Interestingly, figure 22.5c shows that the distribution of humans across the village is much more even

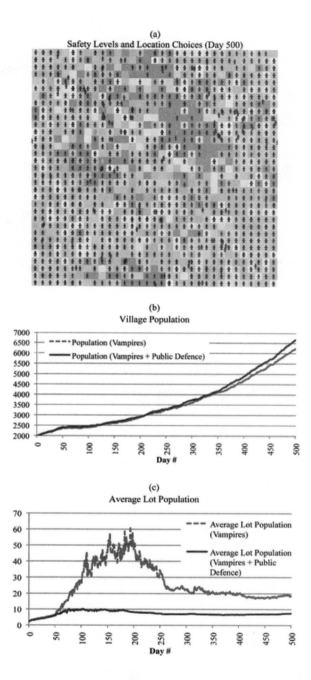

Figure 22.5. Simulated Population Dynamics for the Virtual Village with Vampires and Public Defense, Safety Levels and Location Choices (Day 500).

with public defense than without (compared to figure 22.4b). A village-sponsored public-safety program has reduced the incentive to seek safety in numbers, and local areas have become more suburban!

Although this agent-based model is designed to provide insights into how human and vampire communities might evolve together over time, it can also be used to understand how different groups within human communities interact and develop. For example, human criminals behave quite similarly to vampires: they use violence to extract their livelihood from victims. It is no surprise that vampire imagery has made its way into legal documentation in reference to certain types of illicit activity (illustrated by Sutherland [2006] in reference to drug dealers).[17] If we treat the "vampires" in the earlier agent-based model as a metaphor for the criminal element in society, we can draw broader conclusions about how real urban landscapes evolve. As illicit activity occurs, law-abiding citizens respond by either increasing investment into security (alarm systems, gates, etc.) or by moving to safer neighborhoods. These actions impact the urban landscape in a way that produces socioeconomic segmentation. The rich define secure urban spaces in the city while the poor are sequestered in dilapidated neighborhoods. Do we not see the same trends in New York or Los Angeles? Also, as public initiatives in defense (police and other armed forces) develop, a wider sprawl in settlement patterns appears (i.e., suburbanization). Do we not see this also? Again, these patterns are produced by the actions of semi-instinctual, semi-rational, unique individuals attempting to make economic decisions as best they can; perhaps these sorts of agents better represent the city dwellers of today.

BETWEEN GODS AND MONSTERS

Ecological models seem better suited to animals, whose instincts and environment determine their survival. Standard economic models seem better suited to gods, whose perfectly rational choices determine their fates. Neither seems appropriate for vampires or the humans who deal with them. With simulation approaches like agent-based modeling, however, we can fabricate synthetic individuals whose behaviors lie somewhere between totally instinctual and fully rational. By placing artificial vampires and humans together in a virtual environment inspired directly by vampire mythology, we can watch and learn from their developing communities. These types of models have much to offer in the "science of vampires."

Evolution might be driving mankind away from beasts, but we've got some way to go before we become the *homo economicus* portrayed in standard economic models. Perhaps simulation can help us better understand humanity's decisions in the meantime. Whether we make it all the way to godliness, however, is up for debate. In many instances, humans do exhibit vampiric qualities, and using vampires as metaphors in our models might be a useful way to study human choices. If this keeps up, one has to ask: are we really on our way to becoming gods, or are we following the path of monsters?

Chapter Twenty-Three

Killing Time

Dracula *and Social Discoordination*

Hollis Robbins[1]

In Bram Stoker's *Dracula* (1897), Count Dracula first appears as an old man holding an antique silver lamp, standing at the door to a crumbling castle filled with moth-eaten furniture and ancient gold coins. He is fascinated by modern life, so much so that he reads English law books and up-to-date Bradshaw railroad guides and is planning a move to London.[2] But he is also a vampire, a supernatural creature who appears in mist and moonlight, who slips through cracks, and who can turn himself into a bat, a wolf, and fog. Dracula also has the power to put humans in a mental fog so that they lose track of the date and time. "He cannot think of time yet," the wife of Dracula's first victim laments, nursing him to health after a close escape from the vampire's lair. "At first he mixes up not only the month, but the year."[3]

Scholars have long read the fictional Count Dracula as embodying a real, debilitating contemporary threat to the moral and cultural health of the West (specifically Victorian England): perverse sexuality, feminism, racial degeneration, colonialism, and monopoly capitalism.[4] This essay examines the vampire's threat to *economic* health, specifically, his disruption of new civil timekeeping standards and the danger this poses for modern commerce.[5] Britain's economic prosperity in the nineteenth century was largely dependent on the adoption of international standards such as Greenwich Mean Time and the universal day, which ensured smooth coordination for trade, legal transactions, railroad travel, and mail delivery. Dracula, whose powers are governed by the sun and the moon rather than clocks and calendars, works to destabilize social coordination. His objective is not only literally to "fatten on the blood of the living,"[6] but also more broadly to suck the lifeblood of a thriving commercial economy at the dawn of a global age. Under

Dracula's spell, humans forget the time, becoming listless, unproductive, and indifferent to social convention. At heart, the fundamental battle in Stoker's *Dracula* is a death struggle between standard time as an institutional basis for world markets and planetary time governing a primitive, superstitious existence.

DRACULA IN HISTORICAL CONTEXT

The story of *Dracula*, most readers will recall, is about an old-world vampire, Count Dracula, who desires to live in England. "I long to go through the crowded streets of your mighty London, to be in the midst of the whirl and rush of humanity, to share its life, its change, its death, and all that makes it what it is,"[7] he explains to Jonathan Harker, a young solicitor sent by his British firm to Castle Dracula in Transylvania to finalize the purchase of residential property in London. But it must be an old home, the count tells Jonathan: "to live in a new house would kill me."[8] He has acquired books and directories on customs, law, shipping, and transportation routes that he exploits to transport boxes of his native soil (in which he must sleep every night) to England. Dracula and his crates arrive at the Yorkshire port of Whitby, where he wreaks havoc across the countryside, killing animals and humans on his journey to London. He infects a beautiful young woman who becomes a vampire. A group of young, modern professionals—a lawyer, two doctors, a gentleman, a stenographer, and a rich American—organizes themselves to kill the female vampire and chase Dracula out of England and back to his castle, where they slay him in his coffin at sunset.

Stoker's novel is composed of a series of dated journal entries, letters, captains' logs, newspaper articles, and other records, all in strict chronological order.[9] On his journey to Transylvania, Jonathan Harker writes to his fiancée Mina about his travels and Castle Dracula. Mina writes to her girlhood friend, the beautiful Lucy Westenra, about Jonathan. Lucy writes to Mina about her three beaux: Arthur Holmwood, a young aristocrat; Quincey Morris, a Texan; and Dr. John Seward, head of a lunatic asylum. The captain of the Russian ship *Demeter*, laden with boxes of Transylvanian soil, writes in his log of fearful happenings at night. Newspapers in England chronicle a ship crashing ashore, wolf sightings, and a series of midnight murders. Mina writes in her diary about Lucy's sleepwalking. Seward writes to his old professor, Abraham Van Helsing, in Amsterdam, for help identifying strange bite marks on Lucy's neck. And so on.

To follow Stoker's tale, readers need a basic understanding of date- and timekeeping systems, particularly standard time (based on Greenwich Mean Time) and the Gregorian calendar, the standard temporal reference framework of the modern world.[10] Standard time concepts such as units of time (seconds, minutes, hours), along with time reckoning and dating frameworks (clocks and calendars), are now so widely accepted that they seem inevitable, but it was not always so. The universal authority of these systems is essential to the plot of *Dracula*, which alternates between modern time specificity and the fog of temporal uncertainty that surrounds Count Dracula.

Clearly, institutional time and date agreement is essential to legal and commercial transactions as well as for certain aspects of social intercourse. A simple agreement as to when the day begins allows events to be assigned to a particular date without confusion. For some cultures, the new day begins at sunset; for others, dawn; for others, midnight. The adoption of universal rules for marking and measuring time is just one example of the need for agreed-upon standards to coordinate behavior—a need that became increasingly relevant in the nineteenth century. Expanding trade and commerce encouraged the adoption of national standards for weights, measures, typewriter keyboards, railway track gauges, and traffic lights, for example.

The economic function of standards is to coordinate behavior in ways that maximize benefits for all parties and minimize loss from mismatched expectations. In the language of game theory, a standard is a solution to a *coordination game*. One simple example of a coordination game is the choice of which side of the road to drive on. In principle, the choice of left or right doesn't matter. What matters crucially is that everyone in a given region makes the same choice; if they do not, wrecks will occur.

There are cases, however, where some standards are considered to be objectively better than others. The metric system is often deemed superior to the English system of weights and measures because it's easier to learn. A society that has adopted an inferior system (perhaps by historical accident or because the standard had once been superior) may oppose calls to switch to a better system. Standard switching nearly always generates confusion, transition costs, and psychological resistance.

Arguably, that was precisely the situation with respect to time conventions in the nineteenth century. In 1897, when *Dracula* first appeared, the notion of a standard time was still very new in Britain. For most of history, people kept local time, marked by sundials and tolled by church bells. But the advent of modern commerce made local time an inferior standard, which gradually gave way to superior—that is, more universal—standards that allowed coordination over greater distances. After the development of the mechanical clock in the thirteenth and fourteenth centuries, clock towers were introduced in cities around Europe to standardize the workday and regulate sessions of municipal courts, assemblies, and university lectures; hourglasses soon joined smaller mechanical clocks in schools and homes.[11] Minute hands became widely used in the eighteenth century. The expansion of postal routes and railway lines necessitated national (and soon international) time standards and timetables. Railway companies, recognizing the need for a standard time, as networks of tracks and lines were shared by dozens of railway companies with their own schedules, adopted an industry standard, Railway Time, in 1840. Greenwich Mean Time (based on time measured in the Greenwich Observatory, situated on the Greenwich meridian, zero degrees longitude) replaced Railway Time for British railways in 1847. In 1859, Big Ben was installed in London, tolling Greenwich time and encouraging watches to be set to national time. In 1880, Greenwich Mean Time became legal time in Britain. In 1884 the International Meridian Conference in Washington, D.C., recommended that all countries adopt Universal Time (with Greenwich as prime meridian) and the universal twenty-four-hour day, to begin at midnight. Of particular relevance to Dracula's story, two of the delegations voting "no" to this resolution were Austria-Hungary and Turkey, on either side of Transylvania, both of which backed a resolution starting the day at noon.[12]

The calendar too was not fully standard across Europe in Bram Stoker's lifetime. The Gregorian calendar had been in use by Roman Catholic countries in Western Europe since the sixteenth century, while the Eastern Orthodox regions of Eastern Europe, including the regions surrounding Transylvania, still followed the Julian calendar. Instituted by Julius Caesar in 45 BCE, the Julian calendar, adopted as the basis of the official church calendar at the Council of Nicaea in 325, had slowly drifted away from its biblical, seasonal, and astronomical footings. In 725, the English monk Bede observed in his treatise "The Reckoning of Time" (*De temporum ratione*) that the vernal equinox (a crucial variable for fixing the date of Easter) was becoming irreconcilable with the calendar. By the fifteenth century, the vernal equinox had drifted eleven days, falling on March 10 instead of March 21. In 1583 Pope Gregory XIII authorized a new calendar that would fix the vernal equinox on March 21. The Gregorian calendar was adopted almost immediately in Italy, Portugal, Spain, Poland, Luxembourg, France, Belgium, Austria, Catholic Germany, Catholic Switzerland, and Catholic Holland. Hungary followed in 1587.

The adoption of the Gregorian calendar by Protestant nations took more than a century. Elizabethan England, newly split from the Catholic Church, was initially wary; Protestant Germany rejected it out of hand. "We do not recognize this Lycurgus (or rather Draco, whose laws were said to be written in blood)," wrote James Heerbrand, a professor of theology at Tübingen in 1584; "we do not recognize this legislator, this calendar-maker, just as we do not hear the shepherd of the flock of the Lord, but a howling wolf."[13] A serious concern for adoption of the reformed calendar was the loss of ten days (which would grow to eleven by 1700, when Germany, Denmark, and Switzerland made the transition).[14] Merchants, tradesmen, astronomers, and scientists in England repeatedly advocated for unification of the calendar with the Continent, but internal political and theological disputes delayed change. Gradually, economic and scientific interests eclipsed theological concerns.[15] Finally, in 1752, Great Britain and her colonies (including America) adopted the "new style" calendar with a mandate that Wednesday, September 2, would be followed by Thursday, September 14, and that the new year would begin on January 1.[16]

Clearly, calendar agreement across Europe would facilitate trade and communication among nations via shared terms and a standard temporal framework. But countries and regions following the Eastern Orthodox Church, including Romania, did not adopt the new calendar until 1918.[17] At the time Stoker was writing *Dracula*, Transylvania, on the border of Romania and Hungary, had been caught between two competing calendars for centuries.

DRACULA AND TIME/DATE CONFUSION

Stoker's novel depicts the new expectations for promptness and efficiency that were established by unified time standards and a common calendar in Britain and most of Western Europe but not the East. Jonathan Harker's first journal entry—the opening lines of *Dracula*—reads: "Left Munich at 8.35 p.m. on 1st May, arriving in Vienna early next morning; should have arrived at 6.46 but train was an hour late."[18] The next day, entering the region of Transylvania, Harker notes: "After rushing to the station at 7:30 I had to sit in the carriage for more than an hour before we began to move. It seems to me that the further East you go the more unpunctual are the trains."[19] Indeed, Transylvania was not party to British time protocols.

Stoker's novel also depicts the region's calendar confusion. In Jonathan Harker's second diary entry, an old woman accosts him on his way to Castle Dracula to ask, hysterically, "Do you know what day it is?" Harker replies that it is the fourth of May.

> "Oh yes! I know that, I know that! But do you know what day it is?" On my saying that I did not understand, she went on:
> "It is the eve of St. George's Day. Do you not know that tonight, when the clock strikes midnight, all the evil things in the world will have full sway? Do you know where you are going, and what you are going to?"[20]

The misunderstanding here is significant: The feast of St. George is celebrated on April 23 under both the Julian and Gregorian calendars. The old woman's claim that it is St. George's Day indicates that she is using the Julian calendar: April 23 is exactly eleven days behind May 4.

Recent scholarship suggests that dating discrepancies may have provoked popular belief in the undead throughout Eastern Europe. Consider that a person who died on April 1 and was buried on April 3 under the Julian

calendar could be remembered strolling about by a Gregorian calendar fol-
lower on, say, April 7 (March 28 under the Julian calendar). Citing Dom
Augustin Calmet, author of a 1746 French study of Eastern European vampire infestations, Gabriel Ronay writes that in Catholic Poland, "the first
reports of un-dead people returning from the grave came from the eastern
territories taken from Orthodox Muscovy. . . . In the occupied lands conquer-
ing Catholicism and crusading Orthodoxy found themselves in enforced
physical contact for the first time," and rumors of "dead men who, while
already in their graves, are lustful" soon followed.[21] The majority of vampire
sightings were in border areas, where both the Julian and Gregorian calendars were in use. While Dracula's origins are left vague in Stoker's novel, it
is clear that he emerges at a time and in a place (late medieval Transylvania)
where there was little agreement about the date and time. Stoker had taken
careful notes on the brutal history of Moldavia, Wallachia, and Transylvania,
particularly the centuries of bloody battles over religion and rule, and com-
prehended the mischief of calendar conflict.[22]

Count Dracula has a complex relationship with modern calendar and
timekeeping systems. In part, he is indifferent to them: he is immortal and
unconcerned with his age or eventual death. His activities are regulated by
celestial cycles rather than by social convention. Yet in his castle, after
keeping Jonathan Harker up all night talking of business, Dracula knows to
seek pardon for his unorthodox hours when he disappears at sunrise. Dracula
appreciates the utility of shipping and railway schedules and uses these networks to transport his soil overseas without mishap, but he creates uncertainty for his own advantage. Under Dracula's influence, Jonathan forgets to
wind his watch. Dracula compels Jonathan to postdate letters, puzzling his
correspondents before Dracula sets sail for England, leaving the lawyer im-
prisoned in the castle. In these respects, Dracula exploits modern time conventions to manipulate and control humans. For four months, Jonathan never
notes the time of day in his journal until he escapes and is nursed to health by
Mina. He has no sense of modern time, though he observes the sun's movements and keeps a running chronology of passing days.

Dracula's presence on the sea journey to England likewise provokes temporal bewilderment. The captain of the Russian ship *Demeter*, transporting
Dracula and fifty boxes of Transylvanian soil to England, uncharacteristical-
ly falters in timekeeping. The captain notes the exact time in his log on July
11 ("Under way at 4 p.m.") and July 16 ("Took larboard watch eight bells
last night"), but for the rest of the trip (through his death soon after August 4)
he only mentions natural time:

> 28 July.—Four days in hell, knocking about in a sort of maelstrom, and the
> wind a tempest. No sleep for any one. Men all worn out. Hardly know how to
> set a watch, since no one fit to go on. . . .

2 August, midnight.—Woke up from few minutes sleep by hearing a cry, seemingly outside my port. Could see nothing in fog. Rushed on deck, and ran against mate. Tells me he heard cry and ran, but no sign of man on watch. One more gone. Lord, help us!. . . .

4 August.—Still fog, which the sunrise cannot pierce, I know there is sunrise because I am a sailor, why else I know not. I dared not go below, I dared not leave the helm, so here all night I stayed, and in the dimness of the night I saw it, Him! [23]

Quite deliberately and literally, Dracula brings the fog of time confusion with him to England.

Dracula fully understands, however, that British compliance with standards and laws will ensure that his legal and commercial transactions will be carried out. The unmanned ship, her dead captain lashed to the helm, crashes safely into gravel in the port of Whitby at high tide. A black dog (the vampire, temporarily transformed) leaps off and disappears. But as Dracula clearly anticipated, his cargo is safe: the local officials of the Board of Trade are "most exacting in seeing that every compliance has been made with existing regulations." [24] The Coast Guard, first to board, cannot claim rights of salvage from what seems to be a derelict craft. [25] The boxes of soil are duly sent to a Whitby solicitor named on the manifest, who takes possession and forwards the crates to London.

Dracula's concern with time coordination is also manifested by the vampire's arrival in Whitby, symbolically threatening Britain's first calendar agreement, which, according to the monk Bede, brought civic peace to the nation. Whitby was the site of the first major European calendar conference held in 664 to resolve the problem about the date of Easter in Britain, when two practices of settling the date, Ionan (or Celtic) and Roman (Julian), were both in use. [26] Bede's *Ecclesiastical History of the English People* (731) emphasizes the role of the bishop Wilfrid, who advocated a coordinated worldwide celebration of the Resurrection:

[As is] practiced in Africa, Asia, Egypt, Greece, and all the world, wherever the church of Christ is spread abroad, through several nations and tongues, at one and the same time; except only these and their accomplices in obstinacy, I mean the Picts and the Britons, who foolishly, in these two remote islands of the world, and only in part even of them, oppose all the rest of the universe. [27]

Bede suggests that synchronizing the British celebration of Easter with Rome and the world had unified and coordinated the nation, preventing the tribal bloodshed of earlier eras. [28] A thorough researcher, Stoker knew well Whitby's role in the history of global calendar coordination and the danger that Dracula's arrival here would signify.

THE POWER OF STANDARD TIME

Ultimately, Dracula's natural time constraints become his undoing. A vampire's power wanes with the rising of the sun. Dracula can transform himself from a human-looking figure into an animal or into mist only at midnight, at sunrise, or at sunset exactly. He can pass running water only at the ebb or the flood of the tide. These are natural, not socially coordinated, time rules. Dracula's alienation from social convention becomes a weakness when he is not in his own realm but in England, where his enemies organize a coordinated effort to find and destroy his Transylvanian soil. Dracula must return home to survive.

Dracula's failure to make a permanent home in London suggests that Stoker sees time coordination as key to the nation's social and economic advancement and time confusion as a threat to continued progress. Stoker was not alone in his concern: late Victorian fiction is filled with anxiety about the British race and culture falling into decline.[29] If, as Charles Darwin asserted, man came from apes, then man could slip back into savagery. Thus strict social rules and modern codes of behavior must be followed to prevent decay and degeneracy. Stoker's vampire provokes in his victims unpunctuality and nocturnal behavior: neither one a Victorian virtue. The danger Dracula poses is the danger of market destabilization and social dissolution—a transformation of British modernity into Transylvanian backwardness.

Time notations in *Dracula* indicate whether humans or vampires are in control. When the time is given in natural rather than social terms (sunrise, sunset, moonrise, evening, the sound of the cock crowing), Dracula is growing in power and individual human characters are in danger. When a person looks at his or her watch, notes the hourly time, notes the time of trains or the tolling of bells, or coordinates with others, Dracula's power is waning. The novel signals the death of Lucy Westenra, Dracula's third English victim, by her disregard of timekeeping protocols. Mina grounds her early journal entries in exact time (e.g., "the clock struck six," "the clock has just struck nine"). But after Dracula lands on British soil, Mina notes only noon, night, and sunset. Dr. Seward, whose lunatic asylum is adjacent to Dracula's London residence, generally records clock time scrupulously, but after an inmate, Renfield, falls under Dracula's power, Seward lapses into noon, moonrise, and sunrise, as does Van Helsing. A telegram summoning Dr. Seward to Lucy's bedside is tragically delayed, leaving her unprotected at night. Lucy dies and is transformed into a vampire.

Lucy's friends rally by turning individual memories into calendar events; journals and documents are put into chronological order, enabling a clear assessment of Dracula's activities. Their growing power is indicated by time specificity, such as Mina's note to Van Helsing:

I have this moment, whilst writing, had a wire from Jonathan, saying that he leaves by the 6:25 tonight from Launceston and will be here at 10:18, so that I shall have no fear tonight. Will you, therefore, instead of lunching with us, please come to breakfast at eight o'clock, if this be not too early for you? You can get away, if you are in a hurry, by the 10:30 train, which will bring you to Paddington by 2:35.[30]

The team begins meeting regularly.[31] The paper trail of the consignment of goods (boxes of soil) to various sites in London is followed. All but one is found and purified. Dracula flees back to Transylvania by sea and land, pursued by Van Helsing and his team, as John Seward's diary details:

"When does the next train start for Galatz? [Van Helsing]
"At 6:30 tomorrow morning!" [Mina]
"How on earth do you know?" [Quincey Morris]
"You forget . . . that I am the train fiend." [Mina]
"Wonderful woman . . . Now let us organize." [Van Helsing] "Arthur, go to the train and get the tickets . . . Jonathan, go to the agent of the ship and get from him letters to the agent in Galatz, with authority to search the ship just as it was here. Morris Quincey, you see the Vice-Consul, and get his aid with the fellow in Galatz and all he can do to make our way smooth, so that no times be lost when over the Danube. John will stay with Madam Mina and me, and we shall consult . . . it will not matter when the sun set."[32]

Coordination pays off: knowing the train timetables, the authorizing environment of the transportation network, and the vampire's limitations, the heroes are able to overtake Dracula just in time. Lying powerless in his coffin, he is stabbed in the heart, outside his castle, at sunset.

TIME AND ECONOMIC ORGANIZATION

The Marxist critic Franco Moretti famously reads *Dracula* as representing the danger of monopoly capitalism, a reading that seems unwarranted given Dracula's disruptive effect on commerce and his indifference to government support. Nineteenth-century Britain had shown itself to be an agent of economic growth via its promotion of standard time, a crucial institutional basis for market creation. Sensibly, Dracula does not provoke temporal confusion in his agents—actors in the coordination game of international trade—while transactions that are important to his plans are ongoing. However, key figures in Dracula's purchase of property and transport of goods die after completion of their tasks: the captain of the *Demeter* (arrives dead in Whitby), his legal advisor and estate agent Peter Hawkins (dies suddenly), and Romanian shipping agent Petrof Skinsky (found with his throat torn open). Moretti argues that: "like capital, Dracula is impelled towards a continuous growth, an unlimited expansion of his domain: accumulation is inherent in his nature."[33] But expansion of Dracula's domain would require a certain kind of corporate organization—establishing a network of business associates, for instance—of which Dracula seems incapable beyond the execution of a single transaction. Even the vampires he creates are not partners.[34] Expansion is impossible; accumulation of anything—power, gold—is limited by his inability to put together a reliable management team.

Global timekeeping is universal, communitarian, official, and mechanical. Dracula, governed by natural cycles, can only occasionally be party to this social contract. He will never be modern. Nineteenth-century opponents of standard time argued for the importance of local control and the health benefits of "natural" cycles and against globalized "machine time." Yet Dracula's disruption of clock time is cast as decadent and atavistic rather than pastoral or Romantic. Stoker's novel promotes modern British industriousness broadly by its scrupulous attention to the importance of chronology and time conventions. The Count cannot violate the rules that regulate his behavior; he cannot adapt to the new conventions and standards of the modern age. Wounded and alone in his coffin, his body turns to dust.

Pop Culture Bibliography

To list every movie, TV show, book, video game, role-playing game, or website associated with the undead would be an insurmountable task. We have therefore limited ourselves to those works actually referenced somewhere in this book.

We have listed members of a series together rather than individually, provided that the series has a well-known title (e.g., Anne Rice's *Vampire Chronicles*, Stephenie Meyer's *Twilight* saga). When the series lacks a clear and well-established title, we have listed the works separately. In the case of the (many) book series with more than four volumes, we have limited ourselves to the first three, trusting that you can Google the rest.

All sources unrelated to pop culture, including economics books and articles, are cited in the endnotes to the relevant chapter.

MOVIES

28 Days Later. Directed by Danny Boyle. Twentieth Century Fox Film Corporation, 2002.

30 Days of Night. Directed by David Slade. Sony Pictures, 2007.

Abraham Lincoln: Vampire Hunter. Directed by Timur Bekmambetov. Twentieth Century Fox Film Corporation, 2012.

American Zombie. Directed by Grace Lee. Cinema Libre Studio, 2007.

Bram Stoker's Dracula. Directed by Francis Ford Coppola. Columbia Pictures, 1992.

The *Blade* trilogy:

Blade. Directed by David S. Goyer. New Line Cinema, 1998.

Blade II. Directed by Guillermo del Toro. New Line Cinema, 2002.

Blade Trinity. Directed by David S. Goyer. New Line Cinema, 2004.

City of the Living Dead (*Paura nella città dei morti viventi*). Directed by Lucio Fulci. Medusa Distribuzione, 1980; Motion Picture Marketing, 1983.

Daybreakers. Directed by Michael Spierig and Peter Spierig. Lionsgate, 2009.

Dawn of the Dead. Directed by George A. Romero. United Film Distribution Company, 1978.

Dawn of the Dead. Directed by Zack Snyder. Universal Studios, 2004.

249

Day of the Dead. Directed by Steve Miner. Millennium Films, 2008.

Day of the Dead. Directed by George A. Romero. United Film Distribution Company, 1985.

Diary of the Dead. Directed by George A. Romero. Third Rail Releasing, 2007.

Dracula 2000. Directed by Patrick Lussier. Dimension Films, 2000.

Fido. Directed by Andrew Currie. Lionsgate, 2006.

Ghost. Directed by Jerry Tucker. Paramount Pictures, 1990.

Hillbilly Bob Zombie. Directed by Ray Basham. Basham Productions, 2009.

The Hunger. Directed by Tony Scott. MGM/UA Entertainment Company, 1983.

I Am Legend. Directed by Francis Lawrence. Warner Bros., 2007.

Interview with the Vampire: The Vampire Chronicles. Directed by Neil Jordan. Geffen Pictures and Warner Bros., 1994.

I Walked with a Zombie. Directed by Jacques Tourneur. RKO Radio Pictures, 1943.

Land of the Dead. Directed by George A. Romero. Universal Pictures, 2005.

Near Dark. Directed by Kathryn Bigelow. De Laurentiis Entertainment Group, 1987.

Night of the Living Dead. Directed by George A. Romero. Continental Distributing, 1968.

Nosferatu. Directed by F. W. Murnau. Centraal Bureau voor Ligafilms, 1922; Film Arts Guild, 1929.

The Omega Man. Directed by Boris Sagal. Warner Bros Pictures, 1971.

Pirates of the Caribbean: The Curse of the Black Pearl. Directed by Gore Verbinski. The Walt Disney Company, 2003.

Plague of the Zombies. Directed by John Gilling. Twentieth Century Fox Film Corporation, 1966.

Plan 9 from Outer Space. Directed by Edward D. Wood. Distributors Corporation of America, 1959.

Prince of Darkness. Directed by John Carpenter. Universal Pictures, 1987.

Pulp Fiction. Directed by Quentin Tarantino. Miramax Films, 1994.

The Queen of the Damned. Directed by Michael Rymer. Warner Bros., 2002.

The *Resident Evil* series:

Resident Evil. Directed by Paul W. S. Anderson. Screen Gems and Sony Pictures, 2002.

Resident Evil: Apocalypse. Directed by Alexander Witt. Screen Gems and Sony Pictures, 2004.

Resident Evil: Extinction. Directed by Russell Mulcahy. Screen Gems and Sony Pictures, 2007.

Resident Evil: Afterlife. Directed by Paul W. S. Anderson. Screen Gems and Sony Pictures, 2010.

Resident Evil: Retribution. Directed by Paul W. S. Anderson. Screen Gems and Sony Pictures, 2012.

Return of the Living Dead. Directed by Dan O'Bannon. Orion Pictures Corporation, 1985.

Return of the Living Dead III. Directed by Brian Yuzna. Trimark Pictures, 1993.

Romero, George A. See *Night of the Living Dead*, *Dawn of the Dead* (1978), *Day of the Dead* (1985), *Land of the Dead*, *Diary of the Dead*, and *Survival of the Dead*.

The Serpent and the Rainbow. Directed by Wes Craven. Universal Pictures, 1988.

Shaun of the Dead. Directed by Edgar Wright. Focus Features, 2004.

Survival of the Dead. Directed by George A. Romero. Magnet Releasing, 2009.

The *Trancers* series:

Trancers. Directed by Charles Band. Empire Pictures, 1985.

Trancers II. Directed by Charles Band. Full Moon Entertainment, 1991, video.

Trancers III. Directed by C. Courtney Joyner. Full Moon Entertainment, 1992, video.

Trancers 4: Jack of Swords. Directed by David Nutter. Full Moon Entertainment, 1994, video.

Trancers 5: Sudden Deth. Directed by David Nutter. Paramount Home Video, 1994, video.

Trancers 6. Directed by Jay Woelfel. Shadow Entertainment, 2002, video.

The *Twilight* saga:

Twilight. Directed by Catherine Hardwicke. Summit Entertainment, 2008.

The Twilight Saga: New Moon. Directed by Chris Weitz. Summit Entertainment, 2009.

The Twilight Saga: Eclipse. Directed by David Slade. Summit Entertainment, 2010.

The Twilight Saga: Breaking Dawn—Part 1. Directed by Bill Condon. Summit Entertainment,

2011.

The Twilight Saga: Breaking Dawn—Part 2. Directed by Bill Condon. Summit Entertainment, 2012.

The *Underworld* series:

Underworld. Directed by Len Wiseman. Screen Gems, 2003.

Underworld: Evolution. Directed by Len Wiseman. Screen Gems, 2006.

Underworld: Rise of the Lycans. Directed by Patrick Tatopoulos. Sony Pictures, 2009.

Underworld: Awakening. Directed by Måns Mårlind. Screen Gems, 2012.

Vampire Hookers. Directed by Cirio H. Santiago. Caprican 3, 1978.

Van Helsing. Directed by Stephen Sommers. Universal Pictures 2004.

Warm Bodies. Directed by Jonathan Levine. Summit Entertainment, 2013.

World War Z. Directed by Marc Foster. Paramount Pictures, 2013.

Zombie. Directed by Lucio Fulci. The Jerry Gross Organization, 1980 (1979).

Zombieland. Directed by Reuben Fleischer. Sony Pictures, 2009.

Zombie Strippers! Directed by Jay Lee. Sony Pictures, 2008.

Zombies vs. Strippers. Directed by Alex Nicolaou. Full Moon Features, 2012, video.

Zombies Zombies Zombies: Strippers vs. Zombies. Directed by Jason Murphy. Passion River Films, 2008, video.

TELEVISION SHOWS

Angel. Created by David Greenwalt and Joss Whedon. WB Television Network, 1999–2004.

Being Human. Created by Toby Whithouse. BBC, 2008–2013.

Buffy the Vampire Slayer. Created by Joss Whedon. WB Television Network, 1997–2001; United Paramount Network, 2001–2003.

Dark Shadows. Created by Dan Curtis. ABC, 1966–1971.

Dead Like Me. Created by Bryan Fuller. Showtime, 2003–2004.

Dead Set. Directed by Yann Demange. Created by Charlie Brooker. BBC, 2008.

Falling Skies. Created by Robert Rodat. TNT, 2011– .

In the Flesh. Created by Dominic Mitchell. BBC Three, 2013– .

Revolution. Created by Eric Kripke. NBC, 2012– .

Sesame Street. Created by Joan Ganz Cooney. PBS, 1969– .

True Blood. Created by Alan Ball. HBO, 2008.

The Vampire Diaries. Created by Julie Plec and Kevin Williamson. CW Network, 2009– .

The Walking Dead. Created by Frank Darabont. AMC, 2010– .

BOOKS

Becker, Robin. *Brains: A Zombie Memoir*. New York: HarperCollins, 2010.

Brooks, Max. *World War Z: An Oral History of the Zombie War*. New York: Broadway Books, 2007.

Brooks, Max. *The Zombie Survival Guide: Complete Protection from the Living Dead*. New York: Three Rivers Press, 2003.

Clines, Peter. The Ex series:

Ex-Heroes. New York: Broadway Books, 2010.

Ex-Patriots. New York: Broadway Books, 2011.

Ex-Communication. New York: Broadway Books, 2013.

. . . and two others.

Conrad, Pat. *Stonewords: A Ghost Story*. New York: HarperCollins, 1990.

Cronin, Justin. *The Passage*. New York: Ballantine, 2010.

Del Toro, Guillermo, and Chuck Hogan. *The Strain*. New York: HarperCollins, 2009.

Grahame-Smith, Seth. *Abraham Lincoln: Vampire Hunter*. New York: Grand Central Publishing, 2011.

Hamilton, Laurell K. The Anita Blake series:

Guilty Pleasures. Jove Publishing Group, 2002.

The Laughing Corpse. Jove Publishing Group, 2002.

Circus of the Damned. Jove Publishing Group, 2002.

. . . and many others.

Harris, Charlaine. The *Sookie Stackhouse* series:

Dead until Dark: A Sookie Stackhouse Novel. New York: Penguin, 2001.
Living Dead in Dallas: A Sookie Stackhouse Novel. New York: Penguin, 2002.

Club Dead: A Sookie Stackhouse Novel. New York: Penguin, 2003.

. . . and many others.

Huston, Charlie. *Already Dead*. New York: Ballantine, 2007.

Kadrey, Richard. *Sandman Slim*. New York: HarperCollins, 2010.

Mancusi, Mari. The Blood Coven series:

Boys That Bite. New York: Berkley Jam Books, 2006.

Stake That. New York: Berkley Jam Books, 2006.

Girls That Growl. New York: Berkley Jam Books, 2007.

. . . and many others.

Matheson, Richard. *I Am Legend*. Greenwich, CT: Gold Medal, 1954.

Mead, Richelle. *Vampire Academy*. New York: Penguin, 2007.

Meyer, Stephenie. The *Twilight* saga:

Twilight. New York: Little, Brown and Company, 2005.

New Moon. New York: Little, Brown and Company, 2006.

Eclipse. New York: Little, Brown and Company, 2007.

Breaking Dawn. New York: Little, Brown and Company, 2008.

Pratchett, Terry. The *Discworld* series:

The Color of Magic. New York: HarperCollins, 1983.

The Light Fantastic. New York: HarperCollins, 1986.

Equal Rites. New York: HarperCollins, 1987.

. . . and many others.

Rice, Anne. The *Vampire Chronicles*:

Interview with the Vampire. New York: Ballantine, 1976.

The Vampire Lestat. New York: Ballantine, 1985.

The Queen of the Damned. New York: Ballantine, 1989.

. . . and many others.

Rowling, J. K. The *Harry Potter* series:

Harry Potter and the Sorcerer's Stone. New York: Scholastic, 1997.

Harry Potter and the Chamber of Secrets. New York: Scholastic, 1998.

Harry Potter and the Prisoner of Azkaban. New York: Scholastic, 1999.

. . . and four others.

Rymer, Malcolm. *Varney the Vampire; or the Feast of Blood*. Maryland: Wildside Press, 2011 (1847).

Schlozman, Steven C. *The Zombie Autopsies: Secret Notebooks from the Apocalypse*. New York: Grand Central Publishing, 2011.

Shan, Darren. The *Cirque Du Freak* series:

Cirque Du Freak: A Living Nightmare. New York: Hachette Book Group, 2001.

Cirque Du Freak: The Vampire's Assistant. New York: Hachette Book Group, 2001.

Cirque Du Freak: Tunnels of Blood. New York: Hachette Book Group, 2002.

. . . and many others.

Sheridan Le Fanu, Joseph. *Carmilla*. Amazon Digital Services, Inc., 2012 (1872).

Smith, L. J. The *Vampire Diaries* series:

The Awakening. New York: HarperTeen, 2009.

The Struggle. New York: HarperCollins, 2010.

The Fury. New York: HarperCollins, 2010.

. . . and many others.

Stoker, Bram. *Dracula*. Norton Critical Edition. New York: W. W. Norton, 1997 (1897).

Strieber, Whitley. *The Hunger*. New York: Simon & Schuster, Inc., 1981.

Wellington, David. The Laura Caxton Vampire series:

13 Bullets: A Vampire Tale. New York: Three Rivers Press, 2007.

99 Coffins: A Historical Vampire Tale. Three Rivers Press, 2007.

Vampire Zero: A Gruesome Vampire Tale. Three Rivers Press, 2008.

. . . and two others.

Whitehead, Colson. *Zone One*. New York: Anchor Publishers, 2011.

OTHER

American Vampire. Comic book series. Created by Scott Snyder and Rafael Albuquerque. Vertigo, 2010– .

Blade: The Vampire Hunter. Comic book series. Created by Ian Edginton and Doug Wheatley. Marvel Comics, 1994–1995. First appearance of character: *The Tomb of Dracula* 10. Marv Wolfman and Gene Colan. Marvel Comics, 1973.

BloodRayne. Video game. Terminal Reality, 2002.

Christabel. Poem by Samuel Taylor Coleridge, 1816.

Left 4 Dead. Video game. Turtle Rock Studios, 2008.

Resident Evil. Video game. Capcom, 1996.

Resident Evil 3: Nemesis. Video game. Capcom, 1999.

"The Undeading." Internet short video. Heart & Stroke Foundation of Canada, 2012. www. theundeading.ca/.

The Walking Dead. Comic book series. Created by Robert Kirkman and Tony Moore. Image Comics, 2003– .

The Walking Dead: The Game. Telltale Games, 2012.

World of Darkness. Role-playing game. White Wolf Gaming Studio, 1991–2003.

Y: The Last Man. Comic book series. Created by Brian K. Vaughan and Pia Guerra. Vertigo, 2002–2008.

Zombie Research Society. Website. www.zombieresearch.org/.

Notes

INTRODUCTION: LIVING DEAD AND THE MODERN ECONOMY

1. *Buffy the Vampire Slayer*, "Into the Woods," season 5, episode 10.
2. William Irwin, ed., *Seinfeld and Philosophy: A Book about Everything and Nothing* (Chicago: Open Court, 2000).
3. Douglas Glen Whitman, "The Political Economy of Non-Coercive Vampire Lifestyles," in *Zombies, Vampires, and Philosophy: New Life for the Undead*, ed. Richard Greene and K. Silem Mohammed (Chicago: Open Court, 2010).
4. See David M. Levy and Sandra M. Peart, "The Secret History of the Dismal Science. Part I. Economics, Religion and Race in the 19th Century," Library of Economics and Liberty, 2001, accessed October 31, 2013, www.econlib.org/library/Columns/LevyPeartdismal.html.

1. HUMAN GIRLS AND VAMPIRE BOYS, PART 1

1. Gary Becker, "A Theory of Marriage, Part I," *Journal of Political Economy* 81, no. 4 (1973): 814.
2. For an exception, see *Vampire Hookers*.
3. Alex Williams, "The New Math on Campus," *New York Times*, February 5, 2010, accessed October 18, 2013, www.nytimes.com/2010/02/07/fashion/07campus.html.
4. Karensa Cadenas, "Twilight: *Breaking Dawn Part 2* Crushes the Box Office," Indiewire.com, November 19, 2012, accessed October 18, 2013, http://blogs.indiewire.com/womenandhollywood/twilight-breaking-dawn-part-2-crushes-the-box-office.
5. Peter Diamond, Dale Mortensen, and Christopher Pissarides, citation for Nobel Committee's report. See "Markets with Search Frictions," Economic Sciences Prize Committee of the Royal Swedish Academy of Sciences, October 11, 2010.
6. Or their own great-great-great-great-granddaughter, as came perilously close to happening to Bill Compton in *True Blood*, "I'm Alive and On Fire," season 4, episode 4.
7. Michael J. Rosenfeld and Reuben J. Thomas, "Searching for a Mate: The Rise of the Internet As a Social Intermediary," *American Sociological Review* 77, no. 4 (2012): 523–47.
8. L. Rachel Ngai and Silvana Tenreyro, "Hot and Cold Seasons in the Housing Market," CEP Discussion Papers dp0922, Centre for Economic Performance, LSE (2009).

255

9. David D. Friedman, *Law's Order: What Economics Has to Do with Law* (Princeton, NJ: Princeton University Press, 2001), 172.

2. HUMAN GIRLS AND VAMPIRE BOYS, PART 2

1. Oliver E. Williamson, *The Economic Institutions of Capitalism* (New York: The Free Press, 1985), 61.
2. Ibid., 30.
3. This is assuming that scalping the ticket is not an option.
4. Williamson, *The Economic Institutions of Capitalism*, 47.
5. *The Vampire Diaries*, "Miss Mystic Falls," season 1, episode 19.
6. *True Blood*, "Evil Is Going On," season 3, episode 12.

3. PACKING FOR THE ZOMBIE APOCALYPSE

1. *The Zombie Survival Guide* is a very popular source of information for what to do, although a quick Google search will also give you many good pieces of advice.
2. Max Brooks, *World War Z*, 145.
3. This is not the only zombie creation myth involving alcohol. Donn Beach, sometimes known as Don the Beachcomber after his successful Polynesian restaurants, was one of the early promoters of the "tiki" style that was very popular in the forties and fifties. Once he prepared a special high-alcohol cocktail for a customer who later returned and complained of being turned into a "zombie," and so the zombie cocktail was born (http://en.wikipedia.org/wiki/Zombie_(cocktail)). One version of the recipe combined three and a half parts of various kinds of rum, one part brandy, and two parts fruit juice, and so it's not surprising that the drinker would be reduced to staggering around moaning incoherently. This may be the first example of a zombie created by nonmystical means, and so I would argue that Donn Beach is the true originator of the modern zombie.
4. It's called *physical* capital to distinguish it from financial capital, the money or financial assets that you can use to support your business.
5. For more about trade and specialization, see Darwyyn Deyo and David T. Mitchell's "Trading with the Undead: A Study in Specialization and Comparative Advantage" in this volume.
6. George J. Stigler and Gary S. Becker, "De Gustibus Non Est Disputandum," *American Economic Review* 67, no. 2 (1977): 76–90.
7. Brooks, *World War Z*, 142.
8. Ibid.
9. For another example of how even the most commonplace items require complicated economic interrelationships, see Thomas Thwaites's TED talk, available at www.ted.com/talks/thomas_thwaites_how_i_built_a_toaster_from_scratch.html.
10. For more about specialization and economic growth, see Brian Hollar's "To Truck, Barter . . . and Eat Your Brains!!! Pursuing Prosperity in a Post-productive World" in this volume.

4. EATING BRAINS AND BREAKING WINDOWS

1. Frédéric Bastiat, "What Is Seen and What Is Not Seen," in *Selected Essays on Political Economy*, trans. Seymour Cain (Library of Economics and Liberty, 1995), accessed July 22, 2013, www.econlib.org/library/Bastiat/basEss1.html.

2. Agustino Fontevecchia, "Despite $50b in Damages, Hurricane Sandy Will Be Good for the Economy, Goldman Says," *Forbes.com*, November 6, 2012, accessed October 17, 2013, www.forbes.com/sites/afontevecchia/2012/11/06/despite-50b-in-damages-hurricane-sandy-will-be-good-for-the-economy-goldman-says/.

3. Jack Mirkinson, "Paul Krugman: Fake Alien Invasion Would End Economic Slump (VIDEO)," *Huffington Post*, October 15, 2011, accessed October 17, 2013, www.huffingtonpost.com/2011/08/15/paul-krugman-fake-alien-invasion_n_926995.html.

4. Max Brooks, *World War Z*, 13.

5. Ibid., 13.

6. Ibid., 16.

7. Ibid., 85.

8. Ibid., 58.

9. Ibid., 142.

10. Dwight D. Eisenhower, "The Chance for Peace," address delivered before the American Society of Newspaper Editors, April 16, 1953, www.eisenhower.archives.gov/all_about_ike/speeches/chance_for_peace.pdf.

11. Ludwig von Mises, *Nation, State, and Economy* (New York: New York University Press, 1983), 154.

12. Wayne A. Leighton and Edward J. Lopez, *Madmen, Intellectuals, and Academic Scribblers: The Economic Engine of Political Change* (Stanford, CA: Stanford University Press, 2013), 96.

13. Brooks, *World War Z*, 2.

14. For more on the role of specialization and division of labor in economic development, see Brian Hollar's "To Truck, Barter . . . and Eat Your Brains!!! Pursuing Prosperity in a Post-productive World" in this volume.

15. Brooks, *World War Z*, 143.

16. Ibid., 337.

17. Steven Horwitz, "Stimulus Spending and Jigsaw Puzzles," *Coordination Problem* (blog), March 16, 2011, www.coordinationproblem.org/2011/03/stimulus-spending-and-jigsaw-puzzles.html.

18. Brooks, *World War Z*, 340.

19. For more on the tragedy of the commons, see Glen Whitman's "Tragedy of the Blood Commons: The Case for Privatizing the Humans" in this volume.

20. Scott Edelman, "The Last Supper," *Lightspeed Magazine*, September 2012, accessed July 19, 2013, www.lightspeedmagazine.com/fiction/the-last-supper/.

5. TO TRUCK, BARTER . . . AND EAT YOUR BRAINS!!!

1. Adam Smith, *An Inquiry into the Nature and Causes of Wealth of Nations*, 5th ed., ed. Edwin Cannan (London: Methuen & Co., Ltd., 1904 [1776]), Library of Economics and Liberty e-book, www.econlib.org/library/Smith/smWN.html.

2. Ibid., I.2.1.

3. Ibid., I.4.2.

4. Ibid., I.4.2.

5. Ibid., I.4.2.

6. Postage stamps in contemporary U.S. prisons are another, more recent example of commodity money.

7. Smith, *The Wealth of Nations*, I.1.5.

8. This is similar to the story of the pin factory Adam Smith describes in book 1, chapter 1 of *The Wealth of Nations*, in which ten people working together are able to produce 48,000 pins per day by dividing the operation into ten distinct tasks each assigned to a different person. By dividing the tasks and working together, the workers are able to produce hundreds, if not thousands more pins than if they were trying to produce them on their own. For more on how specialization improves productivity, see Darwyyn Deyo and David T. Mitchell's "Trading with the Undead: A Study in Specialization and Comparative Advantage" in this volume.

9. Smith, *The Wealth of Nations*, I.3.1.

6. WHAT HAPPENS NEXT?

1. This is subtly different from earlier narratives in which corpses reanimated due to something other than having died with a latent infection.

2. Philip Munz, Ioan Hudea, Joe Imad, and Robert J. Smith, "When Zombies Attack! Mathematical Modelling of an Outbreak of Zombie Infection," in *Infectious Disease Modelling Research Progress* (Hauppage, NY: Nova Science Publishers, 2009), 133–50.

3. *Night of the Living Dead*, directed by George A. Romero (Continental Distributing, 1968).

4. Such as Romero's other films, as well as *Shaun of the Dead* and *The Walking Dead*.

5. Respectively *Night of the Living Dead*, *Dawn of the Dead*, *Day of the Dead*, and *Shaun of the Dead*.

6. Marc Nerlove and Lakshmi K. Raut, "Growth Models with Endogenous Population: A General Framework," in *Handbook of Population and Family Economics, Volume 1* (Amsterdam: Elsevier, 1997), 1117–74.

7. United Nations, Department of Economic and Social Affairs, Population Division, Population Estimates and Projections Section, "World Population Prospects: The 2012 Revision" (2012), http://esa.un.org/wpp/.

8. *Night of the Living Dead* established many features common to the zombie apocalypse narrative.

9. Exceptions exist, of course, such as *Shaun of the Dead* and a handful of ultimately successful institutions in *World War Z*.

10. In fact, many of these steady states are possible, each with a different population of zombies, but all with zero humans.

11. Robert E. Lucas Jr., "Econometric Policy Evaluation: A Critique," *Carnegie-Rochester Conference Series on Public Policy* 1, no. 1 (1976): 19–46.

12. Kyle William Bishop, "The Idle Proletariat: *Dawn of the Dead*, Consumer Ideology, and the Loss of Productive Labor," *Journal of Popular Culture* 43, no. 2 (2010): 234–48.

13. For more on the tragedy of the commons, see Glen Whitman's "Tragedy of the Blood Commons: The Case for Privatizing the Humans" in this volume.

14. Robert E. Ricklefs, *Ecology*, 3rd ed. (New York: W. H. Freeman, 1990).

15. Further, it is well documented that in some real-world populations, host behavior is dramatically changed by the parasitic infection. See Sandra B. Andersen, Sylvia Gerritsma, Kalsum M. Yusah, David Mayntz, Nigel L. Hywel-Jones, Johan Billen, Jacobus J. Boomsma, and David P. Hughes, "The Life of a Dead Ant: The Expression of an Adaptive Extended Phenotype," *American Naturalist* 174, no. 3 (2009): 424–33.

16. E. Fuller Torrey and Robert H. Yolken, "*Toxoplasma gondii* and Schizophrenia," *Emerging Infectious Diseases* 9, no. 11 (2003), http://wwwnc.cdc.gov/eid/article/9/11/03-0143.htm.

17. The relevance of real-world infection to this discussion of zombies is that humans are an intermediate host to *T. gondii*, and infection leads to suboptimal psychoses and harmful behaviors. Infection of humans with a zombie vector could affect the part of the brain that controls decision making, leading humans to behave in a manner that subtly decreases their own fitness but perpetuates the life cycle of the zombie parasite by allowing more zombies to develop, thus

completing the life cycle of the zombie parasite. Creators of zombie narratives may already be anticipating this: the behaviors outlined here are found in both versions of *World War Z*, both versions of *The Walking Dead*, and *The Walking Dead: The Game* (Telltale Games, 2012).

7. ORDER, COORDINATION, AND COLLECTIVE ACTION AMONG THE UNDEAD

1. Norman Barry, "The Tradition of Spontaneous Order," *Literature of Liberty* 5, no. 2 (1982): 7–58.

2. Friedrich Hayek contrasted "spontaneous order" with "organization." See Friedrich A. Hayek, "Economics and Knowledge," *Economica* 4, no. 13 (1937): 33–54; "The Use of Knowledge in Society," *American Economic Review* 35, no. 4 (1945): 519–30; "Kinds of Order in Society," *New Individualist Review* 3, no. 2 (1965): 3–12; and *Law, Legislation and Liberty* (Chicago: University of Chicago Press, 1973).

3. Hayek, "Kinds of Order in Society," 5.

4. In the *World War Z* book and movie, zombies make a moan that communicates to other zombies the presence of humans. It seems to be an involuntary response but serves as a coordination device.

5. "Why Zombies Will Win: Altruism," *Zombie Research Society*, undated, accessed March 20, 2013, http://zombieresearchsociety.com/archives/6292.

6. Even if it is not part of our analysis, we can note that this refers to a classical problem of "optimal growth" in economics. The ability for an economy to grow depends on its ability to spare now a bit of the current product in order to invest it for later, so that the economy can, in subsequent periods, produce (and consume) more. The later benefits of this investment (subsequent consumption in the future) are to be balanced with individuals' craving for present consumption in order to find the optimal rate of growth. The same goes for zombies, who should, first, attempt not to eat totally the bodies of human beings (just infect them) and, second, not to eat all humans in order to let them reproduce and allow for the possibility of later infecting larger cohorts of human bodies.

7. Based on Richard Matheson's novel *I Am Legend*, *The Omega Man* departs significantly from it precisely in terms of groups and socialized forms of collective life.

8. Joseph A. Schumpeter, *Business Cycles: A Theoretical, Historical and Statistical Analysis of the Capitalist Process* (New York: McGraw-Hill, 1939), 100.

9. Schumpeter, *Business Cycles*.

10. See Israel Kirzner, *Competition and Entrepreneurship* (Chicago: University of Chicago Press, 1973) and *Perception, Opportunity, and Profit—Studies in the Theory of Entrepreneurship* (Chicago: University of Chicago Press, 1979).

11. "Biography for Big Daddy," Internet Movie Database, undated, accessed March 29, 2013, www.imdb.com/character/ch0077315/bio.

BLOOD MONEY

1. Alfred Marshall, *Principles of Economics* (London: MacMillan, 1920 [1890]), I.I.1, available in the Library of Economics & Liberty, http://econlib.org/library/Marshall/marPCover.html.

8. INVESTING SECRETS OF THE UNDEAD

1. Michael Noer, "The Forbes Fictional Fifteen," *Forbes.com*, April 14, 2010, accessed November 11, 2013, http://www.forbes.com/2010/04/13/richest-fictional-characters-opinions-wealth.html.

2. Stephenie Meyer, *New Moon*, in *The Twilight Saga Collection* (Kindle edition), 510–11.

3. Charlaine Harris, *Dead until Dark* (Kindle edition), 224.

4. Laura Miller, "Real Men Have Fangs," *Wall Street Journal*, October 31, 2008, accessed November 11, 2013, http://online.wsj.com/article/SB122540672952785957.html.

5. Elroy Dimson, Paul Marsh, and Mike Staunton, *Triumph of the Optimists: 101 Years of Global Investment Returns* (Princeton, NJ: Princeton University Press, 2002).

6. *Buffy the Vampire Slayer*, "Flooded," season 6, episode 4.

7. In practice, money this year is different from money next year for two reasons: the total amount you consume in a particular year can affect the satisfaction you get from spending an additional dollar in that year, and also consumption in the future may be discounted. For more on vampires and discounting, see Fabien Medvecky's "Sinking Our Teeth into Public Policy Economics: A Taste of Immortality" in this volume.

8. Dimson, Marsh, and Staunton did adjust for survivorship bias within countries (the fact that companies in a particular country failed during the time period).

9. Stephenie Meyer, *Breaking Dawn*, in *The Twilight Saga Collection* (Kindle edition), 647.

10. *Buffy the Vampire Slayer*, "The Freshman," season 4, episode 1.

11. Formally, the standard deviation of your wealth increases with the square root of the amount of time. However, as the Count would point out, this is slower than if it increased linearly with time.

12. See Seth Grahame-Smith, *Abraham Lincoln: Vampire Hunter* (New York: Grand Central Publishing).

13. Harris, *Dead until Dark*, 213.

9. ZOMBIFICATION INSURANCE

1. Beryl Markham, *West with the Night* (New York: North Point Press, 2013), 217.

2. For more on the circumstances in which such a "stalemate" might occur, see Kyle William Bishop, David Tufte, and Mary Jo Tufte's "What Happens Next? Endgames of a Zombie Apocalypse" in this volume.

3. Burial insurance as we see it today is actually more interesting than a simple risk-pooling arrangement. It is designed to meet the financial planning needs of households in which there's not a lot of money to spare, a circumstance under which it can be hard to set money aside for future expenses. A *whole life* burial insurance policy is part insurance (against dying young without enough time to save for a funeral) and part savings plan, providing a way to protect money earmarked for the future against the pressing demands of the present. Free-standing zombification insurance is likely to be sold as the simpler *term* insurance, where an annual premium provides coverage for a year and then must be renewed or dropped.

4. See *Shaun of the Dead* and *Survival of the Dead* respectively. Feminist viewers of the latter are likely to demand clauses in insurance policies that do not allow husbands to chain their undead wives to the kitchen.

5. A nonviolent end to zombie existence is said (for example, in *World War Z*) to arrive with the gradual breakdown of the body, spurred in colder climates by repeated freezing and thawing and in warmer climates by disease vectors for which the zombie body is a viable host.

6. "Alcor's 117th Patient," Alcor Life Extension Foundation, undated, accessed June 5, 2013, www.alcor.org/blog/?p=2735&utm_source=feedburner&utm_medium=feed&utm_campaign=Feed%3A+AlcorNews+%28Alcor+News%29.

7. A slower response time would be satisfactory for persons who demand cryonic services even after zombification has occurred, hoping not just for an antibiotic agent to destroy the virus but for a cure that would reverse the extensive physiological reorganization of the zombification process. We fear that unscrupulous cryonics providers might take advantage of persons who cannot separate anti-zombification science from fantasy.

8. Or, if attacked, are not left in a state that could reasonably be characterized as whole-body.

9. Strictly speaking, the relevant question is whether anyone might seek a zombie encounter once they are insured who in the absence of insurance would not have sought one. In *Return of the Living Dead*, encounters are sought by the obviously insane, and in the *Land of the Dead* they are sought by the already infected. We can safely surmise that neither group is displaying a rational reaction to the presence of insurance.

10. The cancer example brings up the question of preexisting conditions. Because the incubation period involved in zombification is only a day or so, zombification insurance can sidestep the preexisting infection problem by requiring a forty-eight-hour waiting period before a new policy goes into effect. If the zombie presence becomes epidemic and preexisting conditions come to include your apartment building's being surrounded while you're trying to buy insurance over the Internet, then a somewhat longer waiting period (or a requirement that you appear in person at the insurance office) is likely to be imposed. In the case of contracts covering cryonic services, we expect clauses governing a wider array of preexisting conditions that will be addressed not through imposing waiting periods but rather by denying insurance coverage. While in medical markets more generally we have seen the government step in to limit the denial of coverage, such intervention is unusual in the case of high-end procedures such as cryonic preservation.

11. *Return of the Living Dead III* reminds us of the military's interest in zombies' destructive power.

12. Scholars have yet to agree on the legal status of zombie combatants. In a private communication to the authors of this essay, human rights specialist Christopher Einolf summarizes the issues as follows: "The 3rd Geneva Convention (Article 4) defines prisoners of war as 'persons' who are 'members of the armed forces of a Party to the conflict' and 'persons who accompany the armed forces without actually being members thereof,' provided that they 'have received authorization from the armed forces which they accompany.' The Conventions are silent on whether the 'persons' have to be alive. If one takes the view that zombies are alive, it would seem that they are covered by the 3rd Geneva Convention. If one takes the view that they are dead, then they are covered by Article 17 of the 1st Geneva Convention, which sets out 'Prescriptions regarding the dead.' States who wish to use zombie armies cannot argue that they are inanimate objects, as zombies would then be classified as self-propelled disease vectors, which are prohibited by the 1972 Convention on Biological Weapons."

13. Tim Carney and Dick Patten, "Life Insurance Cash Cow: An Issue Brief on the Hidden Side of Estate Tax Lobbying," American Family Business Foundation, November 30, 2010, accessed June 12, 2013, http://nodeathtax.org/uploads/view/2313/life_insurance_brief.pdf.

10. MONSTERS OF CAPITAL

1. Karl Marx, *Capital*, vol. 1 (Harmondsworth, UK: Penguin, 1990), 342

2. Marx, *Capital*, 245. Marx is clearly applying here the pre-Romero, folkloristic interpretation of the "zombie," a soulless being whose mind and body had been enslaved and controlled, often through magic, by a powerful individual.

3. Stuart and Elizabeth Ewen, *Channels of Desire: Mass Images and the Shaping of American Consciousness* (New York: McGraw-Hill, 1982), 75.

4. And even when the democratization of brands has made it possible for middle-class consumers to purchase less exclusive items from designer collections, layers of commercialization still exist, so that the prestige and social status that used to be associated with possession

itself have now shifted to the realm of specialization, personalization, and, more often than not, location experience.

5. It must be noted, of course, that this form of engagement is not a prerogative of the working and middle classes only. Rich people, too, will partake of some mass-produced and branded consumer products.

6. Tzvetan Todorov, *The Fantastic: A Structural Approach to a Literary Genre* (Ithaca, NY: Cornell University Press, 1975), 52

7. For more on how vampires manage to amass such fortunes, see James Dow's "Investing Secrets of the Undead" in this volume.

8. Jean Baudrillard, *For a Critique of the Political Economy of the Sign* (Prestatyn, UK: Telos, 1981).

9. Lorna Piatti-Farnell, *The Vampire in Contemporary Popular Literature* (New York: Routledge, 2013), 189.

10. Thorstein Veblen, *The Theory of the Leisure Class* (New York: Dover Publications, 1994 [1899]).

11. The term "masstige" was introduced and popularized by Michael Silverstein and Neil Fiske in their article "Luxury for the Masses," *Harvard Business Review* 81, no. 4 (2003): 48–57, and their book *Trading Up: Why Consumers Want New Luxury Goods—and How Companies Create Them* (New York: Portfolio, 2005). Masstige is portmanteau of the words "mass" and "prestige," and means literally "prestige for the masses." Masstige items are defined by Silverstein and Fiske as "premium but attainable" and fill the gap between mid-market and superpremium.

12. Of course, examples still exist, especially in the literary world, in which vampires do not live a luxury, extravagant, commodity-filled existence, but prefer anonymity and even dwell in caves or abandoned crypts, recalling more aptly the vampiric creatures of folklore. One need only think of David Wellington's *Laura Caxton Vampire* series (2007–2012) or Justin Cronin's *The Passage* (2010) as evocative examples here. Recent cinematic examples of this category of "common vampires" include, among others, *Near Dark* (1987), *30 Days of Night* (2007), and *Daybreakers* (2009).

13. Rob Latham, *Consuming Youth: Vampires, Cyborgs, and the Culture of Consumption* (Chicago: University of Chicago Press, 2002), 156 and 1.

14. "The Fictional 15," *Forbes*, April 14, 2010, April 1, 2011, and April 23, 2012.

15. Mark Tungate, *Luxury Goods: The Past, Present, and Future of Luxury Brands* (London: Kogan Page, 2009), 26.

16. Robert Frank, *Choosing the Right Pond: Human Behavior and the Quest for Status* (New York: Oxford University Press, 1985), and *The Darwin Economy: Liberty, Competition and the Common Good* (Princeton, NJ: Princeton University Press, 2011).

17. Stephanie Boluk and Wylie Lenz, "Introduction: Generation Z, the Age of Apocalypse," in *Generation Zombie: Essays on the Living Dead in Modern Culture*, ed. Stephanie Boluk and Wylie Lenz (Jefferson, NC: McFarland, 2011), 5.

18. Matt Bailey, "Dawn of the Shopping Dead," in *Braaaiiinnnsss! From Academics to Zombies*, ed. Robert Smith (Ottawa: University of Ottawa Press, 2011), 195.

19. Bailey, "Dawn of the Shopping Dead," 199.

20. Bailey, "Dawn of the Shopping Dead," 195.

21. John Quiggin, *Zombie Economics: How Dead Ideas Still Walk among Us* (Princeton, NJ: Princeton University Press, 2012), 5.

22. Michel de Certeau, "The Practice of Everyday Life," in *Cultural Theory and Popular Culture: A Reader*, ed. John Storey (New York: Harvester Wheatsheaf, 1994), 474–75.

23. Grant McCracken, *Culture and Consumption: New Approaches to the Symbolic Character of Consumer Goods and Activities* (Bloomington: Indiana University Press, 1991), 85.

24. McCracken, *Culture and Consumption*, 85.

25. Mihaly Csikszentmihalyi, *Flow* (New York: Harper Perennial, 1991), 19.

26. Csikszentmihalyi, *Flow*, 19.

27. Csikszentmihalyi, *Flow*, 18.

28. David McNally, *Monsters of the Market: Zombies, Vampires and Global Capitalism* (Leiden: Martinus Nijhoff, 2011), 113.

11. TRADING WITH THE UNDEAD

1. Spike, a vampire, "trades" his assistance by helping Buffy defeat Angelus in exchange for Buffy sparing Drusilla because Spike plans to get out of town with Drusilla forever ("Becoming, Part 2," season 2, episode 22). Throughout most of seasons 4 and 5, Spike helps the "Scoobies" in return for a straightforward cash payment. In "Fool for Love" (season 5, episode 7), Buffy throws her promised payment onto the ground as Spike weeps. In later seasons, Spike has a chip implanted into him that prevents him from directly harming mortals. While Spike is chipped, Buffy often makes deals with him.

2. For more on the importance of specialization for our standard of living, see Brian Hollar's "To Truck, Barter . . . and Eat Your Brains!!! Pursuing Prosperity in a Post-productive World" and James Dow's "Packing for the Zombie Apocalypse," both in this volume.

3. Though we know from Claudia in *Interview with the Vampire* that it isn't a good idea to turn a child into a vampire.

4. If only Jules and Vincent had zombies in the movie *Pulp Fiction*. Zombies could clean up even better than the Wolf. And zombies don't care if the victim had hepatitis or anything else.

5. It wouldn't have to be for sadistic reasons. Farmers pay veterinarians to help their animals even though the animals will eventually end up at the slaughterhouse.

6. Opportunity cost is the *benefit* you would gain if you did something else. For example, if you weren't reading this, you might be starting a flame war on reddit.com. The benefits of starting a flame war on Reddit are the opportunity cost of reading this.

7. *Buffy the Vampire Slayer*, "Becoming, Part 2," season 2, episode 22.

8. Freddy speaking to Tina in *Return of the Living Dead* (1985).

9. The origins of this particular phrasing are unknown, but Frederic Bastiat and Otto T. Mallery both said similar things.

10. For more on the question of exploitation versus voluntary trade, see Enrique Guerra-Pujol's "Buy or Bite?" in this volume.

11. Benjamin Powell, *Sweatshops: Improving Lives and Economic Growth* (New York: Cambridge University Press, forthcoming 2014). Paul Krugman, "In Praise of Cheap Labor: Bad Jobs at Bad Wages Are Better Than No Jobs at All," *Slate*, March 21, 1997, accessed October 8, 2013, www.slate.com/articles/business/the_dismal_science/1997/03/in_praise_of_cheap_labor.html.

12. For another example of how glamouring/compelling might reduce the value of trade, see Glen Whitman's "Human Girls and Vampire Boys, Part 2: 'Til Death Do Us Part" in this volume.

13. *Buffy the Vampire Slayer*, "Welcome to the Hellmouth," season 1, episode 1.

12. BUY OR BITE?

1. This strange title is the correct spelling of Professor Haraway's thought-provoking but unorthodox book.

2. For the standard economic treatment of the market forces of supply and demand, see, e.g., N. Gregory Mankiw, *Principles of Microeconomics*, 6th ed. (Stamford, CT: South-Western Cengage Learning, 2012), 65–84.

3. One alternative to markets is altruism or a system of voluntary donations of blood, but for the reasons I discuss later, a voluntary system of blood donations is unlikely to meet the demand for blood by vampires.

4. See "Ending the Drug War Would End the Violence," Marijuana Policy Project, undated, accessed September 26, 2013, www.mpp.org/states/pennsylvania/news/ending-the-drug-war-would-end.html.

5. It is worth noting that blood is not the only resource with this renewable property. Many other natural resources are also renewable, like forests, rivers, and love—consumption of such renewable resources does not necessarily reduce their stock because such renewable resources can be replenished. See, e.g., Robert D. Cooter, *The Falcon's Gyre: Legal Foundations of Economic Innovation and Growth* (Berkeley, CA: Berkeley Law Books, 2013), 6–7.

6. Murray N. Rothbard, "Free Market," in *Concise Encyclopedia of Economics*, 2nd ed. (2008), accessed September 26, 2013, http://www.econlib.org/library/Enc/FreeMarket.html.

7. For the standard economic treatment of public goods and common resources, see, e.g., Mankiw, *Principles of Microeconomics*, 217–29.

8. For an in-depth economic analysis of the problem of uncertainty in law, see, e.g., Giuseppe Dari-Mattiacci and Bruno Deffains, "Uncertainty of Law and the Legal Process," *Journal of Institutional and Theoretical Economics* 163, no. 4 (2007): 627–56.

9. Of course, as the economist Ronald Coase specified, where the costs of contracting exceed the gains from trade, there will be no trade, even when markets are fully legal or property rights fully defined and enforced. See R. H. Coase, "The Nature of the Firm," *Economica* 4, no. 16 (1937): 386–405.

10. Or, stated formally, a market failure occurs when a "market on its own fails to produce an efficient allocation of resources." See Mankiw, *Principles of Microeconomics*, 12.

11. For an in-depth analysis of property rights in blood, see generally Jasper A. Bovenberg, *Property Rights in Blood, Genes, and Data: Naturally Yours?* (Leiden, Netherlands: Martinus Nijhoff Publishers, 2006). As an aside, the leading law case in the United States illustrating this legal failure is *Moore v. UC Regents*, 793 P.2d 479 (Cal. 1990). For some background into the *Moore* case and the current state of the law, see Rebecca Skloot, "Taking the Least of You: The Tissue-Industrial Complex," *New York Times*, April 16, 2006, accessed September 26, 2013, www.nytimes.com/2006/04/16/magazine/16tissue.html?_r=1&oref=slogin. In addition, for a dramatic example of legal failure regarding the ownership of rights to blood in Australia, see Diana M. Bowman and David M. Studdert, "Newborn Screening Cards: A Legal Quagmire," *Medical Journal of Australia* 194, no. 6 (2011): 319–22.

12. World Health Organization, "World Blood Donor Day 2006," June 12, 2006, accessed October 15, 2013, www.who.int/mediacentre/news/releases/2006/pr33/en/index.html.

13. Gordon Ansell, "Is Selling Blood Legal?," EHow UK, undated, accessed October 15, 2013, www.ehow.co.uk/info_12283047_selling-blood-legal.html.

14. The primary federal law relating to the purchase or sale of human tissues is the National Organ Transplant Act of 1984, which prohibits on pain of fine or imprisonment the buying or selling of human organs, including kidneys, livers, hearts, lungs, bone marrows, corneas, bones, and skin or "any subpart thereof." See 42 U.S.C. § 274e(c)(1) (2000). But there is some uncertainty as to whether this prohibition applies to blood. Specifically, there is an internal conflict in this law between its letter and its spirit—for although this law excludes renewable tissues, such as blood or sperm, from its letter, its spirit suggests otherwise, since the inclusion in the statute's text of any "subpart" of any listed organ means that even a single skin cell or a single drop of blood could arguably fall under the federal prohibition on sales.

15. See generally Bovenberg, *Property Rights in Blood, Genes, and Data*.

16. Richard Morris Titmuss, *The Gift Relationship: From Human Blood to Social Policy*, expanded and updated edition (New York: The New Press, 1997).

17. Indeed, in large part because of the force of Professor Titmuss's arguments, the medical industry in the United States and in many other countries has adopted a nonmarket or "all-volunteer" blood donation system in place of a market system.

18. Titmuss, *The Gift Relationship*, 237–46.

19. See Nicola Lacetera, Mario Macis, and Robert Slonim, "Economic Rewards to Motivate Blood Donations," *Science* 340, no. 6135 (2013): 927–28.

20. Titmuss, *The Gift Relationship*, 142–127.

21. See Lacetera, Macis, and Slonim "Economic Rewards to Motivate Blood Donations," 927–28.

22. The author thanks James Dow for raising this point in a previous draft of this chapter.

23. Titmuss, *The Gift Relationship*, 90–119.

24. See Daniel Engber, "The Business of Blood: Does the Red Cross Sell Your Frozen Plasma?" *Slate*, September 11, 2006, accessed September 26, 2013, www.slate.com/articles/ news_and_politics/explainer/2006/09/the_business_of_blood.html.

25. For more on the question of exploitation versus voluntary trade, see Darwyyn Deyo and David T. Mitchell's "Trading with the Undead: A Study in Specialization and Comparative Advantage" in this volume.

13. TO SHOOT OR TO STAKE, THAT IS THE QUESTION

1. Jeffrey R. Church and Roger Ware, "Industrial Organization: A Strategic Approach," selected work of Jeffrey Church (January 2000), accessed October 7, 2013, http://works. bepress.com/jeffrey_church/23/.

2. Craig Parsons, "Towards an Empirical Industrial Organization Analysis (New and Old) of the Japanese Beer Industry," Center for International Trade Studies, Faculty of Economics Yokohama National University (February 2007), accessed October 7, 2013, http://www.econ. ynu.ac.jp/cits/publications/pdf/CITSWP2007-01.pdf.

3. Keith O. Fuglie et al. "Root Crops, Starch and Agro-industrialization in Asia," International Potato Center, 2006, http://cipotato.org/publications/pdf/003222.pdf.

4. Margaret Pierson et al., "How Much Is a Reduction of Your Customers' Wait Worth? An Empirical Study of the Fast-Food Drive-Thru Industry Based on Structural Estimation Methods," *Manufacturing & Service Operations Management* 13, no. 4 (2011): 489–507.

5. Douglas A. McIntyre et al., "America's Most Profitable Products," finance.yahoo.com, May 3, 2013, accessed October 28, 2013, http://finance.yahoo.com/news/ america%E2%80%99s-most-profitable-products-183025482.html.

6. "Improvised Weapon: Literature," tvtropes.org, undated, accessed October 7, 2013, http://tvtropes.org/pmwiki/pmwiki.php/ImprovisedWeapon/Literature.

7. Jurgen Brauer, "The US Firearms Industry Production and Supply," working paper, The Small Arms Survey, 2013.

8. "Silver Bullet," *Wikipedia*, accessed October 7, 2013, http://en.wikipedia.org/wiki/ Silver_bullet.

9. "Physical Characteristics of Silver Bullets," Patriciabriggs.com, undated, accessed October 7, 2013, http://www.patriciabriggs.com/articles/silver/silverbullet4.shtml.

10. Christopher Eger, "Wooden Bullets Used in Peace and War," suite101.com, undated, accessed October 7, 2013, http://suite101.com/a/wooden-bullets-used-in-peace-and-war-a141786.

11. On March 6, 2009, the Federal Trade Commission announced a settlement ending the litigation and requiring Whole Foods to sell thirty-two stores and the Wild Oats brand.

12. Contrary to the Whole Foods and Wild Oats case described earlier, this merger was finally rejected by the authorities, despite the proposition by Staples and Office Depot to sell sixty-three stores to Office Max in areas that didn't already have a rival office-supply superstore.

13. "List of Vampire Traits in Folklore and Fiction," *Wikipedia*, accessed October 7, 2013, http://en.wikipedia.org/wiki/List_of_vampire_traits_in_folklore_and_fiction.

14. Richelle Mead, *Vampire Academy* (New York: Razorbill, 2007).

15. "List of Vampire Traits in Folklore and Fiction," *Wikipedia*.

16. *Buffy the Vampire Slayer*, "A New Man," season 4, episode 12.

17. Paul Haufer et al., "The Economics of Market Definition Analysis in Theory and in Practice," *The Asia-Pacific Antitrust Review* (2007): 10–13.

18. United Brands case 27/76, United Brands Co and United Brands Continental Bv v. Commission (1978), ECR 207 (1978) 1 CMLR 429.

14. TAXATION OF THE UNDEAD

1. See Adam Chodorow, "Death and Taxes and Zombies," *Iowa Law Review* 98 (2013): 1207–31.
2. Amy Wilentz, "A Zombie Is a Slave Forever," *New York Times*, October 30, 2012, accessed November 17, 2013, http://www.nytimes.com/2012/10/31/opinion/a-zombie-is-a-slave-forever.html.

15. TRAGEDY OF THE BLOOD COMMONS

1. Here is a typical prisoners' dilemma set-up. If both prisoners stay quiet, they'll both be convicted of a minor crime and get one year in prison each. If both confess, they'll both be convicted of a major crime and get five years in prison each. If one confesses and the other does not, the confessing prisoner will be set free (zero years in prison) in exchange for testifying against the nonconfessing prisoner, who will go to prison for eight years. In this scenario, both prisoners have a dominant strategy of confessing.
2. Garrett Hardin, "The Tragedy of the Commons," *Science* 162 (1968): 1243–48.
3. Other thinkers had noticed it before Hardin, but without giving it a catchy name. Gordon's (1954) analysis of a common fishery is just one example. H. Scott Gordon, "The Economic Theory of a Common-Property Resource: The Fishery," *Journal of Political Economy* 62, no. 2 (1954): 124–42.
4. Hardin, "The Tragedy of the Commons," 1244.
5. The classic work on the subject is William T. Hornaday, *The Extermination of the American Bison* (Washington, DC: Government Printing Office, 1889).
6. The National Geographic Society, "Overfishing: Plenty of Fish in the Sea? Not Always," undated, accessed April 23, 2012, http://ocean.nationalgeographic.com/ocean/critical-issues-overfishing/.
7. Elinor Ostrom, *Governing the Commons: The Evolution of Institutions for Collective Action* (Cambridge: Cambridge University Press, 1990).
8. Harold Demsetz, "Toward a Theory of Property Rights," *American Economic Review* 57, no. 2 (1967), Papers and Proceedings of the Seventy-ninth Annual Meeting of the American Economic Association, 347–59, at 351–53.
9. Terry L. Anderson and Donald R. Leal, *Free Market Environmentalism*, rev. ed. (New York: Palgrave, 2001), 29–31.
10. Nevertheless, there have been some moderately successful efforts at fishery privatization via the allocation of transferable catch shares. See Christopher Costello, Steven D. Gaines, and John Lynham, "Can Catch Shares Prevent Fishery Collapse?" *Science* 321, no. 5896 (2008):1678–81.
11. F. A. Hayek, "The Use of Knowledge in Society," *American Economic Review* 35, no. 4 (1945): 519–30.
12. Robert Ellickson, *Order without Law* (Cambridge, MA: Harvard University Press, 1991).
13. For examples, see Hernando De Soto, *The Mystery of Capital: Why Capitalism Triumphs in the West and Fails Everywhere Else* (New York: Basic Books, 2000), 135–47.
14. Diego Gambetta, *The Sicilian Mafia: The Business of Private Protection* (Cambridge, MA: Harvard University Press, 1996).
15. David D. Friedman, "A Positive Account of Property Rights," *Social Philosophy & Policy* 11, no. 2 (1994): 1–16.

16. ZOMBIES AS AN INVASIVE SPECIES

1. Lucy Emerton and Geoffrey Howard, *A Toolkit for the Economic Analysis of Invasive Species* (Nairobi: Global Invasive Species Programme, 2008), 9.

2. Ibid., 10.

3. Ibid., 15.

4. Mark Williamson and Alastair Fritter, "The Varying Success of Invaders," *Ecology* 77, no. 6 (1996): 1661–66.

5. Jonathan M. Jeschke and David L. Strayer, "Invasion Success of Vertebrates in Europe and North America," *Proceedings of the National Academy of Sciences of the United States of America* 102, no. 20 (2005): 7198–7202.

6. Robert Costanza and Charles Perrings, "A Flexible Assurance Bonding System for Improved Environmental Management," *Ecological Economics* 2 (1990): 57–76.

7. Charles Perrings, "Environmental Bonds and Environmental Research in Innovative Activities," *Ecological Economics* 1 (1989): 95–110.

8. Not to be confused with *Zombies vs. Strippers*, in which the cause of the zombie outbreak is never revealed. In *Zombie Strippers!*, the cause is a secret government-manufactured virus (see above).

9. "Why Are Feral Pigs So Hard to Control?" *The Economist Explains*, May 15, 2013, accessed October 14, 2013, http://www.economist.com/blogs/economist-explains/2013/05/economist-explains-why-feral-pigs-hard-control.

10. "Feral Pigs: Pork, Chopped," *The Economist*, May 4, 2013, accessed October 14, 2013, http://www.economist.com/news/united-states/21577096-pesky-tasty-addition-landscape-pork-chopped.

17. POST-APOCALYPTIC LAW

1. Common law is the foundation of the legal systems in the United States and Great Britain.

2. "When the Dead Come Knocking," season 3, episode 7.

3. Formalized by Judge Learned Hand in *United States v. Carroll Towing Co.*, 159 F.2d 169 (2d. Cir. 1947).

4. This doctrine is based on the court case *Vincent v. Lake Erie Transportation Co.*, 124 N.W. 221 (Minn. 1910).

5. While there would be a problem of recording deeds in this new world, that is a matter of proof of ownership and not a change in principles of law.

6. Robert Cooter and Thomas Ulen, *Law and Economics*, 6th ed. (Boston: Pearson, 2012).

7. Economists refer to harm to third parties as *negative externalities*. Benefits to third parties are called *positive externalities*.

8. The lack of a monetary system would also be problematic for torts and property but probably less so. It comes into play for torts in determining compensation for accidental damage. In property law, specific performance is arguably easier to implement than under contract law.

9. "Save the Last One," season 2, episode 3.

10. In ancient times, such as in Ancient Greece, ostracism was considered one of the worst punishments. An ostracized person was likely to be robbed and killed by bandits. This would also be true of someone left on his own to defend himself against a world full of zombies.

18. BRAIN-DEAD VS. UNDEAD

1. *Buffy the Vampire Slayer*, "The Harvest," season 1, episode 2.
2. See, e.g., Daniel W. Drezner, *Theories of International Politics and Zombies* (Princeton, NJ: Princeton University Press, 2011); David McNally, *Monsters of the Market: Zombies, Vampires and Global Capitalism* (Leiden, the Netherlands: Brill, 2011); Annalee Newitz, *Pretend We're Dead: Capitalist Monsters in American Pop Culture* (Durham, NC: Duke University Press, 2006); Dennis Snower, "Macroeconomic Policy and the Optimal Destruction of Vampires," *Journal of Political Economy* 90 (1982): 647–55.
3. See, e.g., Drezner, *Theories of International Politics and Zombies*.
4. See, e.g., Keith Whittington, "It's Alive! The Persistence of the Constitution," *The Good Society* 11 (2002): 8–12.
5. Snower, "Macroeconomic Policy and the Optimal Destruction of Vampires."
6. David J. Prottas, "The Vampire in the Next Cubicle: The Americans with Disabilities Act and the Undead," *Employee Responsibilities and Rights Journal* 24 (2012): 79–89.
7. Andrew Gelman, Nate Silver, and Aaron Edlin, "What Is the Probability That Your Vote Will Make a Difference?" *Economic Inquiry* 50 (2012): 321–26.
8. For a more detailed discussion of rational political ignorance, see Ilya Somin, *Democracy and Political Ignorance: Why Smaller Government Is Smarter* (Stanford, CA: Stanford University Press, 2013), 62–78. The economist Anthony Downs first formulated the theory of rational ignorance. See Anthony Downs, *An Economic Theory of Democracy* (New York: Harper & Row, 1957), ch. 13.
9. For a recent overview of the evidence, see Somin, *Democracy and Political Ignorance*, ch. 1.
10. Zogby poll, July 21–27, 2006.
11. Carol Bialik, "Americans Stumble on the Math of Big Issues," *Wall Street Journal*, January 7, 2012.
12. For this analogy, see Somin, *Democracy and Political Ignorance*, 78–79.
13. For citations to the relevant literature, see ibid., 78–82.
14. Ibid., 104–5.
15. Diana Mutz, *Hearing the Other Side: Deliberative Versus Participatory Democracy* (New York: Cambridge University Press, 2006), 29–41.
16. Bryan Caplan, *The Myth of the Rational Voter: Why Democracies Choose Bad Policies* (Princeton, NJ: Princeton University Press, 2007), ch. 5.
17. *Buffy*, "The Harvest."
18. *Buffy the Vampire Slayer*, "Gingerbread," season 3, episode 11.
19. This is made clear in *Buffy the Vampire Slayer*, "Homecoming," season 3, episode 5.
20. For a summary of the literature on this kind of "rent-seeking," see Dennis Mueller, *Public Choice III* (Cambridge: Cambridge University Press, 2003), 333–58.
21. *Angel*, "Power Play," season 5, episode 21.
22. Max Brooks, *World War Z*, 32–44.
23. Ibid., 45–67.
24. Ibid., 52–54. The "brushfire war" is a thinly veiled reference to the Iraq War.
25. See Jeffrey Friedman and Wladimir Kraus, *Engineering the Financial Crisis: Systemic Risk and the Failure of Regulation* (Philadelphia: University of Pennsylvania Press, 2011).
26. Brooks, *World War Z*, 93.
27. Ibid., 98–99.
28. Ibid., 104.
29. *Buffy the Vampire Slayer*, "Goodbye Iowa," season 4, episode 14.
30. Somin, *Democracy and Political Ignorance*, ch. 5.
31. See, e.g., David Friedman, *The Machinery of Freedom: A Guide to a Radical Capitalism*, revised ed. (Arlington, VA: Open Court, 1989).
32. Robert Nelson, *Private Neighborhoods and the Transformation of Local Government* (Washington, DC: Urban Institute, 2005), xiii.

33. For a discussion of the informational advantages of private planned communities, see Somin, *Democracy and Political Ignorance*, 137–39.

34. Brooks, *The Zombie Survival Guide*, 159–70.

35. For examples, see Drezner, *Theories of International Politics and Zombies*, 93–94.

36. Brooks, *World War Z*, 55–61.

37. Some of the vampires and demons defeated by Buffy threatened to take over the world if they succeeded in carrying out their plans. But their actual presence was usually limited to Sunnydale.

38. The average American household only donates about 3 percent of its income to charity. Arthur Brooks, *Who Really Cares? America's Charity Divide* (New York: Basic Books, 2006), 3. Very few people routinely risk their lives for the sake of unrelated strangers.

39. Matt Davies, "'You Can't Charge Innocent People for Saving their Lives': Work in *Buffy the Vampire Slayer*," *International Political Sociology* 4 (2010): 178–95.

40. Amartya Sen, *Development As Freedom* (Norwell: Anchor Press, 1999), 178.

41. For a survey of these shortcuts and their limitations, see Somin, *Democracy and Political Ignorance*, ch. 4.

42. Andrew Healy and Neil Malhotra, "Myopic Voters and Natural Disaster Policy," *American Political Science Review* 103 (2009): 387–406.

43. See Ilya Somin, "Democracy, Natural Disasters, and Political Ignorance," *Volokh Conspiracy*, March 14, 2011, http://www.volokh.com/2011/03/14/democracy-natural-disaster-and-political-ignorance/.

44. See Somin, *Democracy and Political Ignorance*, 139–43.

45. On public ignorance about fiscal issues, see, e.g., Bialik, "Americans Stumble on the Math of Big Issues." On immigration and protectionism, see Caplan, *Myth of the Rational Voter,* 36–39, 50–51.

46. Apologists for the orcs are even now taking advantage of public ignorance by trying to persuade gullible readers that orcs have been misunderstood and are not really a threat. See, e.g., Stan Nicholls, *Orcs* (New York: Orbit, 2008). Once the public is lulled into a false sense of security, a full-fledged orc invasion cannot be far behind!

19. SINKING OUR TEETH INTO PUBLIC POLICY ECONOMICS

1. Nicholas Stern, *The Economics of Climate Change: The Stern Review* (Cambridge: Cambridge University Press, 2007).

2. Kenneth J. Arrow, "Global Climate Change: A Challenge to Policy," *The Economists' Voice* 4, no. 3 (2007).

3. Interest compounds, so to work out the returns of investing $1,000 for ten years at 5 percent interest, we need to use the following formula: 1000×1.05^{10}, which equals $1,628.89.

4. Daniel Read and N. L. Read, "Time Discounting over the Lifespan," *Organizational Behavior and Human Decision Processes* 94, no. 1 (2004): 22–32.

5. William D. Nordhaus, "A Review of 'The Stern Review on the Economics of Climate Change,'" *Journal of Economic Literature* 45, no. 3 (2007):686–702.

6. John Quiggin, "Stern and His Critics on Discounting and Climate Change: An Editorial Essay," *Climatic Change* 89, no. 3 (2008): 195–205.

7. Laura B. Shrestha and Elayne J. Heisler, *The Changing Demographic Profile of the United States*, CRS Report RL 32701 (Washington, DC: Congressional Research Service, 2006).

8. Angus Maddison, *The World Economy: A Millennial Perspective* (Paris: OECD Publishing, 2001).

20. WHERE, OH WHERE HAVE
THE VAMPIRES GONE?

1. Charles M. Tiebout, "A Pure Theory of Local Expenditures," *Journal of Political Economy* 64, no. 5 (1956): 416–24.

2. "The 'Banner Democratic Ward' Voted Dead Men and Absentees," *Chicago Daily Tribune*, April 11, 1891, 1.

3. E.g., Raymond Lahr, "GOP Plans Drive: Tombstone Vote Fought in Cities," *Bakersfield Californian*, September 22, 1964, 3; *Masters of Horror*, "Homecoming," season 1, episode 6, directed by Joe Dante, aired December 2, 2005; Susan Trausch, "Perot: He's the Last Hope for Keeping Us from Becoming Zombies," *Logansport Pharos-Tribune*, April 21, 1992, 6. It should also be noted that some commentators dismiss the reality of the graveyard vote as simple voter fraud. Given the evidence in popular culture that the undead do walk among us, however, it is clear that this interpretation is merely wishful thinking.

4. Robert Weisbrot, *Freedom Bound: A History of America's Civil Rights Movement* (New York: W. W. Norton, 1990), 48.

5. Lahr, "GOP Plans Drive," 3.

6. *Masters of Horror*, "Homecoming."

7. Dave Mundy, "Complaint Alleges Widespread Voter Fraud in South Texas," *Gonzales Cannon*, November 2, 2012, accessed June 22, 2013, www.gonzalescannon.com/node/11637.

8. "Politics," *Lebanon Daily News*, August 8, 1963, 10.

9. "Attack Up-State Voting," *New York Times*, February 6, 1922, 15.

10. "Dead Votes," *Daily Messenger*, November 11, 1938, 1.

11. "Counting the Electoral Vote in Joint Convention," *Chicago Daily Tribune*, February 13, 1873, 2.

12. Associated Press, "Voters Nix 'Dead' Vote," *Indiana Gazette*, May 17, 1961, 49.

13. Bruce Hutchison. *The Incredible Canadian: A Candid Portrait of Mackenzie King: His Works, His Times, and His Nation* (New York: Longmans Green, 1953), 371–72. Note: the authors reject claims that the Canadian government referred to certain types of living soldiers as "zombies" during that time period as an unfortunate and misguided attempt to soothe public sensibilities into believing that the undead do not actually exist.

14. Seth Greheme-Smith,*Abraham Lincoln: Vampire Hunter* (New York: Grand Central Publishing, 2011).

15. "The County Court," *Galveston Daily News*, May 26, 1874, 1; Joseph F. Zimmerman and Wilma Rule, *The U.S. House of Representatives: Reform or Rebuild?* (Westport, CT: Praeger Publishers, 2000), 101.

16. Tex Easley, "Texans in Washington," *Baytown Sun*, February 20, 1964, 18.

17. N. M. Gallup, "Surprisingly the Dead Vote," *Hope Star*, October 2, 1968, 2.

18. Stephen Ansolabhere and Eitan Hersh, "The Quality of Voter Registration Records: A State-by-State Analysis," Harvard University Department of Government Working Paper, July 14, 2010; "Inaccurate, Costly, and Inefficient," Pew Center on the States, IssueBrief, February 2012, www.pewstates.org/uploadedFiles/PCS_Assets/2012/Pew_Upgrading_Voter_Registration.pdf.

19. Statistical test results: $X2 = 12.0$, $p = .002$

20. Statistical test results: $t = 21.6$, $p = .0001$

21. Stephenie Meyer, *Twilight* (New York: Little Brown, 2005).

22. *Buffy the Vampire Slayer*, WB, 1997-2001; United Paramount, 2001-2003.

23. *True Blood*, HBO, 2008.

24. *Pirates of the Caribbean*, directed by Gore Verbinski (Walt Disney Pictures, 2003).

25. *Buffy the Vampire Slayer*, "Go Fish," season 2, episode 20.

26. *World of Darkness* role-playing game; see "Vampire," The Unofficial White Wolf Wiki, undated, accessed July 25, 2013, http://whitewolf.wikia.com/wiki/Vampire.

27. Bram Stoker, *Dracula* (New York: Norton, 1997).

21. THE ECONOMICS OF BLOODLUST

1. For one example of this type of analysis, see Frans Spinnewyn, "Rational Habit Formation," *European Economic Review* 15, no. 1 (1981): 91–109.

2. Gary S. Becker and Kevin Murphy, "A Theory of Rational Addiction," *Journal of Political Economy* 96, no. 4 (1988): 675–700.

3. John Tierney, "The Rational Choices of Crack Addicts," *New York Times,* September 13, 2013, accessed September 29, 2013, http://www.nytimes.com/2013/09/17/science/the-rational-choices-of-crack-addicts.html?ref=science&_r=2&.

4. Anne Rice, *Interview with the Vampire* (New York: Bellantine, 1997), 41.

5. See Gary Becker, Michael Grossman, and Kevin Murphy, "Rational Addiction and the Effect of Price on Consumption," *AER Papers and Proceedings* 81 (1991): 237–41; Gary Becker, Michael Grossman, and Kevin Murphy, "An Empirical Analysis of Cigarette Addiction," *American Economic Review* 84 (1994): 396–418; and Nilss Olekalns and Peter Bardsley, "Rational Addiction to Caffeine: An Analysis of Coffee Consumption," *Journal of Political Economy* 104, no. 5 (1996): 1100–1104.

6. This can also be a willing participant in several more romantic mythoi. See the *Twilight* collection of works and several instances in the novels of Anne Rice.

7. Becker and Murphy, 691.

8. *The Vampire Diaries*, "Brave New World," season 2, episode 2. In this mythos, vampires are created if a human is killed with vampire blood in her system, so newly changed vampires often awake from this deadly encounter with little memory of the details of the attack.

9. *The Vampire Diaries*, "As I Lay Dying," season 2, episode 22. While Stefan lives his life in a mostly vegetarian manner, his past includes numerous blood binges; Stefan has gone through a number of cycles of bloodlust throughout his undead life. These binges can also be explained in an alternative framework as well. See Becker and Murphy, 692–94.

10. Anne Rice, *Interview with the Vampire*, 28.

22. BETWEEN GODS AND MONSTERS

1. Agent-based modeling has been used to study many problems in the social sciences, particularly those where one-to-one interaction is paramount. For samples, see Michael W. Macy and Robert Willer, "From Factors to Actors: Computational Sociology and Agent-based Modeling," *Annual Review of Sociology* 28 (2002): 143–66; Philippe Mathieu, Bruno Beaufils, and Oliver Brandouy, *Artificial Economics: Agent-based Methods in Finance, Game Theory and Their Applications* (New York: Springer, 2005); Leigh Tesfatsion, "Agent-based Computational Economics: Growing Economies from the Bottom Up," *Artificial Life* 8, no. 1 (2002): 55–82; Leigh Tesfatsion, "Agents Come to Bits: Towards a Constructive Comprehensive Taxonomy of Economic Entities," *Journal of Economic Behavior & Organization* 63, no. 2 (2007): 333–46.

2. For further discussions, see Joshua M. Epstein, "Agent-based Computational Models and Generative Social Science," *Complexity* 4, no. 5 (1999): 41–60; Joshua M. Epstein, "Remarks on the Foundations of Agent-based Generative Social Science," in *Handbook of Computational Economics*, vol. 2, ed. Leigh Tesfatsion and Kenneth L. Judd (Amsterdam: North-Holland, 2006), 1585–1604.

3. For a full description of the standard predator-prey model, the mathematically inclined reader can consult Elizabeth S. Allman and John A. Rhodes, *Mathematical Models in Biology: An Introduction* (Cambridge: Cambridge University Press, 2004).

4. For more on the overexploitation of renewable resources, see Glen Whitman's "Tragedy of the Blood Commons: The Case for Privatizing the Humans" in this volume.

5. Richard F. Hartl, Alexander Mehlmann, and Andreas Novak, "Cycles of Fear: Periodic Bloodsucking Rates for Vampires," *Journal of Optimization Theory and Applications* 75, no. 3

(1992): 559–68; Richard F. Hartl and Alexander Mehlmann, "The Transylvanian Problem of Renewable Resources," *Operations Research* 16, no. 4 (1982): 379–90.

6. Dennis J. Snower, "Macroeconomic Policy and the Optimal Destruction of Vampires," *Journal of Political Economy* 90, no. 3 (1982): 647–55.

7. Sandra Tomc, "Dieting and Damnation: Anne Rice's *Interview with the Vampire*," in *Blood Read: The Vampire As Metaphor in Contemporary Culture*, ed. Joan Gordon, Veronica Hollinger, and Brian Aldiss (Philadelphia: University of Pennsylvania Press, 1997), 95–114.

8. For further discussions, see Colin. F. Camerer, George Loewenstein, and Matthew Rabin, eds., *Advances in Behavioral Economics* (Princeton, NJ: Princeton University Press, 2011).

9. This includes cases where the human *looks* like a love interest the vampire once had. Both Stefan and Damon exhibit this sort of connection to Elena in *The Vampire Diaries*, as does Barnabas Collins with Maggie in *Dark Shadows*.

10. In many cases, vampires become protective of their human companions and engage in conflicts with other vampires to defend them, a prominent theme in *Buffy the Vampire Slayer*, *True Blood*, the *Twilight* saga, and *The Vampire Diaries*.

11. Romantic relationships tend to stay a hunter's hand; Buffy and Angel in *Buffy the Vampire Slayer* is an obvious example. A hunter's efforts may be more extreme when dealing with a nemesis or archenemy; in *Dracula 2000*, for example, Van Helsing injects himself with Dracula's blood for a century to find a sure way to destroy his enemy. Occasionally, a hunter does not kill a vampire because of some good deed the vampire has done or to form an alliance against a greater threat; for example, Buffy unites with Spike against Drusilla and Angelus at the end of season 2 of *Buffy the Vampire Slayer* despite his many previous offenses in Sunnydale.

12. Many pieces of vampire lore are missing: humans do not actively hunt vampires, vampires are never successfully destroyed, vampires never reproduce (via infection), and nobody starves (neither vampires nor humans). These can be added with little impediment to create an even more complex artificial ecosystem. I have constructed one of these more detailed models. See Dan Farhat, "The Economics of Vampires: An Agent-based Perspective," *University of Otago Economics Discussion Papers* no. 1301 (2013), www.business.otago.ac.nz/econ/research/discussionpapers/.

13. The computer program used here is NetLogo, a modeling environment with an easy-to-learn programming language designed specifically for agent-based modeling. NetLogo software is freely available. For more information, see Uri Wilensky, NetLogo, Center for Connected Learning and Computer-based Modeling, Northwestern University, Evanston, IL, 1999, ccl.northwestern.edu/netlogo.

14. These details are available in an online technical appendix available at https://sites.google.com/site/undeadeconomics/vampires/artificial-vampires.

15. To see this more clearly from figure 22.4, compare lot sizes when the human population in both the vampire-free and vampire-laden village is 4,000. The vampire-free village has a human population of approximately 4,000 by day 200 (figure 22.4a). On this day, average populated lot size was about 60 people (figure 22.4b). The vampire-laden village had a population of about 4,000 by day 350. On this day, average populated lot size was much lower (about 20 people). Again, this is due to how safety levels and rental prices change as vampires feed.

16. For added realism, the security purchased with tax dollars is made to be less effective than that which is purchased by private individuals. The tax program only comes into effect if a vampire has managed to kill a human the previous day. Additional details are available in the technical appendix online.

17. Sharon Sutherland, "Piercing the Corporate Veil—With a Stake? Vampire Imagery and the Law," in *Vampires: Myths and Metaphors of Enduring Evil*, ed. Peter Day (Amsterdam: Rodopi, 2006), 143–57.

23. KILLING TIME

1. I wish to thank Kelly Hurley, Bill Gleason, Jennifer Waldron, Julie Barmazel, Paul Kelleher, Dan Novak, Erwin Rosinberg, Howard Rhodes, Diana Fuss, James Bowley, Peter Jelavich, Meg Guroff, Will Hays, and Linda DeLibero for useful suggestions on earlier drafts of this essay.

2. *Bradshaw's Monthly Railroad Guide*, published in Manchester, England, from 1839 to 1961, was the standard reference for railway timetables in Great Britain and the Continent.

3. Bram Stoker, *Dracula* (New York: W. W. Norton, 1997), 100.

4. Cf. Christopher Craft, "'Kiss Me with Those Red Lips': Gender and Inversion in Bram Stoker's *Dracula*," *Representations* 8 (1994): 107–33; Talia Schaffer, "'A Wilde Desire Took Me': The Homoerotic History of Dracula," *English Literary History* 61, no. 2 (1994): 381–425; Carol A. Senf, *The Vampire in Nineteenth-Century English Literature* (Bowling Green, OH: Popular Press, 1988); Stephen D. Arata, "The Occidental Tourist: *Dracula* and the Anxiety of Reverse Colonization," *Victorian Studies* 33, no. 4 (1990): 622; Franco Moretti, "The Dialectic of Fear," *New Left Review* 136 (1982): 67–85; and Barbara Belford, *Bram Stoker: A Biography of the Author of* Dracula (New York: Alfred A. Knopf, 1996).

5. Recall the concerns over Y2K.

6. Stoker, *Dracula*, 211.

7. Stoker, *Dracula*, 26.

8. Stoker, *Dracula*, 29.

9. Stoker's manuscript notes (at the Rosenbach Museum & Library in Philadelphia), particularly his careful plotting on a daily calendar, indicate an intense authorial concern with chronology. See also David Seed, "The Narrative Method of *Dracula*," *Nineteenth-Century Fiction* 40, no. 1 (June 1985): 61–75.

10. See Eviatar Zerubavel, "The Standardization of Time: A Sociohistorical Perspective," *American Journal of Sociology*, 88, no. 1 (July 1982): 1–23, and Derek Howse, *Greenwich Time and the Discovery of the Longitude* (Oxford: Oxford University Press, 1980). See also W. N. Osborough, "The Dublin Castle Career (1866–78) of Bram Stoker," *Gothic Studies* 1, no. 2 (1999): 222–40, which explores Stoker's first book, *The Duties of Clerks of Petty Sessions in Ireland* (1879). One of the key responsibilities of the clerks of Dublin Castle was to reconcile and clarify calendar terms in the official records. Stoker writes in his introduction: "Experience has shown me that with several hundred men performing daily a multitude of acts of greater or lesser importance, a certain uniformity of method is necessary to lighten their own labour and the labour of those to whom is entrusted the auditing of their accounts and returns. Such subjects as the advisability of uniform filing of papers or folding of returns, of using dots instead of o's in money columns, or of forwarding returns at the earliest instead of the latest date allowable" (unpaginated).

11. See Gerhard Dohrn-van Rossum, *History of the Hour: Clocks and Modern Temporal Orders*, trans. Thomas Dunlap (Chicago: University of Chicago, 1996).

12. Howse, *Greenwich Time,* 148.

13. G. V. Coyne, M. A. Hoskin, and O. Pederson, eds., *Gregorian Reform of the Calendar: Proceedings of the Vatican Conference to Commemorate its 400th Anniversary, 1582–1982* (Città del Vaticano: Pontifica Academia Scientiarum, Specola Vaticana, 1983), 260.

14. The dates to be lost according to Rome were October 5–14.

15. Personal interests, too: Lord Chesterfield, the leading advocate for the new calendar in the House of Lords, wrote that the complications of corresponding across the dateline with his mistress in France had convinced him of the necessity of reform. Robert Poole, *Time's Alteration: Calendar Reform in Early Modern England* (London: UCL Press, 1998), 114.

16. Isaac Newton earlier advocated a plan that would ease financial disruption, proposing directives "for performance of all covenants duties and services and payment of interest, rents, salaries, pensions, wages, and all other debts and dues whatsoever with an abatement . . . proportional unto eleven days" (Poole, *Time's Alteration*, 131). Newton's advice was not followed by those in charge of implementing the new calendar; rather, a gradual system was

used. Still, official tables of abatements were published in the press and in almanacs so that landlords, tenants, and tradesmen could muddle through.

17. Japan adopted the newer calendar in 1873 and Egypt in 1875.

18. Stoker, *Dracula*, 9. Jonathan and Mina both write in their journals in shorthand. Dr. Seward, later in the novel, uses a phonograph. Contemporary reviews commented on the "up-to-dateness" of *Dracula*. See *The Spectator* 79, July 31, 1897, 151.

19. Stoker, *Dracula*, 11.

20. Stoker, *Dracula*, 12–13.

21. Gabriel Ronay, *The Truth about Dracula* (New York: Stein and Day Publishers, 1972), 16.

22. Cf. Arata, "The Occidental Tourist," and Belford, *Bram Stoker*. Stoker spent countless hours in the Whitby library and took extensive notes on the history of Whitby as well as the history of Transylvania, particularly William Wilkinson's *An Account of the Principalities of Wallachia and Moldavia* (1820), for example.

23. Stoker, *Dracula*, 81–84.

24. Stoker, *Dracula*, 80.

25. Stoker, a lawyer, has fun with this episode: "Already, however, the legal tongues are wagging, and one young law student is loudly asserting that the rights of the owner are already completely sacrificed, his property being held in contravention of the statutes of mortmain, since the tiller, as emblemship, if not proof, of delegated possession, is held in a dead hand" (*Dracula*, 79).

26. For most Catholics and Protestants, Easter is observed on the first Sunday following the full moon that occurs on or following the spring equinox (March 21). Eastern Orthodox followers observe Easter according to the date of the Passover festival. There is no controversy when the moon rises on the fourteenth day of the month after the spring equinox when the fifteenth day is a Sunday. But because the cycles of the sun and the moon are not easily aligned with the cycle of the days of the week, trouble arises when the fourteenth falls on any other day but a Saturday. The dispute is longstanding. Saint John celebrated Easter on the fifteenth of the month regardless of the day of the week, while Saint Peter, according to Bede, "tarried for the Sunday."

27. Bede, *The Ecclesiastical History of the English People*, trans. Bertram Colgrave, ed. Judith McClure and Roger Collins (Oxford: Oxford University Press, 2008), 155.

28. See Richard Abels, "The Council of Whitby: A Study in Early Anglo-Saxon Politics," *Journal of British Studies* 23, no. 1 (Autumn 1983): 1–25 for political background.

29. See Arata, "The Occidental Tourist," 622.

30. *Dracula*, 167–68.

31. As Seed notes, "Characters become proportionately less vulnerable the more they act together" ("Narrative Method"), 73.

32. Stoker, *Dracula*, 293–94.

33. Moretti, "Dialectic of Fear," 73.

34. Cf. Herbert Marcuse, *One-Dimensional Man* (Boston: Beacon Press, 1964). Dracula, not man in an industrial civilization, better exemplifies the estranged individual. Dracula is not a team player.

Index

Contributor Biographies

Kyle William Bishop, when not fighting the hordes of undead, teaches American literature and film studies at Southern Utah University. He has written articles and book chapters on such diverse works as *Metropolis, Night of the Living Dead, Fight Club, Dawn of the Dead, The Birds, Zombieland*, and *The Walking Dead*. Of late, he has been asked to share his survival tips and understanding of zombies across the globe, drawing from his book *American Zombie Gothic: The Rise and Fall (and Rise) of the Walking Dead in Popular Culture*, published in 2010. If he can fend off the monsters long enough, he hopes to have a new book on the twenty-first-century zombie out soon.

Eleanor Brown is the James Irvine Professor of Economics at Pomona College. Her research usually focuses on altruism, and she is currently president of the Association for the Study of Generosity in Economics, as well as a coeditor of the *Review of Economics of the Household*. Born in 1954, she is a member of the generation that rushed home from school to begin their undead education watching *Dark Shadows*. The zombie side of her undead experience is due entirely to the influence of her older son Robert, who is her coauthor in this volume.

Ian Chadd is a doctoral economics student at the University of Maryland, College Park. His coffin is located in the District of Columbia, where he moved after his coven in Ohio was disbanded. His research interests include behavioral and experimental approaches to macroeconomics and neuroeconomics—a field he entered primarily for culinary reasons.

Darwyyn Deyo is a doctoral economics student at George Mason University and does most of her work after the sun has safely gone down. She has a forthcoming article on teaching economics using Harry Potter in the *Journal of Economics and Finance Education*. Darwyyn also works as a research manager at the American Road and Transportation Builders Association in Washington, D.C.

James Dow is a professor of finance, as well as chair of finance, real estate, and insurance, at California State University, Northridge. His research interests include household financial management, the implementation of monetary policy, and macroeconomics. He tries to go to bed early, stay in the light, and eat lots of garlic, because you can never be too sure.

Daniel Farhat is a faculty member in the Economics Department at Otago University in Dunedin, New Zealand. Much like Dr. Frankenstein, he spends much his time bringing things to life . . . artificial life. Using computer simulation techniques to build virtual environments populated by heterogeneous interacting agents, he seeks to explain the emergence of social patterns in a variety of market settings. So far, he has studied education and economic growth, fluctuations in consumption spending, and scientific progress. Dan's greatest accomplishment: not one of his creations has ever escaped to terrorize the villagers . . . yet.

Jean-Baptiste Fleury is an associate professor of economics at the University of Cergy-Pontoise, where he started to study zombie behavior simply by looking at (a few!) sleepy students during his microeconomics lectures. He has published papers in *History of Political Economy* and the *Journal of Economic Methodology* about the history of recent economics and more specifically on how economists have expanded the scope of their discipline to study crime, marriage, discrimination, and now . . . zombies!

Enrique Guerra-Pujol, a law professor, father of four, and versatile vampire scholar, has taught at Barry Law School in Orlando, Florida, and at the Pontifical Catholic University of Puerto Rico. He is a member of the American Association for the Advancement of Science (AAAS), and his work has been published in legal journals across the United States, Europe, Australia, India, and the Caribbean, all places (coincidentally enough) where vampires are known to dwell. When he is not researching the formal properties of conflict and cooperation in the vampire world, Professor Guerra-Pujol devotes his time to his family and to the study of mathematics, technology, and the legal process. He also blogs regularly at priorprobability.com.

Brian Hollar is a professor of economics at Marymount University, where he routinely feeds economics to the brains of undergraduates. He is director of Marymount's economics program and does research on the economics of religion—studying the behavioral effects of belief in the supernatural. He lives and works in Arlington, Virginia—just outside Washington, D.C.—the very last place on earth zombies would look for functioning brains.

Steven Horwitz slays the demons of economic ignorance as the Charles A. Dana Professor of Economics at St. Lawrence University in Canton, New York. He is also a senior fellow at the Fraser Institute in Canada and an affiliated senior scholar at the Mercatus Center in Arlington, Virginia. He is the author of two books, *Microfoundations and Macroeconomics: An Austrian Perspective* (2000) and *Monetary Evolution, Free Banking, and Economic Order* (1992), and he has written extensively on Austrian economics, Hayekian political economy, monetary theory and history, and the economics and social theory of gender and the family. His work has been published in professional journals such as *History of Political Economy*, *Southern Economic Journal*, and *Cambridge Journal of Economics*. He has also done public policy research for the Mercatus Center, Heartland Institute, Citizens for a Sound Economy, and the Cato Institute. Rumors of his undeath have been greatly exaggerated.

Sébastien Lécou holds a PhD in economics from the Sorbonne University. He was born in the late nineteenth century, during the most active period of the Count's life. As a baby, he was turned into a vampire (this is why he looks so young), but his kindness forced him to fight the devil inside him. Sébastien has always tried to do good things; for example, he recently resigned from his position as an economist for the French postal services (a well-known residence of demonic forces). His secret ambition is to become more famous as a good vampire than Angel.

Joseph Mandarino is a partner with the law firm of Stanley Esrey & Buckley, LLP, in Atlanta, Georgia, not far from that army tank in *The Walking Dead*. His practice focuses primarily on tax and financial planning, and he keeps a thirty-day water supply in his panic room. Mr. Mandarino's articles have appeared in the *National Law Journal*, *Mergers & Acquisitions* magazine, *Tax Notes Today*, *Journal of Real Estate Taxation*, *Journal of S Corporation Taxation*, *Journal of Multistate Taxation*, and *Tax & Finance Newsletter*, none of which will matter in the least when the undead walk the earth.

Alain Marciano is an associate professor at the University of Montpellier 1. His interest in the history of economic thought—his main area of research—comes from a natural fascination with dead souls and dead bodies. The great economists of the past, for him, are not dead at all but sufficiently alive to haunt the corridors of his mind. His acquaintance with the undead of economic thought allowed him to publish some of their stories in journals such as *History of Political Economy*, *Journal of the History of Economic Thought*, *International Review of Law and Economics*, and *Journal of Economic Behavior and Organization*.

Fabien Medvecky is a philosopher of economics at the University of Queensland in Australia, a land drenched in sun and largely devoid of the undead. His work is largely concerned with economics and social environmental decision making, and he has published in the *Erasmus Journal for Philosophy of Economics*, *Applied Ecology*, and *Science and Engineering Ethics*, among others. He has a well-established connection with the undead as his family, the Medvecky, were originally minor nobles at Orava Castle, Count Orlok's abode in Murnau's *Nosferatu*. Unlike Orlok, Fabien doesn't feed on humans, preferring the rich red blood of vines instead.

David T. Mitchell is a professor of economics at the University of Central Arkansas. He has published in the *Southern Economic Journal*, *Journal of Small Business Management*, and *Journal of Economic Education*, among other journals. He is the associate editor of both the *American Journal of Entrepreneurship* and *Journal of Entrepreneurship and Public Policy*. He fiendishly uses his knowledge of macroeconomics and statistics to transform bright and hopeful students into the mindless undead zombies of the corporate and political worlds.

Michael O'Hara is an assistant professor of economics at Colgate University, where he teaches and publishes in environmental and resource economics and econometrics. He looks forward to the zombie apocalypse, or tenure, whichever should come first.

A. L. Phillips is a PhD student in marketing at the University of Nebraska–Lincoln. Her published works include a fantasy novel as well as multiple academic articles in venues such as the *Hastings Business Law Journal* and *Journal of Financial Service Professionals*. While this is her first foray into writing about the undead, she has worked with undergraduate and graduate students for the past six years. She can attest from personal experience that at 8:00 a.m. in a statistics class, these populations are nearly identical.

G. M. Phillips is a professor of finance, financial planning, and insurance at California State University, Northridge. An econometrician by training, he has worked on numerous research projects, including the optimal statistical sampling of cemeteries' population density. Students leaving his lectures have been known to resemble zombies.

M. C. Phillips is a graduate of Grove City College, where she focused on political science and the computational arts (mathematics, computer science, and business analytics). She is a research programmer at the Center for Computationally Advanced Statistical Techniques in Pasadena, California, and also an avid cook best known for her "brain Jell-O."

Lorna Piatti-Farnell is a senior lecturer in communication studies at Auckland University of Technology. Known as "the Gothmother" in Gothic circles, she takes advantage of the long nights by writing journal articles and book chapters on popular culture, contemporary literature, animation, and film. While dwelling in the crypt of knowledge, she has also written three books: *Food and Culture in Contemporary American Fiction* (2011), *Beef: A Global History* (2013), and, more recently, *The Vampire in Contemporary Popular Literature* (2013). Her third book is rumored to be autobiographical.

Robert Prag is a software engineer. He spends much time staring blankly forward and muttering how he needs more brains. His zombie-preparedness credentials include movie premieres, elaborate disguises, and a survival plan signed by *The Zombie Survival Guide* author Max Brooks. He owes any good sense he demonstrates, in this volume or elsewhere, to his mother.

Hollis Robbins is chair of the Humanities Department at the Peabody Institute of Johns Hopkins University, with an appointment in the Center for Africana Studies. When not paralyzing students and colleagues with fear, she publishes articles on the intersection of literature and government bureaucracy, including "William Wordsworth's 'We Are Seven' and the First British Census" (*English Language Notes* 48, no. 2 [2010]) and "Fugitive Mail: Henry 'Box' Brown and Antebellum Postal Politics" (*American Studies* 50, nos. 1–2 [2009]). She is currently completing a book on the African American sonnet tradition and can be found writing every dusk to dawn, by candlelight, wearing a cape.

Sarah Skwire is a fellow at Liberty Fund, Inc., a private, nonprofit educational foundation. Her research is primarily focused on the unholy alliance of literature and economics and has been published in a range of academic and popular outlets. She torments the souls of undergraduates with her college writing textbook, *Writing with a Thesis*, now in its twelfth edition, and furthers her dark agenda as a blogger for *Bleeding Heart Libertarians* and as a regular columnist for *The Freeman*. She was educated at the University of Chicago and Wesleyan University, and she hails from Cleveland, widely acknowledged as the locus for a great deal of demonic activity and a Hell-mouth second only to that of Sunnydale.

Ilya Somin is a professor of law at George Mason University School of Law in Arlington, Virginia, just across the river from some of the nation's most dangerous vampires and zombies. He is the author of *Democracy and Political Ignorance: Why Smaller Government Is Smarter* (2013) and coauthor of *A Conspiracy against Obamacare: The Volokh Conspiracy and the Health Care Case* (2013). His work has appeared in numerous academic journals and popular publications, including *Yale Law Journal, Stanford Law Review*, the *Los Angeles Times*, the *New York Times*, and *USA Today*. Somin is a regular contributor to the popular *Volokh Conspiracy* blog. His research focuses on constitutional law, property law, and political participation. But he has also written on much more important issues, such as the portrayal of federalism and socialism in *Star Trek*, libertarianism and science fiction, and the politics of *The Hunger Games*.

David Tufte is an associate professor of economics at Southern Utah University, where his students discuss Robinson Crusoe's fate when Friday goes zombie. He has published articles in the *Journal of Macroeconomics, Southern Economic Journal, Journal of Applied Econometrics, World Development*, and other outlets. Zombies are actually the undead storyline he's least familiar with, so he's counting on Mary Jo Tufte's vocational skills to help him make it through a zombie apocalypse.

Mary Jo Tufte is a lecturer in biology at Southern Utah University. Her preferred organisms of study are human cadavers. As subjects, she finds the cadavers endlessly fascinating, always educational, and usually better behaved than zombies. Students describe Mary Jo as "the perfect kind of creepy" for cadaver and zombie work. One day she hopes to put all of her on-the-job training to work for her by transitioning into a more permanent cadaver and/or zombie state of being, as she continually finds them the best kind of people to deal with on a daily basis.

Charlotte Weil, born in the French volcanic region of Auvergne, decided early to dedicate her life to evil and fire. After some experience in the energy sector, she suddenly went postal. She now works as a regulatory economist for the French postal services, where she uses her demonic talents to obtain ever-increasing stamp tariffs. At night, she is a supervillain in front of her TV, encouraging the First, the Count, and monopolistic firms.

Glen Whitman is a professor of economics at California State University, Northridge, where he feeds on state taxpayers. He has published in such journals as the *UCLA Law Review*, *Journal of Legal Studies*, and *Journal of Economic Behavior and Organization*. In his second career as a screenwriter, he has written for the Fox series *Fringe* and the El Rey series *Matador*. His academic office is located in Juniper Hall, which doubled as Sunnydale High in the final season of *Buffy the Vampire Slayer*—which, as dedicated Buffy fans know, sits atop a Hellmouth. Needless to say, he prefers to work at home.